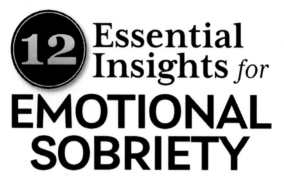

12 Essential Insights *for* EMOTIONAL SOBRIETY

Getting Your Recovery Unstuck

ALLEN BERGER, Ph.D.

4th Dimension Publishing

4th Dimension Publishing
Los Angeles, CA
4dphd.com

Includes bibliographical references.

ISBN 978-1-955415-12-5 (softcover) — 978-1-955415-13-2 (e-book)
Library of Congress Cataloging-in-Publication Data on file at the Library
of Congress

Contents

Foreword Herb Kaighan 9

Acknowledgments 13

Chapter 1: Being Stuck and Getting Unstuck 17

Chapter 2: Exploring Emotional Sobriety 27

Chapter 3: Waking Up from Our Sleepwalking 53

Chapter 4: Living Life Consciously 69

Chapter 5: Discerning Our Emotional Dependency ... 87

Chapter 6: Knowing It's Not Personal 109

Chapter 7: Realizing That No One Is Coming 129

Chapter 8: Accepting What Is 145

Chapter 9: Living Life on Life's Terms 169

Chapter 10: Discovering Novel Solutions 185

Chapter 11: Breaking the Bonds of Perfectionism ... 205

Chapter 12: Healing through Forgiveness 221

Chapter 13: Living a Purposeful Life 241

Chapter 14: Holding On to Ourself in Relationships . 261

Chapter 15: Paddling Your Own Canoe 293

Appendix A 303
Bill Wilson's 1958 *Grapevine* Article:
"Emotional Sobriety – The Next Frontier"

Appendix B 307
The Emotional Sobriety Inventory Form

References 309
About the Author 311

Foreword

12 Essential Insights for Emotional Sobriety is written by re-nowned psychotherapist Dr. Allen Berger. In what will become a definitive work on emotional sobriety, he attempts to place the heart inside the mind, free reality from illusion, and associate recovery with the pilgrimage for truth and emotional freedom.

Dr. Berger has changed the lives of hundreds of thousands of individuals with his work on emotional sobriety, paving a new path to recovery for both the addict and their families. His tireless work and contributions have been long acknowledged and revered by fellow professionals and the recovery community. Most importantly, he has created a large following among the truth-seekers and patients alike due to his innovative approach to life, therapy, sobriety, and recovery.

In what is the fifth addition to Dr. Berger's Twelve Series of popular recovery books, he will take you on an incredible personal journey that will introduce you to a process that will lead to incorporating emotional sobriety into your life and into your recovery. So, what is emotional sobriety?

Emotional sobriety is emotional freedom, a true independence of spirit. It is the transcendence of other validated self-esteem to self-validated self-esteem. It is the evolution from emotional dependency to self-support. It is the outcome of a successful personal journey from an unrealistic, childish outlook on life (one all too common among many adults today) to a realistic, mature perspective of living life on life's terms. Dr. Berger confirms the rite of passage to emotional maturity – an authentic and effective alignment with and coping with reality as it actually is.

Assuming we already have a solid foundation or freedom from addiction, this new book describes how we can improve our ability to cope with and navigate our unmanageability ... practically ... one day at a time. Reading this book will be like taking a graduate course in life. A must needed introduction to coping with life as it is.

Dr. Berger explores the long and winding road of human development, helping us understand the veers we have taken along the way, and pointing us back to the way to optimal living while, at the same time, confronting our often delayed and arrested transition into adulthood and emotional maturity. He engages and motivates the reader to translate theory and knowledge into action by sharing the journey that many of his patients have taken on his couch and also his own personal journey applying these principles to the challenges he faced in his own life.

One couldn't have a better guide for this odyssey into the world of emotional sobriety. Dr. Berger is highly qualified for this role with over five decades of personal recovery and a doctorate in clinical psychology from UC Davis. His perspective is unique. He integrates modern psychotherapy with Twelve Step recovery unlike anyone else I've encountered in my own personal journey. He is considered a pioneer in bringing this important issue to the forefront of recovery and is also considered the foremost authority on the subject. The reader will see how he has earned this reputation.

He works with the number 12 in all of his writing. This seems to represent a cosmic order. It is applied here in 12 Essential Insights to help us create an "inner cosmic order" in our lives, forged by our personal experiences, sufferings and the 12 essential insights he so skillfully and thoughtfully provides.

Dr. Berger's new methodology helps us build a truthful existence, find emotional freedom, and recover our integrity. He demystifies certain aspects of recovery fraught with conflict and thoughts of "Is this all there is?" He helps us see that trouble doesn't mean something is wrong but rather see it as an invitation to our growth. And finally, this book will help the reader experience a practical approach to shift from self-centered chaos to self-conscious contentment, connection and efficacy.

Dr. Berger's new book invites everyone to read, absorb, ponder, question, discuss, experiment, incorporate, and especially to practice living optimally. It is a beacon for those of us making the journey from darkness into light!

Herb Kaighan,
Author/Spiritual Guide

Acknowledgments

An author is often thought of as the person who writes a book. My experience is that this is misleading. There are many people who have been involved with the effort to bring this book into being. They deserve to be recognized and appreciated for their contributions.

My appreciation also goes to Glenn Rader and Karen Bartos for their helpful feedback on the opening chapters of this book. Your support of my work and dedication to spreading the word about the importance of emotional sobriety mean a lot to me.

Two of my colleagues deserve special recognition: Herb and Thom. The emotional sobriety workshops I have been cofacilitating with Herb Kaighan for the past two decades, as well as our numerous conversations about this vital topic, were instrumental in helping me develop the concepts I discuss in this book. Thank you, Herb

Thom Rutledge and I have been meeting regularly since the coronavirus pandemic interrupted all of our lives. We provided support for those in recovery during the initial phases of the pandemic, and we continued carrying the message with our podcast, "Start Right Here: Conversations about What Matters Most." Our new podcast on emotional sobriety will continue developing the concept of this critical component of full recovery. Thom's influence permeates my writing. Thank you, Thom, for your professional wisdom and personal support during these trying times.

My sponsor, Tom McCall, made a significant contribution to this work by giving me permission to share his recovery story, but his contribution to my recovery goes far beyond sharing his experience, strength and hope here. His ongoing, unconditional love and wisdom continue to inform the way I live my life today and laid the early foundations for my emotional sobriety.

It is said that when one door closes another one opens. This is what happened in the eleventh hour when my previous publisher decided to not publish this current work. In the space between what happened and what would come next Kristin Witzenburg appeared and encouraged me to move forward with this project. Kristin, you have been a good friend and supporter of my professional career for over a decade and now you are a partner in this new adventure. I appreciate and respect your professionalism, talent, and enthusiasm. Thank you for helping me turn this vision of emotional sobriety into a reality.

Last, but not least: Vince Hyman. Vince, you are an incredibly talented writer. There are times when I think you possess magical powers. You were an inspiration to my writing and tireless in your efforts to help me produce a book that I believe will help countless people. Your ability to express my concepts and ideas in a cogent and succinct way blows my mind. Your contributions to this work go far beyond editing. You have become my muse and good friend. Thank you.

Chapter 1:
Being Stuck and
Getting Unstuck

Roger trudged into my office with a look of shame and resignation on his face. He slumped down into his chair, rubbed his hand back and forth across his brow, and emitted a long, slow sigh. He couldn't quite look at me and barely said hello.

"Well, Roger," I said with a smile. "It's good to see you too!"

I had last worked with Roger about seven years ago. He had a serious problem with alcohol and cocaine. Getting clean and sober was tough for him. He relapsed several times before being able to maintain physical sobriety. Eventually, he accepted his addiction and developed a solid commitment to himself and his recovery. But as you are going to find out, there's more to recovery than physical sobriety. The trouble that had brought Roger back to therapy was inviting him to take the next step in his recovery. He simply hadn't discovered that yet.

I sensed Roger's struggle. "You seem to be having a hard time looking at me, Roger."

Roger responded with an insecure laugh, sort of a snort. He raised his head and looked at me for a long moment, his face a shifting combination of bemusement, sadness, a touch of shame, frustration, and more than a little resignation.

"I am," he said.

"What's going on? What's happening inside that makes it hard to face me?"

"I've hit a wall," Roger said, sighing again. "I keep asking myself, 'Is this it? Is this all there is to recovery?' I've been doing all the right things for a long time. And the fact is—and I mean no disrespect, Dr. Berger, you've been a help, you really have—I feel like I've been on a treadmill for a while now. I feel like I've let you down and that maybe I'm a phony."

We sat for a moment, quiet. I could tell Roger was formulating his thoughts.

"I'm not joyous and free, even though I act like it. I work this great program, but I feel like I don't. You wouldn't know that I am feeling so dissatisfied about my recovery if you heard me share in a meeting."

I needed to address the shame Roger felt about letting me down. This was important for our work together. But I also needed to help him recognize the expectations he had regarding his recovery. It struck me that Roger's expectations about what it meant to be in long-term recovery were unreasonable. I suspected that he defined his recovery in a way that was quite limiting for him. I saw why Roger felt confused. There wasn't room in Roger's "great program" for his own recovery.

Roger's plight is an all-too-common experience for those who have achieved physical sobriety but have not yet developed much emotional sobriety.

"Roger, I want you to know what it means to me that you've come back to see me. I'm touched. It means a lot to me," I told him. "I also want you to know that I am not disappointed in your recovery. I would have felt that I'd failed you if you had been unable to turn to me when you needed help. I expected you to encounter problems that will baffle you as you walk the road of recovery. The fact that you reached out to get some additional help says to me you are working a good program. It means that you need help to take the next step in your recovery.

"But here's the problem as I see it: You have defined your recovery in a way that excludes you and your authenticity from it. This seems to be at the heart of the problem you are experiencing."

Roger appeared to be taken aback. I don't know what he expected from me, but this response wasn't it. "Wow," he said. "That is a very different way to look at things."

I let Roger sit for a moment, digesting the idea that he was not allowing himself to be authentic in recovery. "Roger," I said, "what is really going on in your recovery?"

"I'm not sure. Something has changed. It's like the longer I've been in recovery, the more I expect of myself."

"Yes, I sense that," I said. "I wonder what expectations you have of yourself because you have been in recovery for over seven years. In fact, let's sort this out. We need some clarity. Remember the sentence completion exercises we used to do? Let me remind you. I'll give you an incomplete sentence and you repeat it, ending with the first thought that comes to your mind. Here we go: 'Because I have been in recovery for seven years I should _____.'"

We repeated the sentence six times. Here are Roger's responses:

> "I should be more together."
> "I should be happy, all the time."
> "I should know how to deal with all of my problems."
> "I should be content with my life."
> "I should get along with my wife better than I do."
> "I should be excited about being in recovery, all the time."

Roger took a big breath, then blew it all out through pursed lips, his cheeks billowing like sails. "Wow that is quite an order. I expect a lot of myself. I can't believe I said all that. It's no wonder I've been struggling. It's no wonder I feel stuck! I am stuck. I'm stuck!"

•••

I'm stuck. I've heard this, or variations on it, many times before. We get into recovery, and it's exciting. Our life gets better than we ever imagined it would. And then that becomes normal. In time, we become aware of other issues in our life. Roger's concern is one I have heard voiced by many who have become bored with recovery or who have hit a plateau.

> Getting stuck is common in recovery. Unfortunately, most of us interpret an impasse as a sign that we are not working a "good" program.

Getting stuck is common in recovery. Unfortunately, most of us interpret an impasse as a sign that we are not working a "good" program. This is utter nonsense. Getting stuck in recovery does not mean something is wrong with your program. In fact, it's usually the opposite.

Please pause for a moment and really absorb what I am saying: Getting stuck in recovery does not mean something is wrong with your program.

Working a good program is not a magical vaccine that renders us immune to problems. This is not how recovery works. Recovery isn't a shield against the problems of being human. It's a human being grower. Recovery restores the emotional development that our addiction stunted. It grows us by helping us mature and realize our full potential. In recovery we face "who we've become" in order to become "what we can be." Who we've become, as you'll learn in this book, is a false self—a person we've constructed to make us lovable.

This false self gets us along in life for a while—years even—but as recovery progresses, we begin to sense that there's a more authentic self inside us. That's our true self, the feeling of "what we can be." Our long-neglected true self grates against that false self. That grating was once dulled by alcohol and other drugs, but sobriety enables us to feel it. And we feel it as trouble—as something wrong.

But as you'll see, in this case, trouble doesn't mean something is wrong. Quite the contrary. Trouble means something is right. Getting stuck is our signal that it's time to learn something new. The trouble we are experiencing, wherever it's showing up in our lives, is highlighting the next step in our development, the next step in our emotional maturity, the next step in our recovery. That step is the journey of emotional sobriety.

If it is met with the right attitude and processed in a healthy way, trouble grows people. Emotional sobriety provides the mind-set and tools that help us digest disturbing experiences and convert them to growth opportunities. On this journey, we learn to take what will grow and nourish us from these experiences and get rid of the rest. We learn to claim the experience we are having, rather than letting the experience claim us.

Every emotional disturbance and conflict—every moment of "stuckness"—contains an opportunity for spiritual progress and emotional growth. Once you start to see that, you've achieved a major shift in consciousness. You are on the path of emotional sobriety.

A New Movement in Recovery

I have been in recovery since 1971. That's a lot of years. I've seen a lot too—many movements in psychotherapy, New Age stuff, Landmark Forum, Tony Robbins, Back to the Basics of Recovery—you name it. I've watched the fads, some of them truly crazy (in hindsight), come and go. I've seen and participated in enough of them to be very skeptical of any promising new movements.

But there is a movement afoot that's different from these fads, and it is adding a new vitality to recovery. What is this trend? Emotional sobriety!

It's odd that this is a new movement, since it was first mentioned in the late 1940s by Bill Wilson, one of the cofounders of Alcoholics Anonymous. For decades, most people in recovery skipped this part of his message. We (myself included) were primarily focused on sobriety. Our measure of sobriety was years without relapse. We didn't talk much about emotions or how our emotional lives were related to our idea of success in recovery.

> Emotional sobriety is the key to complete recovery. It sets the stage for real maturity and fulfillment in our lives. It's like finding the key that opens the door to a better life, a happier life, a more fully realized existence.

And yet emotional sobriety is the key to complete recovery. It sets the stage for real maturity and fulfillment in our lives. It's like finding the key that opens the door to a better life, a happier life, a more fully realized existence. The personal work it takes to practice emotional sobriety amplifies recovery as nothing else can.

Bill W. would be pleased. Really pleased. This current trend is fulfilling his vision. He hoped that emotional sobriety would become the next frontier in recovery, that emotional sobriety would spearhead "the development of much more real maturity and balance (which is to say, humility) in our relations with ourselves, with our fellows, and with God" (1988, 236).

Bill W. deeply understood the importance of emotional maturity in his own recovery. It helped him deal with his crippling and chronic depression. His personal reflections on the underlying cause of his depression and its cure provided us with many important insights into emotional sobriety.

When Bill W. wrote *Twelve Steps and Twelve Traditions* in the early 1950s, he noted that living according to the spiritual principles set forth in the Twelve Steps would help us achieve emotional sobriety. In the chapter on Step Twelve, Bill wrote, "Here we begin to practice all Twelve Steps of the program in our daily lives so that we and those about us may find emotional sobriety" (Alcoholics Anonymous World Services 1981, 106).

Take a moment and let this sink in. Bill W. concluded that the ultimate purpose of working the Twelve Steps was to achieve emotional sobriety. There is good reason for this. Emotional sobriety helps us discover the answers to the many challenges that life sets before us as we walk our recovery road.

Emotional sobriety provides a way to unpack and understand our emotional reactions. What's more, it provides a way for us to recover our balance when a situation doesn't go the way we want it to or when someone or something doesn't live up to our expectations. It helps us learn how to hold on to ourselves—that is, how to avoid being overly influenced by others and less emotionally reactive to what happens around us or even to us.

When we gain emotional sobriety, we don't personalize the things other people say and do. We are no longer dependent on their behavior for our happiness. We set ourselves free from the often ridiculous expectations that we had of others. And the result is that we are free to find what has long been lost to us: a deep, honest sense of emotional balance and maturity. We discover we have the potential to be what we can be. We discover our "true self." The inner peace and emotional freedom we achieve is what Bill W. was pointing us to with the concept of emotional sobriety.

Getting Unstuck

If you have been active in recovery for a while but now seem stuck, this book is an opportunity to find your way out of that. It will describe twelve essential insights for emotional sobriety—insights that offer actions that can help you get unstuck. These insights are not associated with any one approach to recovery. Some are influenced by Bill Wilson's reflections on emotional sobriety, but they also include powerful psychological and spiritual insights from psychotherapists into finding true peace of mind and fulfillment in life.

Whether you are following a traditional Twelve Step program or an alternative solution like SMART Recovery, Rational Recovery, Recovery Dharma, or psychotherapy, you will be able to use these insights to grow yourself in the direction of emotional sobriety. This work will help you sustain and amplify your recovery.

Here are the twelve essential insights for emotional sobriety:

1. Waking up from our sleepwalking
2. Living life consciously
3. Discerning our emotional dependency

4. Knowing that it's not personal
5. Realizing that no one is coming
6. Accepting what is
7. Living life on life's terms
8. Discovering novel solutions
9. Breaking the bonds of perfectionism
10. Healing through forgiveness
11. Living a purposeful life
12. Holding on to ourself in relationships

As we integrate these insights into our recovery, we discover not only the places where we have been stuck but also a whole new world of possibilities for happiness and growth in all areas of life.

So, how did Roger take to these insights? It would make for a happy story if I told you Roger left my office revitalized, excited, and ready for a great new life. Well, life doesn't work that way. But we did begin discussing the practice of emotional sobriety. Several of the insights were helpful to Roger. Each is a different way to get at the core of emotional sobriety, which is to know our true self, release our expectations, and embrace life on life's terms. My hope is that you will find some of the insights useful and that, like Roger, you'll gradually incorporate them into your life as you work on the practice of emotional sobriety. You may be quite surprised by the positive changes you see in yourself months and years after you begin this journey.

In the next chapter, you'll gain a deeper understanding of emotional sobriety, and I hope you'll feel motivated to try on some of these insights for yourself. You'll learn about how the work of Earnie Larsen—a gifted and talented author and recovery speaker whose work continues to influence recovery today—dovetails with the concepts at the center of emotional sobriety.

And you'll understand more about how Bill W. originally framed the idea and what it might mean for your recovery.

Chapter 2: Exploring Emotional Sobriety

By the time she was thirty-eight, Sam had six years of solid recovery. Then the pandemic hit. She was attending meetings on a regular basis (and continued to do so, even though they shifted to virtual online fellowships), had worked the Steps with her sponsor, made amends, and was sponsoring other women. The social isolation of the coronavirus pandemic presented a challenge for Sam and her recovery. It scared her.

Sam had a complicated, often painful relationship with her mother, Jennifer. In the past, her mother had disowned Sam several times because she just couldn't bear the trouble Sam would get herself into. While their current relationship had healed some of the wounds, the scars were still present.

One Wednesday morning, Sam was depressed and called her mother seeking comfort. When her mother answered the phone, Sam started to tell her about her fears and anxiety. Several of her close friends had tested positive for the coronavirus, and Sam was terrified that she was going to be infected too. In addition to worrying about what this might mean for her own health, she was also concerned about what it could mean for her family if she became sick or even hospitalized. Sam was a single parent with full custody of her two young children, ages two and four. Her ex was currently in a sober living house but was struggling. He would put together a couple of months of sobriety and then relapse, so Sam feared he would be of no help in caring for the children if she became ill.

Sam was worried about testing positive and was hoping her mother would be supportive and possibly offer some assistance if that came to pass. But instead of empathizing with Sam and reassuring her, Jennifer criticized Sam and railed on her ex. She ranted that Sam should have never married that loser, that he would never get well, and that the children would never have a father. Jennifer then chastised Sam, "I warned you that he was a bad seed, but you wouldn't listen to me."

Next, she chided Sam for never listening to her, capping it all off with, "Look what not listening to me has done to your life. It's a terrible waste."

Sam froze up. She lost her voice. Her body trembled violently. She could barely hold the phone. She hung up, shattered, and fell to the floor in a puddle of tears. She berated herself for turning to her mother. "I should have known that she wouldn't be there for me. What was I thinking? Haven't I learned anything in recovery?"

Sam's mother wasn't the safe harbor she had expected and hoped for. Sam felt terribly alone, angry, and frightened.

Consider the following questions about your own experience:

- Do you relate to Sam's experience?
- Have you ever turned to someone for support and received criticism instead?
- Have you been knocked off balance by what someone

said about you?

- [ ] Do you ever lose your ability to speak up for yourself and defend your psychological space?
- [ ] Is your sense of self defined by what other people think of you?
- [ ] Do you let other people "edit your reality"—tell you how things are?
- [ ] Do you take things personally?
- [ ] Do you find yourself questioning how well you are working your program after an incident like Sam experienced?

Have you been knocked off balance by what someone said about you?

Let's turn it around:

- [ ] Do you relate to Jennifer?
- [ ] Has it been hard for you to support people who have turned to you for support after you warned them about the very problems they were going to have if they didn't listen to your advice?
- [ ] Do you have an "I told you so" inside you too?
- [ ] Do you find yourself needing to be right rather than connecting?
- [ ] Do you lose your capacity for empathy because of your anxiety or anger?
- [ ] Do you regret not pausing in certain situations so that you could let the best in you respond?

If we step back from Sam and Jennifer, we can see they are both stuck in a loop. Sam has expectations of her mother. When her mother fails to meet them, Sam reacts. And just the same, Jennifer has expectations of Sam, who fails to meet them. She reacts. It's a sad, predictable cycle.

Sam or Jennifer — ideally, both — need to develop emotional sobriety if they want this cycle to stop and so they can have the kind of healthy relationship they both deserve. We are going to unpack and explore emotional sobriety throughout this book—starting with Sam and her mother. Let's begin with a definition for you to think about:

> Emotional sobriety is a mental state in which we do not react to our changing emotions as though they were the governing facts of our lives.

Take a moment to think about what Sam's life would be like if she still experienced her immediate emotional responses to her mother's statements but did not react to them. What if she let her emotions happen and took her time figuring out which emotions provided useful information about her own life and what next steps would be helpful for her situation? Do you think the conversation would have gone the same? Do you think Sam would have found herself frozen?

Just as physical sobriety emerges as we gain independence from our addictive urges, emotional sobriety emerges as we gain freedom from our emotional storms. But there's a problem here. We know we have a kind of sobriety when we quit using alcohol or drugs, but no one stops having emotional responses—that would be tragic! Emotions provide important information about our life.

Emotional sobriety does not come from stopping emotions; quite the opposite. This kind of sobriety is an emergent condition

— a quality of being and thinking that arises and develops as we learn to pay attention to what our emotions are telling us rather than simply react. Feelings — even powerful ones — still happen, but we don't give them a privileged space. We don't thoughtlessly react to them. We act upon them with the appropriate amount of respect their due. But we don't treat them like they are an infallible guide to reality.

> Feelings—even powerful ones—still happen, but we don't give them a privileged space.

Because emotional sobriety emerges as we change our internal world, it can be a bit difficult to define. It is one of those "I know it when I see it" kind of things. For that reason, in this chapter I am going to write a lot about the factors that influence emotional sobriety before we do more to explore its definition. I should add here that emotional sobriety (as well as the lack of emotional sobriety) is an attribute shared by all human beings. For example, Sam's mother, Jennifer, is not a recovering person or an addict, but she clearly lacks emotional sobriety or she wouldn't be reacting to Sam in the ways she does. And one other note — emotional sobriety is something that is cultivated. It's a practice. We don't just get there and move on to other things. We need to tend to it all the time, as you'll see throughout this book.

Sam and Jennifer probably had this same basic fight a dozen or more times. They seem to get lost in an ancient mother-daughter quarrel before either of them can get to the actual point of the phone call: They need to deal with their fears and plan for what to do should an emergency put those young children at risk. This is typical for all of us. We all struggle with holding on to ourselves in relationships, especially if we lack emotional sobriety. The capacity to stay centered — that is, to know who you are regardless of what others say or do during troubles — is one of the characteristics of emotional sobriety. I think of this as finding and maintaining your emotional center of gravity.

A second characteristic typical of emotional sobriety is emotional independence, which may also be thought of as a lack of emotional dependency or as the capacity to support oneself emotionally rather than requiring support from other people. A third characteristic of emotional sobriety is emotional maturity. Each of these characteristics is almost synonymous with emotional sobriety. If you see a person who behaves in a way that is centered, emotionally independent, and mature, that person has either achieved some sort of emotional sobriety or is a skilled actor.

Our Emotional Center of Gravity

We must become aware of and manage our emotional center of gravity if we are going to achieve emotional sobriety. In a bit, we will examine where Sam and Jennifer put their emotional centers of gravity in the scene described earlier. But before we do, let me illustrate this concept.

We all have a physical center of gravity. Visualize a vertical line in a three-dimensional space. This line represents the force of gravity. Now imagine the line extends through your body, rooting you to the earth. If you spread your feet about shoulder width apart and slightly bend your knees, then your center of gravity is right on this imaginary line, midway between both feet, centered in your pelvis. In this stance your weight would be equally distributed between both of your feet, giving you a strong feeling of being physically grounded. All your weight is balanced around that central point, low in your body. If you shifted to one leg or the other, or backward or forward even a little bit, you'd be off balance. Your center of gravity would have shifted.

Skilled athletes learn to manage their center of gravity so they are always balanced. This allows them to execute complex and difficult athletic skills. Watch female gymnasts when they perform on the balance beam. Their complete control over their center of gravity enables them to perform flips, handstands, and other amazing moves while standing on a wooden beam measuring a mere four inches in width.

> If our emotional center of gravity is focused on other people and their reactions, external conditions, or other things outside our firm and flexible inner self, we can be impulsive, unbalanced, and even reckless.

Our emotional center of gravity is analogous to our physical center of gravity. Emotions have a "pull" just like gravity. Our emotional center of gravity is that point where our emotions converge around a firm and flexible inner sense of self. When our emotional center of gravity is positioned well ("centered"), we exhibit an emotional balance in our lives that comes from self-awareness. Our emotional responses become less reactive and more tied to this firm and flexible sense of self. If our emotional center of gravity is focused on other people and their reactions, external conditions, or other things outside our firm and flexible inner self, we can be impulsive, unbalanced, and even reckless. People with emotional sobriety will be emotionally balanced; their emotional center of gravity properly converges around what they can control — their actions and attitudes, as chosen by their true or authentic self.

Having a solid but flexible sense of self means we know who we are and who we aren't. This suggests we have reached a certain level of self-awareness, self-acceptance, and self-support. It's important to note that accepting our self doesn't mean we stop striving to be what we can be; it just means we know who we are now, and we start with where we are at.

Emotional Autonomy

When I relocate my emotional center of gravity outside myself — in a situation or in another person — then I become emotionally dependent on that situation or person: I depend on outside conditions to maintain emotional well-being. That sets up situations like we saw with Sam and her mother. Sam expected certain kinds of support from her mother, Jennifer, in order to feel okay. When Sam's mother failed to provide the support Sam wanted, she froze up and then melted down. She was completely dependent on her mother for her emotional well-being. This is emotional dependence. It can happen to anyone (addict or not). It's not good for anyone, and it is especially dangerous for people in recovery from addiction to alcohol or other drugs.

Emotional autonomy, or emotional independence, is the opposite of emotional dependence. People who are emotionally independent do not give away their balance to the whims of the world or the words and emotional states of other people. As I noted, emotional autonomy or emotional independence is a characteristic of emotional sobriety. It requires that we are capable of self-support.

Let me explain what I mean when I use the phrase self-support. When we support ourselves, we mobilize our potential to cope with the world. We learn to use our own resources to cope with life. This is not to be confused with defiant individuality, a term well-known to many people in recovery, where we falsely claim that we don't need anyone, that we can do it ourselves. (This is utter nonsense, especially when it comes to addressing an issue that blocks us.)

Self-support is much different from this sort of false, defiant individuality. It means we take responsibility to ask for help when we need it. When we support ourselves, we ask for help rather than projecting our need for help onto others. We request, but not demand. Then we gratefully receive, not take. Receiving is different than taking. Loving is giving and receiving.

We understand, when asking for help, that the person may be unable to provide the help, and we work to avoid forcing an expectation of such help on that person. The more we take responsibility and support ourselves to change, the less we demand that our loved one's change.

Take a breath for a moment to let this sink in. Okay? Ready?

Now think how Sam's conversation might have gone if she had asked for support directly from her mother without the expectation that her mother could or would provide it. What if Sam had simply listened to her mother without reacting — or even expressed some empathy for her mother's concern? How would this change the relationship? What would this say about Sam's emotional center of gravity and emotional independence?

Self-support creates self-validation and self-acceptance. We don't let other people tell us what's real and what's not. What other people say about us doesn't define us. We learn how to manage the parts of ourselves that are self-critical and blaming so they don't sabotage our recovery by telling us we're worthless and might as well go back to drinking and using. When we can support ourselves, we become the sifter of our own experience. This doesn't mean we are closed to feedback. We remain open and flexible, but we decide what fits and what doesn't.

Emotional Maturity

We can now define emotional maturity as "the movement away from emotional dependency toward self-support." When we are emotionally dependent on others, we feel driven to manipulate them to support us. Think again about Sam. Her opening bid to her mother, Jennifer, was a litany of her fears and worries about getting sick, being unable to care for her children (her mother's grandchildren!), and her ex-husband's inability to help. She hoped for support and assistance but didn't ask Jennifer for it directly. Is there any sort of manipulation going on here? Is there a kind of emotional blackmail going on?

Emotional maturation will provide us with actions we can take, directly, to support ourselves, and diminish our impulse to manipulate other people into supporting us. This, of course, is an ongoing process throughout our recovery. Old habits die hard, if at all. (It's more likely that we set old habits aside for better habits, but the old habits are still there.)

As we transcend emotional dependency and move toward self-support, we are laying the foundation for emotional sobriety. When we are emotionally centered, then it is difficult for anything or anyone to knock us off balance. Regardless of what others are doing or not doing, we keep our cool. We roll with the punches. We let the best in us run the show. Regardless of what challenges, disappointments, or ordeals life sets before us, we find a way to cope. When things don't go our way, we accept them, because they are what they are.

But when our emotional center of gravity is pushed or pulled outside of ourselves, we lose our balance. It becomes impossible to support ourselves.

Whenever we depend on our environment to satisfy our needs or take care of us, we lose influence over our emotional well-being. In these cases, our emotions become determined by what happens or doesn't happen to us, rather than by what we do or how we cope with what happens to us. As Bill Wilson said, this is putting "the cart before the horse" (1988, 236). This means that we depend on life to conform to our expectations for our happiness and joy. The cart is before the horse. Not a good idea if you want to real happiness and joy in your life.

So, here's the problem in a nutshell. If we lack emotional sobriety, if we are emotionally dependent, our well-being will depend on the graciousness and goodwill of others — and even of life itself. Our personal value will rely on the validation of others.

When we put our emotional center of gravity in another person, then that person's mood and behavior exerts undue influence over our feelings and actions. We become like emotional conjoined twins. Our relationship becomes too dependent on the other person. How the other person feels and behaves will either make us feel okay, meaning emotionally balanced, or not okay, off balance.

In these situations, our immaturity is reflected in our consciousness, which is in turn reflected in our language. Our language will define us as victims. We blame others for what we are experiencing. "You hurt me, or you made me angry, or you make me feel insecure," will mirror how we experience ourselves in relationships.

> When our emotional center of gravity is located in an expectation of how things are supposed to be, then our happiness is determined by whether or not things go our way.

When our emotional center of gravity is located in an expectation of how things are supposed to be, then our happiness is determined by whether or not things go our way. Life happens, and when it doesn't conform to our expectations, we object. Blaming becomes second nature. This is an impossible way of life. When we fight reality, we lose. Emotional sobriety is achieved when we align ourselves with reality not fight it.

Do you see how our emotional center of gravity, emotional independence, and emotional maturity are intertwined?

Sam and Her Mother

Sam and Jennifer showed none of the characteristics of emotional sobriety. They both put their emotional center of gravity outside themselves. They were both emotionally dependent on each other, showing no ability to support themselves. They were emotionally immature, and these characteristics are revealed in their interactions. They each gave the other authority over their own emotional center of gravity and therefore over their emotional well-being.

Because of Sam's emotional dependency, she had an unspoken demand that her mother respond to her "request" in the way she was "supposed to." We call such an unspoken demand an unenforceable rule. This is a rule we make regarding how other people are supposed to act or feel or how the world is supposed to work. We make this rule to make ourselves feel safe, and we make it regardless of whether we have any viable or honest way to enforce it. (You'll be hearing a lot more about unenforceable rules throughout this book.)

Sam had several unenforceable rules at work here: Mothers should always be reassuring and supportive to their children, including adult children; you should put differences aside when there is a crisis; and if you love someone, you will automatically forgive that person. When Jennifer responded to Sam's inquiry by venting her resentment and ranting about old, unfinished business, she violated several of Sam's unenforceable rules. Sam felt hurt and rejected. Sam set herself up for this reaction. Expectations are premeditated disasters. Sam's expectations were frustrated. Jennifer didn't respond the way a "good mother" or a "good person" should, and so Sam was devastated.

The reality is that Sam did not make a request for her mother's support and reassurance. She demanded it. How can we know this? If Sam made a request, then when Jennifer rejected it, Sam may have felt disappointed but not devastated. Sam took what her mother said personally. To her it meant that her mother didn't love her, that she didn't care. She took it personally. This devastated Sam.

Sam put her emotional center of gravity in Jennifer and in the narrow expectations of how her mother should behave. Had she kept her emotional center of gravity over her own two feet, she would have felt disappointed at the lack of support, but she would also have wondered what her mother's words had to say about her mother, not Sam. She would have been curious about her mother's position rather than judgmental. She would have seen her mother reflected in her mother's rants rather than seeing a reflection of how her mother felt about her.

Simultaneously, Jennifer put her emotional center of gravity in her daughter. When Sam mentioned that she might have been exposed to the coronavirus, Jennifer became anxious. Instead of being vulnerable and talking to her daughter about this anxiety, she attacked her. Her reaction was saying something like, "I hate being anxious and feeling out of control, and I am blaming you for this feeling. If you had listened to me in the first place, you might be safe, and I wouldn't be feeling like this."

If Jennifer had kept her emotional center of gravity over her own two feet, she would not have attacked and blamed Sam for making her feel anxious. Instead, she would have been equipped to take responsibility for what she was experiencing. Jennifer might have said something to Sam like, "I understand that you are concerned. I am feeling anxious too. I start to imagine all of the things you should have done to protect yourself so I wouldn't feel this way, but this line of thought is irrelevant. You are concerned and I can hear that. I hope you don't have the virus, but I will do what I can to support you. It won't do you or me any good to think about all the things you should have done."

This is what conversations can sound like when we stay connected to someone and take responsibility for our feelings. Even when there is tension, emotional sobriety enables us to hold on to who we are and speak from that, rather than being trapped and activated by our expectations and projections. When we achieve emotional sobriety the best in us speaks for the rest of us.

Recognizing and tending this basic emotional and spiritual center of gravity at the core of who we are is the essence of the twelve insights that I discuss in this book.

The Roots of Emotional Sobriety

Emotional sobriety is kind of an odd term. We get sober from alcohol, but how do you get sober from emotions? Bill Wilson coined this phrase. The earliest of his writings I found this in was *Twelve Steps and Twelve Traditions*, which was first published in 1952. However, it is quite likely he talked about emotional sobriety well before then.

I noted previously how Bill W. predicted that we would achieve emotional sobriety when we worked the Steps and practiced the principles embodied in the Steps in our daily affairs. But in 1956 he wrote a letter that would further elucidate his understanding of what that meant. That year, Bill responded to an inquiry that the Alcoholics Anonymous (AA) General Service Office in New York received from a member of the AA fellowship. The letter writer asked if the Twelve Steps could help him deal with his depression.

I can only imagine Bill W.'s reaction when he was told about this fellow's letter. He must have been quite excited. This was a chance for Bill to share his personal experience in coping with depression.

Bill W. struggled with depression for most of his life. He took on his depression in recovery. For the first two decades of Bill's recovery, he turned himself inside and out while he learned about what caused and what helped his depression. He shared what he had learned in this letter, which was eventually published in the 1958 AA *Grapevine* titled "The Next Frontier—Emotional Sobriety."[1]

In the letter, Bill W. defined emotional sobriety as "real maturity and balance (which is to say, humility) in our relations with ourselves, with our fellows, [with life], and with God." Notice that Bill leads off with the word maturity. As I have expressed, maturity occurs when we transcend our childish urge to gain environmental support (support by making external conditions conform

---

[1] AA *Grapevine*, a monthly magazine for alcoholics, has been published since 1944. The Grapevine article has been reproduced in its entirety in Appendix A. Please take a moment to read it before you continue reading this chapter.

to our needs) and instead develop self-support (support by accepting reality and others as they are and actively seeking the kind of help we need when appropriate). Real simply means that it's not an idea but has become a pattern of actions and behavior. Real maturity happens when we learn to act on our own behalf without manipulating others to support us or make us feel good about ourselves. Real maturity is achieved when our satisfaction is determined by how we are coping with what is happening in our lives. It is about growing up and learning to respect and respond to our emotions without giving them privilege. A good example of this is courage. Courage is defined as doing something that frightens us. If we gave fear privilege, we would not do what frightened us. We would withdraw or feeze. Feelings are to be respected but not given privilege.

> Real maturity happens when we learn to act on our own behalf without manipulating others to support us or make us feel good about ourselves.

Bill W. also used the word balance in his definition. What kind of balance was Bill referring to? I think he was talking about being emotionally balanced in our lives. Many of us can define our addiction as being "addicted to more." Bill articulated that our primary problem is that our natural instincts have become unbalanced. He elaborated on this notion when he said, "Never was there enough of what we thought we wanted" (Alcoholics Anonymous World Services 1981, 71). So, I believe that Bill used balance to refer to restraining our urge to seek ever more external sources of emotional solace. This means returning ourselves to a place where our emotions are in balance with other kinds of information in our lives (this might include information from our inner wisdom, the support of our fellows in AA and elsewhere, and our relationship with our Higher Power).

This is our dilemma: turning to a material solution for a spiritual problem. This will never work. No matter how much of "more" we get in our lives, at some point we will need to face the reality that we won't find our solution outside ourselves. The solution is within us. This means at some point in our recovery we surrender our expectation that something or someone is coming along to make us okay.

Bill W. equated maturity and balance with humility when he said "real maturity and balance (which is to say, humility)" (1988, 236). That's fascinating, isn't it? What did he mean by humility in this context? Well, surrendering our expectations is where humility comes into emotional sobriety.

Having humility means that we realize we are not that important. I don't mean this in a belittling or negative way. I mean that no one is here on earth to serve us or make us happy. Humility tells us that no one is coming (the subject of chapter 7). No material object and no special person outside us is going to make our lives better. To make our lives better, we must surrender our expectations and show up for ourselves. To get our lives unstuck, we must give up being passive and relinquish the belief that life should be generous or gracious or that some fairy godmother is going to come along and turn a pumpkin into a carriage for us.

Humility disarms our attempt to insist that people and circumstances conform to our demands or invisible unenforceable rules. This will have a big impact on how we relate to other people. We have no business expecting others to live up to our expectations. When we demand that others live up to our expectations, we exclude them from the very relationship we're attempting to have with them! The relationship becomes all about what we want, what we expect, what will make our world "right."

Are you starting to see how humility, emotional maturity, and balance are connected? Why Bill W. carefully chose those three terms?

Perhaps now you can see that humility is the antidote to the poison of emotional dependency. Or, to state it another way, humility is the medicine that leads to emotional sobriety. We have to be humble in order to cast aside the childish belief that we're at the center of the universe and that other people should conform to our expectations.

As Bill W. realized, we need to reorganize the way we think about ourselves, the world around us, and others. We need to humbly surrender our expectations and become better aligned with reality by seeing people for who they are rather than as a source of approval or disapproval.

I will further discuss Bill W.'s letter from the AA *Grapevine* later in the book. For most of this chapter, I've been writing about the characteristics of emotional sobriety. Before we move on to a full definition of emotional sobriety and explore the twelve essential insights, I would like to place emotional sobriety in the context of another important development in recovery literature and history: Earnie Larsen's model of Stage I and Stage II Recovery.

Stages of Recovery

Larsen was teaching and writing about his model of Stage I and Stage II Recovery in the 1980s. He knew about the "stuckness" that my patient Roger and many of us have felt in our journeys. He found that men and women who were committed to their long-term recovery seemed to hit a wall: "The fact is that many people reach a dead end or plateau in their personal recovery;

and if they do not understand what is occurring, they frequently feel they're 'losing' their recovery. Everything that used to be so meaningful no longer is, and their new-found excitement and health no longer feel terrific" (Larsen 1987, 11).

Larsen discovered that the dilemma that so many faced was, "I always believed that once I climbed this mountain, I'd be home free. How come I don't feel free?" (1987, 11). After reflecting on this phenomenon, he realized that recovery could be divided into two stages: Stage I and Stage II Recovery.

Stage I Recovery

Stage I Recovery encompassed the beginning of our journey. This stage of recovery always involves breaking the hold that addiction has on our lives. We recovered the power we had given to our addiction. We sobered up and detoxified our bodies from alcohol and other drugs. But we also broke the hold that our alcoholic self or addict self had on our lives.

Research shows that addiction hijacks the brain by changing the reward center, memory, motivation, and judgment portions of the brain. I am not speaking metaphorically; there are observable changes to these portions of the brain. These areas of the brain are employed by addiction to support the use of alcohol and other drugs.

The changes in our brain show up as changes in our personality. A brain doesn't go out and drink or use; a person does. We'll call this self part of a person the addict self. The addict self emerges as the addiction takes over.

You see, it is through our personality that we make contact with our environment to meet our needs. The addict self develops to serve and fulfill the needs of the changed, addicted brain. As addiction progresses, our addict self changes too. The more addiction hijacks our brain, the more the addict self takes control over our lives. This is why so many people who suffer from addiction hardly recognize who they become.

Once the addict self takes control, it wields significant influence over our behavior. Sadly, it alters our value system. We compromise our integrity. We violate our values. It speaks, and we obey, like puppets on a string. This change can happen slowly over years of alcohol and drug abuse or quickly if someone is using certain drugs like crystal meth, crack, or heroin.

Most readers of this book are familiar with the experience of early recovery, or Stage I Recovery. In this stage of recovery we break free from this hypnotic trance. We woke up and realized we had lost our true self. Admitting our powerlessness over addiction opened the door for discovering a new source of power. Some of us discovered a loving and forgiving God of our understanding. Others found a higher self or a life force as a Higher Power. Some found a spiritual path based on Buddhism. But the bottom line was that we realized we wouldn't be able to figure this out alone. We needed help. We embraced the slogan "I can't, but we can." We realized that the consciousness that was creating our problem couldn't solve it.

As my dear friend, author, and colleague Herb Kaighan notes about Stage I, "We begin to thaw out." We become more honest with ourselves. We start to see things much more clearly as our brain begins to heal and recover some of the capacity it lost when we were actively drinking or using.

Larsen realized this clarity came at a price: "It is never very pleasant to see what we have done and become while we were in the bondage of our addiction. Enormous guilt, however, may accompany that insight and in response to that guilt we may lose so much self-esteem that we also lose any ability to be good to ourselves" (1985, 9–10). This guilt can create a serious obstacle to recovery. How can we feel worthy of the gift of recovery?

One benefit of accepting that we suffer from the disease of addiction is that we may be able to give ourselves a break. We can stop hating and blaming ourselves for all of the things we have done that we deeply regret. There's a great saying in Narcotics Anonymous, "Our disease is not our fault, but recovery is our responsibility." Accepting that we suffer from a medical disease may open the door just enough to free ourselves from self-blame and self-recrimination.

It's also important that we be convinced that we deserve a chance to rebuild our lives. We don't deserve it in the sense that we have earned it. Quite the contrary, many people in recovery are grateful they didn't get what they deserve, as that might have been awful! We deserve a chance at recovery in the sense that we have as much right to get well as anyone else.

This begins the process of developing a new relationship with ourselves. We cast aside our old toxic ideas of who we are for a new set of ideas that are self-affirming and nourishing. We move toward self-acceptance and self-support. We begin to embrace the notion that we have made mistakes but that we aren't a mistake. We are in a process of recovering our lost, true selves—the part that had been hijacked by that body snatcher, our addict self. A new way of being emerges as we begin to trudge the road to recovery.

We set the foundation for our recovery by breaking free from our addict self. But Larsen understood, both personally and professionally, that this was just the beginning of the journey. This is where Stage II Recovery comes into play.

Stage II Recovery

Stage II Recovery is concerned with learning how to function in a healthy and loving relationship. This takes a lot of work, and here, too, a price must be paid. We have to dig deep to face who we aren't in order to become who we can be. We have to find the courage to endure emotional discomfort and pain to increase our capacity to function better.

If we don't change how we show up in our relationships, then nothing will change. We will continue doing the same old dance; we hope that our partners will learn new steps that make things better between us or we simply throw in the towel and give up on our relationship. We may try finding new partners as a way to change ourselves, but we will inevitably find that if we don't change, nothing will change.

Larsen went on to say that this stage of recovery is about "getting on with life by facing those patterns, habits, and attitudes that control your life and which, for perhaps the first time, you are clear-headed, sober, or emotionally sound enough to face" (1987, 11–12).

In this second phase of our recovery, we become aware of our habitual ways of thinking and feeling, we challenge our attitudes to see if they are toxic or nourishing, and we keep an eye out for unhealthy patterns that recur in our life.

For Larsen, a healthy and loving relationship requires that "each party comes to it with adequate self-esteem. . . . Each person must have a solid sense of his or her self apart from the other, so that each can lean without becoming dependent and have differences of opinion that don't lead to win-lose situations" (1987, 14).

We call the kind of love that Larsen referred to adult love or mature love. This kind of love requires emotional maturity and therefore it requires emotional sobriety.

Larsen's vision of what it takes to have a healthy and loving relationship is, as you will see, a description of a person who has achieved emotional sobriety. Stage II Recovery is dependent on achieving emotional sobriety. Emotional sobriety, however, is more than a "stage" of recovery. It is a shift in our consciousness that changes how we function in the world. As with Stage II Recovery, emotional sobriety (or its lack) is very obvious in the "grind" of our partner relationships. But it applies to all of our interactions. Let us now turn our attention to a more in-depth definition of emotional sobriety.

Defining Emotional Sobriety

At the opening of this chapter, I provided a simple definition of emotional sobriety. Let's get back to the definition and expand it. I think you'll see that emotional sobriety promises a better life for you.

> Emotional sobriety is a mental state in which we no longer react to our changing emotions as though they were the governing facts of our lives. This mental state is made possible by the emotional and spiritual maturity that come with humility. In this state, we have an appropriate balance and coordination of all that we are.

Just as alcohol or drug sobriety emerges when we gain independence from our addictive urges, emotional sobriety emerges as we gain freedom from our emotional dependency. We cooperate with integrity, maintain our autonomy in relationships, and let the best in us run the rest of us. Emotional sobriety develops when we accept life on its terms rather than demanding that life (people and situations) conform to our expectations. When we do this, we gain emotional freedom, a true independence of spirit in which our innermost or truest self is the determining force in our lives.

As we achieve emotional sobriety, we discard our old ideas, the conceptualizations of how life is supposed to be, how we are supposed to be, how others are supposed to feel and act. We replace them with a new set of ideas, attitudes, and behaviors that increase our capacity to deal with life, on life's terms.

Emotional sobriety allows us to cast aside toxic expectations that demand life should conform to our specifications and replace them with new conceptualizations and motives that are life-affirming instead of controlling and life denying. This transformation is grounded in a way of life that promotes self-awareness, acceptance, alignment with reality, integrity, empathy, compassion, adult love, authenticity, creativity, self-support, forgiveness, and service.

These new ideas and attitudes create a true independence of spirit. We become autonomous in the way we relate to others, which means we are not overly influenced by our emotions, by what someone wants, by what someone does or says, or by what happens. We hold on to ourselves and maintain our sense of self.

Emotional sobriety results in an appropriate balance and coordination of all that we are. This means we harmonize the discordant parts of ourselves so that they can become joint contributors to our life. It is when the best in us runs the rest of us and when the best in us relates to the best in others.

Emotional sobriety helps us balance our desire for togetherness with our desire for separateness. We do not give unwillingly, nor do we take that which is not given with an open hand. We protect our integrity and encourage others to honor theirs.

> We discover that a healthy relationship is not based on some ideal of what a loving relationship should be like but rather is shaped by who we are as individuals.

Emotional sobriety emerges as we commit to creating healthy relationships and to learning to authentically love another person. We discover that a healthy relationship is not based on some ideal of what a loving relationship should be like but rather is shaped by who we are as individuals. We strive to have a mature love that is characterized by union with the preservation of integrity and individuality. We come to understand that love is neither a plan nor a commitment but rather a result of who we are with each other.

As we achieve emotional sobriety, we strive to respect differences, to enjoy a togetherness that welcomes separation, and to cooperate with integrity.

Emotional sobriety is achieved whenever what we do becomes the determining force in our emotional well-being and happiness. We claim our experiences, rather than letting them claim us.

Emotional sobriety is full recovery. As I love to say, "It doesn't get any better than this, baby."

•••

The twelve essential insights we explore in the following chapters will open some doors and illuminate a path to emotional sobriety. But before we can realize our potential through our practice of emotional sobriety, we need to become more aware of the forces that keep us stuck and emotionally immature. This is a critical step in our growth, but it is a difficult step because it involves seeing who we are not.

The paradoxical law of change states that personal growth occurs when we own who we are, not when we try to be someone we are not. Our ego, our false pride, our false self, our addict self — all conspire to hide the truth from us. But deep down inside we each have a very powerful ally. We possess an inner wisdom to be what we can be. This is the growth force that moves us toward physical, emotional, and spiritual wholeness.

You know this force because you've experienced it. It drove you to want to walk instead of being satisfied with crawling. It drove you to learn to speak instead of being satisfied with babbling. It drove you to wake up to a better life when you started your recovery. So have faith in yourself. The force is always deep within. Your job is to trust it. This is what is meant in Twelve Step groups when we say, "Trust the process."

So let's turn to the first essential insight for emotional sobriety, waking up from our sleepwalking.

Chapter 3: Waking Up from Our Sleepwalking

Harold entered my office wearing standard-issue business professional attire. He had a newly pressed and heavily starched white shirt, a J. Crew blue tie, a smartly matched sport jacket, gray wool trousers, and freshly shined Johnston and Murphy Oxford shoes. Every strand of hair on his head was in its proper place. I don't recall if I have ever seen someone seated so stiffly on my couch.

To say Harold was formal would be an understatement; his demeanor was as rigid as his shirt. I wondered if there was a person inside this automaton of a man.

He started the session in a curious way: "Dr. Berger, I'm not certain why I am here. You see, I don't know what is wrong with me." He adjusted his tie and continued, "On paper I have everything I've ever wanted. I am exceptionally successful in my career. I have a beautiful house overlooking the Pacific Ocean in Palos Verdes. I have a very loyal wife who has been sober for almost five years, and we've raised three great children. I have four years of sobriety, but something isn't right. I am unhappy and it baffles me. I just can't figure this out. I've worked the Steps with my sponsor, I attend meetings on a regular basis, I start the day with a reading from *One Day at a Time*, and I am still dissatisfied. Do you think I am asking for too much and that I should just be grateful for what I have?"

Oftentimes what is obvious to outsiders is not so obvious to us. This was the case with Harold. It was clear that he was lost inside the personality he had constructed. His personality was a kind of prison rather than an expression of his true spirit, but he was blind to the cell he'd built. He was confined by his pervasive lack of self-awareness.

> ## Oftentimes what is obvious to outsiders is not so obvious to us.

I asked Harold to tell me what he was experiencing in my office. He went on and on about his personal philosophy of life and his accomplishments. He regurgitated words he'd read in the Big Book, words we've all heard in Twelve Step meetings, and various platitudes he'd picked up through meditation books. But not once did he touch on what he was experiencing—what he was feeling—as he sat with me. So, I asked again, "Harold, what are you experiencing?"

He looked at me like I was speaking a foreign language. With all the sincerity available to him, he replied, "What do you mean?"

Sometimes a person will avoid answering a question because it is too painful or difficult to address. But this wasn't the case with Harold. He was dead serious. He had no idea what I was asking him to do. He could not describe his experience in my office, nor could he identify the feelings that arose within him.

Harold was out of touch with himself. He lived his life from the shoulders up. He could go on and on about his thoughts and philosophize about recovery or even the state of the economy, but when it came to talking about himself in a more intimate or personal way, he fell mute.

He was unaware of what he was feeling, of what was happening inside his body, of what it was like for him as he turned to me for help. He was unable to find the words that would describe his personal experience because he was desensitized to what he was feeling. He was desensitized to himself. One could almost say that I, a stranger, already knew more about Harold than Harold himself knew. Why?

Harold was asleep, believing that he was awake. He was sleepwalking!

Most of Us Are Sleeping!

Harold isn't alone in this problem. To some degree, all of us are sleepwalking through our days. The famous Russian philosopher George Gurdjieff wrote, "In order to awaken, first of all one must realize that one is in a state of sleep," often paraphrased as we are asleep, thinking we are awake. The rest of Gurdjieff's quote is helpful, too: "To realize that one is indeed in a state of sleep, one must recognize and fully understand the nature of the forces which operate to keep one in the state of sleep, or hypnosis. It is absurd to think that this can be done by seeking information from the very source which induces the hypnosis" (Goodreads n.d.).

Like Harold, we too are asleep. Like the sleepwalker who moves about the house and appears to be awake, we are living in a dream world, although we believe ourselves to be awake. We live our lives driven by internal forces, and we're generally unaware of them. As Gurdjieff suggested, if we wish to wake up, we have to understand these forces. Why have we put ourselves to sleep, and how did we do it? What originally drove us to tuck ourselves into bed and live life as though we were in a state of sleep?

There are many powerful forces at work in our lives in relation to our personal development, but some of the most significant ones are the desires

> to be loved,
> to be accepted, and
> to feel that we belong.

Take a moment to think about the importance of those desires in your current life. Can you feel their pull even now? Do you want someone to love you so much that you make changes to be lovable? Do you want others to accept you so much that you do things to "fit in"? Do you so desire to feel you belong to the world that you conform to expectations that feel uncomfortable? These three basic human needs are as important as the need for food, warmth, and shelter. If you have even a smidgen of self-awareness, you will see that even today you do many things in your life to satisfy these needs.

Children feel these needs even more intensely than we adults. Remember, they are much more vulnerable. They are small creatures living among giants! Unlike adults, children lack the awareness and coping skills to moderate the impact of these needs on their behavior. They feel the risk of not being lovable, acceptable, or belonging as an immediate threat to their survival, and they lack the psychic tools to separate that threat from who they are. The threat creates a basic anxiety at a vulnerable stage of personality development.

I cannot emphasize enough the power inherent in this anxiety. It becomes a central organizing force in our early development. You see, the anxiety that we won't be loved, that we won't be accepted, that we won't belong is so disturbing and intolerable that we must find a solution to it. We have to resolve it to ensure our existence.[2] Dr. Karen Horney called this drive to resolve our anxiety "the search for glory."

This basic anxiety was created by the erroneous belief that we needed to become someone else to be secure as a person. That is, we decided, somehow, that we weren't "right" or deserving of love and acceptance unless we changed who we were. We imagined an idealized self, better than who we were, that would always feel secure, always be liked, always feel loved, and always feel welcomed. The process of adopting this idealized self resulted in us rejecting our true self, our real self. We actualized a concept of who we should be. This was the result of our search for glory: We identified a solution, a kind of blueprint for how we should look and act in the world, to relieve the anxiety we felt. We then began to construct a public personality based on that blueprint.

The idealized self is our blueprint of a personal fantasy of how we should be, how we should look, how we should behave, how we should think and feel. It also includes the various self-imposed rules and goals we believe we should live up to. These *should demands* take over our lives. (A should demand is any one of thousands of things we tell ourselves are necessary for us to do in order to be deserving of love, acceptance, and belonging.) Common should demands among American adults include the expectations that we should be desirable, married, productive, wealthy, smart, athletic, materially successful, conforming, popular, well-groomed, religious, respected, heterosexual, gender-conforming, etc. Look at your to-do list for the day. It likely involves a number of should demands!

Should demands become a tyranny. And as with any tyranny, opposition is silenced, put to sleep. We oppress any part of us

---

2 Though this basic anxiety seems negative, it has a positive side; it activates the force inherent in us to actualize what is possible, to find a creative adaptation that ensures our existence in the most challenging of situations.

that doesn't fit with the design of our idealized self. We should on ourselves over and over again. We become directed by the should demands. The shoulds rule our lives, and over time we lose the capacity to be the determining force in our own lives. We live for what we imagine other people want of us rather than what we want. This is the origin of our sleepwalking.

Here is where the real trouble began for us—a trouble that over time made our lives unmanageable. This trouble began when we were children. We grew a false self to ensure we were going to be loved, to be accepted, and to belong. We put all our energies into becoming someone we weren't in order to feel secure. But this was like building a foundation for a house on someone else's property. It's not our own. It's not who we really are.

> We grew a false self to ensure we were going to be loved, to be accepted, and to belong. We put all our energies into becoming someone we weren't in order to feel secure. But this was like building a foundation for a house on someone else's property. It's not our own. It's not who we really are.

Do you get a sense of who Harold had to become in order to be secure? It was clear to me in the first session that he had to be successful to be okay. He was driven to be the best, to be perfect, to win, to be superior.

The approach he adopted to soothing his basic anxiety was found in embracing what Horney called the expansive solution.

This is one of three primary solutions people select when building a false self. (The other two, which I'll discuss in a moment, are the self-effacing solution and the resignation solution.) The underlying assumption to the expansive solution is "I need to master everything and everyone to be okay. I must be top dog. I must be perfect. I must win all the time."

Horney described this person as "bent on self-glorification, on ambitious pursuits, on vindictive triumph, with the mastery of life through intelligence and will power as the means to actualize their idealized self" (1991, 192).

This is what created the dilemma Harold presented in our first session. He was struggling with facing who he was not—that is, he really wasn't that victorious individual; there was something else inside. Something was wrong, but he couldn't identify it.

Because his solution was based on self-glorification, it left no room for him to have self-doubts, insecurities, feelings of inadequacy, personal problems, or self-contempt. Harold had to disregard any desires or emotions that would threaten this solution. He had to be okay even when he wasn't.

He desensitized himself to any feelings or parts of himself that did not fit with his solution. Another way of saying this is he had to put these genuine parts of himself to sleep in order to play a role that was not supported by, and also in conflict with, his genuine needs. He cut himself off from his true self.

Harold walked, talked, and dressed impeccably; he accomplished many things; and he was considered a success by many. And yet, it was as though he was occupied by someone else. Well—he was! He had put to sleep the other parts of Harold that were flawed, frightened, sloppy, sentimental, carefree, emotional, curious, and ultimately honest. So successfully had he tucked his "unfit parts" into bed that Harold couldn't even remember what they were, let alone wake them up. He couldn't even tell me what he was experiencing as he tried to figure out what he was doing in my office.

The authentic Harold was asleep. The false Harold thought he was the real Harold. That is what we mean when we say, "We were asleep, thinking we were awake." This is sleepwalking!

Themes Underlying the False Self

Like Harold, most of us have tucked our true self under a blanket. Perhaps we're not as fast asleep as Harold, but still, every human on the planet experiences some true-self slumber. Earlier I mentioned Dr. Karen Horney, a brilliant psychotherapist who described the search for glory and Harold's choice, the expansive solution. Horney dug deep into the nature of why and how we tuck away our true self.

Remember, the goal for our solution to our childhood anxiety was to ensure that we would be loved, be accepted, and belong. This meant we had to construct an idealized self with the qualities, traits, values, and characteristics that would support and bring to life our selected blueprint. Any part of our real self that would fit into this blueprint was welcomed and fostered. But there was a different fate for the parts of us that didn't fit with the idealized self. The parts of us that were at odds with who we were supposed to be were rejected. Like a tyrant, we oppressed the parts that did not fit our design. We kept them locked up, hidden, and repressed and only let them emerge when we saw them, sometimes mistakenly, in others. (In fact, we often project our repressed parts on others. Projection occurs when we attribute unwanted traits of ourselves to another person. For example, a bully, having repressed any personal weakness, may see another person's acts of compassion as weakness. A martyr, having repressed selfish feelings, may see another person's self-interest as selfishness rather than self-assertion.)

This was an unconscious process. We weren't aware that we were desensitizing ourselves. Our lack of awareness created the sleeplike state referred to by Gurdjieff.

Sleepwalking Harold was out of touch with his feelings of self-doubt, unhappiness, failure, and helplessness. He feared being inadequate, incompetent, or unsuccessful. His natural self-confidence, on the other hand, was welcomed and integrated into his personality, as were his pride, intelligence, competence, and competitiveness. Any other trait was shunned, exiled, and disowned.

Dr. Alexander Lowen, the father of bioenergetics, gave us a great insight into what happens when we don't deal with our childhood experiences, including our traumas. He stated that when someone "has experienced a loss or trauma in childhood that undermines his feelings of security and self-acceptance, he would project into his image of the future the requirement that it reverse the experiences of his past" (1975, 178). I believe he is saying that we choose a solution or blueprint for our idealized self that will reverse the experiences of our past.

If we weren't loved, we are going to choose the blueprint that will construct a false self that, we hope, will ensure we are loved. Thus, the engineered self is based on the appeal of love. How do we ensure we are going to be loved? We imagine someone will love us if we meet the person's every need. This is what we wanted, so of course this is what someone else would value. And like us, if we got the love we wanted, we would be forever loyal and loving toward this person.

Hiding our true self to become the person we deem lovable is one solution to the anxiety we endured as children, but there are other ways of disowning the true self. Earlier I noted that Horney described three themes for the blueprints of the idealized self. She called this solution—erasing ourselves because the path to being loved is to be whatever the other person needs—the self-effacing solution. We believe that if we meet someone's every need, that person will love us. But this also means we need to deny our own needs. We must erase ourselves to pull this off. Essentially, we are saying to the world, "Your needs are more important than mine, and I will do everything in my power to make you happy and to meet all of your needs. I will always subordinate my needs to yours."

If, as children, we somehow perceived messages that our parents' or caregivers' love is conditioned on pleasing them, we are likely to adopt the self-effacing solution to ease our anxiety. We repress those parts of our true self that don't conform to behaviors our caregivers reward with conditional love and approval, and we integrate those parts that do conform. We attempt to reverse the experience of our past (the withholding of unconditional love) by putting first the needs of whomever we select as a partner.

If the message we received was that we were stupid or that we were a loser, then the expansive solution would entice us. As I noted earlier, this is what happened to Harold. His father was both physically and verbally abusive. He would humiliate Harold in front of his father's friends and announce to them how he couldn't believe he had such a stupid kid.

When Harold made a mistake, his father reacted as though the mistake were catastrophic. He made Harold feel like he was not only stupid but incompetent. Harold longed for praise and love and believed the path to this was through mastery, through winning, by being better than everyone else. Thus, Harold wanted people to adore him, admire him, and respect him. He wanted to reverse the experience of his past. Harold had to succeed at everything, look and behave perfectly, and never act in any way that might risk humiliation, all to resolve the anxiety he felt: that belonging, being loved, and being accepted were conditioned on a kind of success that would satisfy his father.

If we were neglected, with some criticism sprinkled in periodically, then we would be enticed by feeling free from emotions. We don't want to feel. To obtain freedom from our pain, from our inner conflicts, from our anxiety or depression, we give up. We resign. This is what Horney described as the resignation solution. Freedom in this context is created by throwing in the towel. We give up on life, on our self. We become the proverbial underachiever. We bury ambition, desire, and striving of any kind. We shut down our personal desires so we won't come into conflict with our true self or with the world. We become needless and want-less.

•••

So, we have three basic blueprints or solutions for our childhood anxiety: the self-effacing solution (behave like a martyr), the expansive solution (behave like a victor), and the resignation solution (behave like nothing's important and nothing bothers you).

We have three basic blueprints or solutions for our childhood anxiety: the self-effacing solution (behave like a martyr), the expansive solution (behave like a victor), and the resignation solution (behave like nothing's important and nothing bothers you).

Think for a moment about these blueprints. Do you see how they are like the common stereotypes we have for people—saints, winners, and losers? Mother Teresas, James Bonds, and drunken bums/class clowns? In life, very few people fit just one of these blueprints. Most of us have a dominant solution (like Harold), but other solutions emerge at times too. Can you see how people you know live out shades of these solutions—perhaps not as black and white as these but nevertheless with some variation? What solution do you favor?

Remember, in embracing these blueprints we are trying to reverse the experiences we had in our past. Needless to say, this process generates a ton of expectations regarding other people, ourselves, and even life itself.

World-renowned psychotherapist Dr. Frederick (Fritz) Perls summarized the effects of adopting one of these three solutions: "When the individual attempts to live according to preconceived ideas of what the world 'should' be like, he brackets off his own feelings and needs. The result of this alienation from one's senses is the blocking off of his potential and the distortion of his perspective" (1975a, 2).

Each of these three solutions is a form of sleepwalking. Inside that saint is a person who wants to be loved exactly as he or she is, not because of what he or she gives up to be loved. Inside the perfect saleswoman is a person who is terrified she will not belong if she doesn't constantly prove herself to be the very best. Inside that meek staffer cracking bad jokes all day at the water cooler and offloading his work to others is a person who decided that feeling his real feelings of fear, anger, unworthiness, loneliness, or failure was not worth the risk, that he simply was unlovable no matter what.

The true person inside each of these individuals is in such deep slumber that the false person assumes it is the only show in town. Our false self may be completely unaware of the deep needs of the sleeping true self.

Who sleeps inside you? How have these internal forces shaped your recovery?

Realizing We Are Asleep, Beginning to Wake

Perls understood that the process of waking up is not easy. He wrote, "To suffer one's death and to be reborn is not easy" (1969, epigraph). Whatever form of sleep we've chosen, we've relied on this blueprint for our security, even though it came at a huge price. We lost our true self and we lost self-awareness. To achieve emotional sobriety, we need to shatter our reliance on our false self.

The consciousness that flows from our false self cannot help us create emotional sobriety. How can it? The false self seeks only to soothe our anxiety. We will continue to follow the same blueprints. We cannot solve our problems by repeating the same attempts that failed in the past. Painful as it is, we need to begin addressing the real needs of our true self. (This, by the way, is probably what the final part of Gurdjieff's quote meant: "It is absurd to think that this [waking up] can be done by seeking information from the very source which induces the hypnosis.")

As we progressed in recovery from addiction, a curiosity emerged. We began to pay attention to ourselves instead of avoiding ourselves. We practiced self-examination through personal inventories and began to get honest with ourselves. Self-honesty is the cornerstone of emotional sobriety. As Bill Wilson stated when discussing Step Ten, "It is a spiritual axiom that every time we are disturbed, no matter what the cause, there is something wrong with us" (Alcoholics Anonymous World Services 1981, 90). We become curious to discover what is wrong with us. We engage ourselves in the all-important journey of self-discovery.

I like to say, "Only the best in us can see the worst in us." Let me break that down for you in this context. Only the best in us (the consciousness that flows from our true self) can see the worst in us (the tragedy of our sleeping state). When this happens, then the best in us begins to run the rest of us in recovery. Self-awareness is curative. It helps us recover our lost true self and helps us begin the forever journey of becoming what we can be.

As Harold's self-awareness was recovered in therapy and through working his program, he began to stir. He began to see the prison he had constructed for himself. Instead of being in control, as he had deluded himself into believing, he realized that he was controlled by his idealized robotic self and its demands. He discovered he was not the determining force in his life, and as he started to see this, he began to wake up. He started owning the feelings and thoughts that had been taboo. He was taking steps to awaken his true self, and this meant he was grappling with the reality that he had been sleepwalking for much of his life.

Harold's awakening created conflict between his idealized self and his real self. For example, he began to see that his need to win, look great, and be perfect was not authentic. He saw that he'd devoted huge amounts of energy to doing things that satisfied his blueprint as a winner, but they didn't satisfy the desires of (in fact, were often at odds with) the "real Harold." As we worked on the issues that created these conflicts, his potential self began to be revealed. He began to integrate the parts of his idealized self that were useful to who he wanted to be and to let go of the other parts of himself that weren't working in his life, parts like, for example, needing to win and be right all the time.

He became less perfectionistic and began to rigorously and authentically work Step Ten—to take an on-the-spot personal inventory and when he was wrong to promptly admit it. This was a huge shift in the way Harold functioned. Remember, Harold's false self could never be wrong. To be wrong was a real danger, since it meant he would not be loved, be accepted, or belong. Step Ten was a therapeutic response to the problem created by his false self. As he practiced it, he became more fulfilled and alive. He achieved emotional sobriety. His relationships improved, including his marriage, which had been on the rocks.

I saw Harold recently after a gap of many years, and he reported to me that the past years of his marriage were incredible, a big shift from what it had been. What a surprise, to find out that the very things that he feared would make him unworthy of love actually enabled a greater intimacy! He now enjoys more than twenty-one years of recovery.

Sentence Completion Exercise

We all need to wake up. To become more self-aware. How? We wake up by unpacking the information inherent in experiences of trouble. Whenever something disturbs us emotionally, no matter the cause, there is something in us that needs tending. We need to stop blaming ourselves and others and instead approach ourselves with curiosity. More on this later. For now, I want to focus on helping you wake up.

At the end of each of the following chapters, I provide you with a sentence completion exercise to help facilitate and promote your self-awareness. Here's what I'd like you to do. Take each sentence stem and write it at the top of a piece of paper.

Next, repeat it silently (or aloud) to yourself, and then complete the sentence stem with the first thought that comes to mind. Do six to ten completions for each. There are no right or wrong answers. The point in this is for you to become more aware of yourself. Emotional sobriety depends on self-awareness.

Here we go:

> I should _____.
>
> The trouble I've experienced in my life is trying to tell me _____.
>
> The voice, deep inside, of my true self is trying to tell me _____.
>
> The idea of myself that I have to give up in order to be more self-accepting is _____.
>
> The parts of me that I have trouble accepting are _____.
>
> What I do to be loved is _____.
>
> What I do to be accepted is _____.
>
> What I do to belong is _____.
>
> I see my blueprint for the solution to my basic anxiety about life when I _____.

Self-awareness is critical to achieving emotional sobriety. The next chapter explores the importance of living life consciously—that is, how self-awareness contributes to emotional sobriety.

Chapter 4: Living Life Consciously

Recovery is the process of getting back something that was lost.

This raises the question, "What did we lose?" We have lost the capacity to focus our awareness on what is happening right now, in the present moment. This is a serious problem. Consciousness is our basic tool for living a meaningful and happy life. Our awareness is the facet of our consciousness we use to make contact with reality, to sense our own needs and desires, to empathize with the needs of others, and to assess the demands of life. Awareness is essential for regulating ourselves, for keeping our emotional center of gravity over our true self, for self-care, for keeping ourselves safe, for having a healthy relationship, and for living with integrity.

Our awareness was lost when we put ourselves to sleep. We pay a high price for dimming our awareness. Dr. Nathaniel Branden, an expert in the psychology of self-esteem, understood this well. He wrote, "If we do not bring an appropriate level of consciousness to our activities, if we do not live mindfully, the inevitable penalty is a diminished sense of self-efficacy and self-respect" (1994, 68).

Addiction distorted our awareness. Our addiction didn't

want us to see that we were lost, that we had been hijacked and were being held prisoner. Our distorted awareness enabled us to persist in our addictive behaviors.

Our awareness was also diminished much earlier in life, during the construction of our false self. The false-self blueprint compromised and shaped our consciousness to fit with our idealized self. It dictated what we should and shouldn't think, what we should and shouldn't feel, what was okay and not okay to be aware of, and how we should and shouldn't behave. It filtered and distorted reality and kept us from processing appropriate feedback from our experiences. We brought this false self into adulthood. Here are some of the underlying issues that may arise when we live with a diminished and distorted level of awareness:

> I know I am not giving my best to my family, but I don't want to look honestly at my neglect.
>
> I don't need to work all of the Steps because I am sober today, and that is good enough.
>
> I know there are signs that my relationship with my partner is failing, but I don't want to think about it.
>
> I know my children suffer from too little access to me, but I am doing the best I can.
>
> I know I am causing hurt and resentment, but one day I'll change.
>
> I know I am self-destructive, but I can't cope with facing what this means.
>
> I know I am a phony and lie about my accomplishments, but I don't want to admit this to myself.
>
> I think to myself; I am sober. What more do you want from me?
>
> The past is the past. I don't need to address the pain and traumas I experienced—it's best to let sleeping dogs lie.

I know I am not living the life I want to live, but I won't face it.

I don't do what I want to do, and I do what I don't want to.

These examples reveal a disconnect between our better selves and our behavior. They show how we betray ourselves when consciousness is not translated into appropriate action. It is as though we are telling ourselves we are not capable, not worthy of the effort, or likely to fail if we do try. When we tell ourselves this, we invalidate and erase our true self. This creates many self-limiting concepts and beliefs.

We are much more capable than we give ourselves credit for. I have witnessed thousands of people face issues they've been avoiding their whole lives. They fantasize that they will fall apart or have a nervous breakdown, but they don't. They thrive. They empower themselves.

We take the first step toward achieving emotional sobriety when we rouse ourselves from sleepwalking. We realize we've been asleep, believing we were awake. This experience is critical to our recovery because it begins an important change in our consciousness. It cracks us open like an egg on the edge of an omelet pan. Just like an egg, when we split open, out pours our nourishment. The essence that pours out of us when we crack open is awareness.

> As we arise from our sleep, we awaken many different parts of ourselves that we had put into hibernation.

As we arise from our sleep, we awaken many different parts of ourselves that we had put into hibernation. We awaken hope that we can create a better life. We awaken desire—to be what we can be. We awaken our integrity, the instinct to be sincere with ourselves. And we awaken our awareness.

Living consciously means more than seeing and knowing. It means integrating and acting on what we see and come to know. It means using our awareness to let the best in us run the rest of us.

Awareness is critical to our recovery, just as it is critical to having a well-lived life.

I'd like you to meet Shareen. When I met her, she was purposely not living consciously. Let us see how she uses her awareness to break a chronic relapse cycle.

Shareen's Recovery Journey

Shareen was thirty-four years old when we met. What stood out about her in our first conversation was that she had given up on recovery and on herself. She had thrown in the towel. She didn't believe that recovery could ever be a real possibility for her.

For the past four years, she had been drunk more than sober, despite being in three inpatient treatment programs, working with four different individual therapists, five different AA sponsors, two psychiatrists, and four different couples counselors. Her husband coordinated the current intervention as a final attempt, a "last-gasp effort" as he called it, at getting her help. He was at his wits' end.

She was admitted to our inpatient program after the intervention. Alcoholism had physically and cognitively ravaged this once healthy young woman. She looked much older than her age and was unmotivated, cognitively dull, and quite angry. She just wanted everyone to leave her alone.

Shareen didn't hesitate to tell me treatment hadn't worked, never worked, nothing had—none of the therapists, the sponsors, the meetings, or the psychiatrists had made a difference. Nothing helped her. (She said this all with a hint of pride, which I found quite unusual.)

When I asked her what she understood about her difficulty in sustaining abstinence, her response was revealing: "I feel worse when I am not drinking than when I'm drinking. And nobody has been able to help me with that."

I am quite certain that Shareen didn't realize the significance of this statement, but I did. She was unaware of what her words meant because she had dialed down her self-awareness dimmer switch. Oftentimes we don't listen to ourselves; we can't hear what we are saying if we have muted our self-awareness. We won't be able to grasp or sense the significance of what we have said if we are unaware of what it means for us. Needless to say, this would interfere with healthy functioning.

I pondered the following question: "What was this young lady experiencing that made being sober so intolerable?" I knew that the answer to this question was going to be critical for her recovery, but I also had the sense that Shareen didn't want to know what was missing in her life that made her so miserable. She was asleep, thinking she was awake, and she wanted to continue sleepwalking to avoid dealing with what she really wanted, as we will see. She did not want to live consciously.

The Therapeutic Value of Self-Awareness

Self-awareness is critical for healthy functioning. If we are aware of what we want, what we'd like, and what we need, we can take care of ourselves; we can be responsible and interact with our environment to satisfy our needs.

This is called self-support, meaning we take responsibility for what we want and what we would like. We don't manipulate our environment to fulfill our needs; rather, we make the appropriate contact with our environment to fulfill our own needs. This is what makes self-awareness so important in recovery. Awareness helps us move our emotional center of gravity back over our own feet.

Dr. Fritz Perls, a master therapist and cofounder of Gestalt therapy, believed in the therapeutic value of full awareness. He stated, "Awareness per se—by and of itself—can be curative. Because with full awareness you become aware of this organismic self-regulation, you can let the organism take over without interfering, without interrupting; we can rely on the wisdom of the organism. And the contrast to this is the whole pathology of self-manipulation, environmental control, and so on, that interferes with this subtle organismic self-control" (1969, 16–17).

Let's unpack this quote. When we bring full awareness to what we are doing and how we are doing it, we become aware of how we get in our own way. We all get in our own way, which means we interfere with our healthy functioning. Awareness helps us experience how we interrupt or interfere with our healthy functioning. Awareness of our self-sabotage is important information, since it allows us to correct our course.

We, our organisms, are a system that strives to be in balance. When we are out of balance, we mobilize ourselves to correct the imbalance. For example, if I am hungry (out of balance), I eat some food (balance is restored). If I am too hot (out of balance), I start sweating to cool off (balance is restored). If I am lonely (out of balance), I reach out to a friend or partner (balance is restored). We are wired to respond to our emerging most urgent need (out of balance) and to satisfy it (balance restored).

But if the action that would restore our balance is taboo, meaning we shouldn't behave that way, we typically betray ourselves and honor the "should." We will sell ourselves out to cooperate with the tyranny of our should in order to be "a good boy" or "a good girl."

Saving face—preserving the mask that is the outward expression of our false self—becomes more important than saving our life. We fail our responsibility to ourselves.

By owning what we are doing and how we are doing it, we create a new possibility. If, for instance, I am sabotaging myself by listening to my addict self, which is pressuring me to use (out of balance), then the moment I own the truth that I am allowing myself to be pressured, something new becomes possible—I try disagreeing with or disobeying the addict self and feel good about it (restoration of balance).

But if we interfere with this organismic wisdom that would move us toward completion, we become dependent on our environment to take care of us, to do for us what we are not doing for ourselves. We abdicate our personal responsibility and deflect or transfer that responsibility onto others. We become emotionally dependent. Our well-being is now in the hands of others.

This is what Shareen did when she married Butch.

Shareen Struggles to Own Her Truth

Shareen and Butch had been married for ten years by the time I met her. She met Butch when she was a hostess at a high-end steak house. He was a very successful investment banker. They had a short and shaky courtship. She matter-of-factly told me she never fell in love with him, but she had enjoyed dating him. He was "a nice-enough guy," she said. Back when she met Butch, Shareen had recently extracted herself from a horrible relationship and so found Butch to be a breath of fresh air.

Shortly after they started dating, they spent a week partying in Las Vegas. She remembers saying to herself on their way back to Los Angeles, "I think I am pregnant."

A month later, when she didn't get her period, she knew she was right. A pregnancy test confirmed her intuition. Abortion wasn't an option for this Catholic young woman. Butch, being a nice guy, stepped up and convinced her they should get married. She agreed but secretly questioned the wisdom of this decision. Many people get married for the wrong reasons. This doesn't mean they can't stay married for the right reasons (once they figure them out). However, that takes a lot of counseling, which can't take place when someone is in the throes of alcoholism.

Butch had a different experience. He was crazy about Shareen from the start, and when she delivered their beautiful daughter, Eva, he knew he had made the right decision. He was thrilled, and he believed that Shareen was feeling the same way.

Unfortunately, Butch was wrong. She wasn't feeling the same way at all. Shareen felt trapped in the marriage and trapped being a mother. But she kept these feelings a secret. Even though she didn't tell anyone what she was feeling, her feelings showed up in her ambivalent attachment to her daughter. She both loved and resented Eva. Because of her ambivalence about being a wife and being a mom, she felt ashamed of herself, like she was a terrible person. Getting drunk while taking care of Eva also added to her self-hate. The pain from her guilt and shame was unbearable. Drinking was the only way she knew to numb this emotional distress and help her forget about the dilemma she found herself in. She wouldn't dare admit this to anyone.

What stood out about Shareen was the way she presented herself. She was along for the ride. Life happened to her; she didn't make it happen. She was a lost child, wandering through life hoping she'd stumble across something that would give her life meaning.

She was confused when her experience of being a mother or being a wife didn't fix things for her. A part of her hoped it would. It seemed to be the solution for so many of her friends. She berated herself for this too. What kind of an ingrate was she that she couldn't appreciate all that she had? She hated herself for being in the situation where she felt trapped and hated herself for being an alcoholic. She lived with a deadly unconscious injunction: "Don't think or feel, just drink."

Do you get a sense of what was missing in the way that Shareen approached her life? Can you identify the attitudes and beliefs that made it impossible for her to sustain sobriety? Did Shareen adopt the expansive solution, the self-effacing solution, or the attitude of resignation for a solution to her basic anxiety?

If you concluded that she had resigned, you were right. Sometime in her distant past, Shareen had given up and tried to make herself want-less and needless, which resulted in her being cast around in life like a cork in stormy seas. Shareen had to grow up to support her recovery, and that was a tall order for this woman. Why? Because in order to grow up, she was going to need to let herself want again. She was going to need to rescind her letter of resignation and begin showing up in her life.

But before she could start to find out what she wanted, Shareen had to take a beginning step. Shareen had to become aware of what she was doing to be able to open up the possibility of doing something different. The choice to live consciously would be an important step toward recovering herself. To mature, she had to use her awareness to discover unused potential and resources.

> Remember, recovery involves the discovery of new possibilities.

Remember, recovery involves the discovery of new possibilities. This is what had to happen for Shareen. It's what has to happen for all of us. Let's look at what it takes to grow ourselves up so we can achieve emotional sobriety.

Suffering the Pains of Growing Up

Unquestionably, Shareen suffered from alcoholism, but we can also think of her alcoholism as a symptom of an underlying problem. Please don't interpret this as meaning that her alcoholism wasn't a priority to treat, because it was. She needed to get sober before she could address her other problems. Her alcoholism was pathogenic in itself.

The first step in recovery is to break the chains of our addiction. Shareen needed to be free from alcohol, but once she achieved physical sobriety, she needed to immediately get to work on her emotional sobriety. Why? Because Shareen suffered from a growth disorder.

A growth disorder occurs when we let fear run our lives. (To be clear, a growth disorder is not a technical psychological diagnosis. It's just an accurate description of the kind of emotional stunting most of us addicts demonstrate.) We become filled with toxic attitudes and unhealthy behaviors. We fail to honor ourselves and what we want. This means we interfere with our healthy functioning. We get in our own way. We prevent ourselves from moving toward something we want because we have internalized an injunction against honoring our most important personal desires, especially if what we want is not acceptable — meaning that it seems shameful or unpopular.

Shareen was at an impasse in her life, and the only way to resolve it was for her to grow up emotionally. But this wasn't going to be easy. She had to face some issues that she had been avoiding for the past ten years.

Shareen was avoiding the truth that she didn't want to be married to Butch. She liked him, but she wasn't in love with him. It was difficult for her to admit this because Butch was a great guy. She didn't want to hurt him. It didn't help that all of her friends loved Butch. He was a great father, made a good living, was loyal, and so much more. But even though he was great on paper, something was missing for Shareen. She didn't love Butch. She liked him and respected him, but she didn't want to be married to him. This alone was a big issue, but the other secret she had been carrying presented an even greater challenge for Shareen to face. Shareen didn't want to be a mother. She loved her daughter but didn't want to raise her.

You can see just why it was so hard for Shareen to become aware and to begin to live consciously in accord with her true self. She had a lot at stake. But once she became aware, it became increasingly difficult for her not to live consciously. The truth was pushing at her.

I will never forget the session where Shareen broke free from her demons. We were working together in a group. I started the group by asking everyone to complete the following sentence, "One thing that I am ashamed about is _____."

When it was Shareen's turn to complete the sentence, she started to sob. In between sobs she stated that if she shared with the group what came to mind, then everyone would hate her and think she was a terrible person. She trembled as she talked.

I responded to Shareen's dilemma by telling her that what she was thinking about the response from the group was a fantasy. It really wasn't the response of the group members that she was struggling with; it was her judgment toward herself about what she wanted to share. She immediately was able to see that it was her self-hate that she projected onto the group members.

This was an important step in her therapy, but the next step was even more critical. I went on to say that the real problem wasn't that she had a very harsh judge inside of her, which she clearly had; the problem was she didn't know how to deal with that part of herself. It was obvious that she gave that part of herself a lot of authority.

Shareen agreed to try an experiment. I wanted her to become aware of the relationship she had with this part of herself. It's always more effective to role-play or act out this kind of internal conflict than to just talk about it, so I set two chairs out and asked her to sit in one of the chairs, which from then on would represent the judge. I asked her to speak first as the judge. She was ruthless! She attacked herself for marrying Butch and not really loving him: "How could you do that to such a nice guy? You are such a bitch!" Then she really lit into herself for being an alcoholic. "You are so fucking selfish for drinking all the time and not taking care of Eva," her judge railed.

But the worst was yet to come. When her judge went after her for not wanting to be a mother, the self-hate was searing. It cut her to the bone. "You are terrible for treating that innocent child like you do. What kind of a monster are you?" She went on and on berating herself.

When I asked Shareen to switch and become herself, the part of her that had to deal with the judge, she immediately said, "Yes, I am a terrible person," agreeing with the judge. She went on and on about how bad she felt and how sorry she was for being such a loser and user. After seeing the relationship between Shareen and her judge, I immediately knew what the matter was.

I asked her if there was any part of her that disagreed with the judge. She said no, as I had anticipated. Her judge prevented her from living her truth, so she became what she thought she should be. But it wasn't real. She couldn't support herself to live her truth. And there was no part of her up for the task.

> Remember, when a need or desire emerges in us, it takes us out of balance. To restore our balance, we need to be able to appropriately respond to our need.

Remember, when a need or desire emerges in us, it takes us out of balance. To restore our balance, we need to be able to respond to our need. Shareen couldn't restore her balance, because her judge wouldn't let her. She was stuck.

Shareen was now fully aware of her struggle. She was beginning to live consciously! (Note that I never said living consciously was easy.) She didn't want to be married to Butch, but she didn't dare let him know. (Of course, he already had his suspicions. We are often not that good at fooling people.) She also didn't want to be a mother and felt horrible for feeling that way.

The psychologist Abraham Maslow stated that the truth will set us free but only if we have the courage to live it.

That's true, as a start, but we need more than just the courage to live the truth. We also need to give ourselves the necessary support.

The Good Witch Comes to the Rescue

When we are unable to support ourselves, we need to develop a new part of ourselves that is up to the task. I asked Shareen if there was anyone in her life who was there for her and stood up for her. There wasn't. Her mother was quite critical of her, and her father never defended Shareen and never stepped in to buffer her mother's cruelty. At that moment, I understood what happened in Shareen's childhood that contributed to the struggle Shareen was having with her internal judge. No one in Shareen's childhood had ever stood up for her. It was no wonder she couldn't stand up for herself. If she had felt supported by someone, she would have been able to bring that experience into the session to help herself. No such luck.

I sat with the reality of what was missing in Shareen's life for a moment and reflected on the difficulty that not knowing how to support herself had created in her life. It is a major challenge to give ourselves something we've never had.

As I sat with her in this dilemma, a vision of a fairy godmother came to me. Yes, this is what Shareen needed. I asked her if there was a fairy godmother from a fairy tale that protected young women that she liked. There wasn't, but she loved Glinda the Good Witch from The Wizard of Oz. Fantastic. I asked her to describe Glinda. "She helps lost girls" was her first response. I said, "Then she is perfect for you. You are lost and need some help in finding your way." She nodded in full agreement.

What happened next touched the entire group. There wasn't a dry eye to be found, including my own. I had Shareen, as Glinda, stand up between her judge and the "bad" self to intercede on Shareen's behalf. She connected to a firmness and compassion in playing Glinda that was remarkable.

She told the judge to back off, that she wasn't going to let the judge put Shareen down anymore, that criticizing and shaming her wasn't helping her deal with the situation. Glinda told the judge that it was making matters worse. Glinda also thanked the judge for pointing out that something needed to be done, but that was as far as she, the judge, would be able to help.

When Glinda turned to Shareen, she warmly said, "My dear child, you are in lots of pain. I am here to help you figure this out." This is when Shareen broke down and cried in a way that revealed to us all that something was healing deep inside of her. That experience in group helped her change her life.

Shareen took action the following day. She asked to meet with Butch so she could talk to him about how she really felt, both about him and about being a mother. There were many difficult and painful discussions that followed over the next several weeks, but something was changed in Shareen. She recovered her true self. She was living consciously.

Eventually, Butch and Shareen divorced and became great friends. After a year of continuous sobriety, she was given 50 percent custody of Eva. Shareen loved this arrangement, and it gave Eva the mother she had always wanted. Shareen has celebrated ten years of recovery.

Living Consciously

While we are each responsible to discover our own solutions to our problems, we can't do this alone. We need help. But we must use the help to learn to live consciously.

What does it mean to live consciously? Well, remember what we learned in chapter 3: We have all been asleep, thinking we are awake. We have not been living consciously but sleepwalking. Here, I want you to learn to live conscious of something deep within yourself: your individual truth, your true self. Living consciously means living with an awareness of our truth. Living consciously is living with the knowledge that we have the capacity to act in response to our current reality.

> Recovery is a rescue operation. We free our true self from the grips of addiction and from the prison constructed by the blueprint of our false self to achieve emotional freedom.

Living this way requires self-support. Shareen found her source of self-support when she became aware of what she was experiencing and by having the courage to live her truth. She found a place to work from, a place to better cope with her world. As self-help author Dr. Jerry Greenwald points out, "A basic attitude toward relieving our self-poisoning patterns is a willingness to say 'yes' to what we want and 'no' to what we don't want" (1974, 72). He writes, "We discover antidotes to toxic behavior through the process of putting into action our unused potentials and resources" (55). When we become fully adult, we learn to honor our authentic or ture self and therefore clearly state to ourselves, "I want to—or I don't want to," depending on the situation.

Recovery is a rescue operation. We free our true self from the grips of addiction and from the prison constructed by the blueprint of our false self to achieve emotional freedom. Emotional sobriety is the result.

As with all rescue operations, there needs to be a plan of attack. A well-planned strategy. For this rescue operation to succeed, it must involve a commitment to living consciously.

> # Waking up is a practice. With any practice, the key is small, steady effort.

We don't suddenly "live consciously." Waking up is a practice. With any practice, the key is small, steady effort. For example, a weightlifter doesn't get strong overnight; she improves her strength by practicing several times a week, increasing the amount of weight she lifts very gradually over months and years. Similarly, a trumpeter practices his scales and other exercises daily with a metronome, increasing his velocity slowly over time. We use the same strategy in recovery as we learn to live consciously a day at a time. We attempt to make small increases in awareness of the way we feel, the choices we make, the actions we take, our habitual ways of feeling and thinking, and their accord with our innermost self. Over time, these small increases add up. Over time, we realize we are aware of how and why we make the choices and take the actions we do. Over time, we begin to live consciously.

Sentence Completion Exercise

Here is a sentence completion exercise to help you bring more awareness to your life. Take each sentence stem and write it at the top of a piece of paper. Next, repeat it silently (or aloud) to yourself, and then complete the sentence with the first thought that comes to mind. Do six to ten completions for each.

> If I bring 5 percent more awareness to my recovery,
> _____.
>
> If I bring 5 percent more awareness to how I get in my own way, _____.

If I bring 5 percent more awareness to my relationship
with myself, _____.

If I bring 5 percent more awareness to my needs and
wants, _____.

If I bring 5 percent more awareness to my relationships,

_____.

If I bring 5 percent more awareness to living consciously,

_____.

If I bring 5 percent more awareness to my emotions,

_____.

I purposely ended this exercise with bringing more awareness to our emotions. Being able to identify our emotional dependency is a critical element of emotional sobriety. In the next chapter, we explore the meaning of emotional dependency and how to discern it in our reactions, choices, and behaviors.

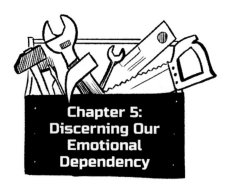

Chapter 5: Discerning Our Emotional Dependency

When I met them, Jamie and his wife, Clarice, were the "perfect" AA couple. Their amazing story started with Clarice hitting bottom, really hard — living on the streets, prostituting herself, getting an intervention, and finally receiving treatment at a well-known recovery center.

Jamie was convinced back then that the problems they were having were related to Clarice's alcoholism. He thought that if she would just get help for her drinking problem, they would have a great marriage. But as more was revealed to Jamie, he understood that the solution to their problem was not as simple as getting sober.

It never is.

After ninety days of treatment, Clarice came home with a new lease on life. She was highly committed to recovery, attended meetings seven days a week, engaged a strong sponsor, worked the Steps, eventually started working with other women, and made her amends to Jamie and the rest of her family. But her marriage was getting worse, not better. She was becoming more and more estranged and alienated from Jamie.

Jamie didn't know how to connect with Clarice once she

stopped drinking. He felt terribly guilty, secretly wishing that she would start drinking again. He missed drinking with her at night. They would sit out on the patio and chat and unwind their days. Drinking together had been the conduit to their connection. Jamie wasn't aware that he was highly dependent on alcohol for their intimacy. He had trouble seeing the role that alcohol played in stabilizing their marriage.

Jamie minimized his own drinking, which was easy for him to do when Clarice was at the worst of her alcoholism. Compared to her, he felt like a model of restraint. But he was drinking more since Clarice got into recovery. He didn't know how to cope with the feelings he was having. He didn't know how to reconnect with Clarice and was hoping she'd take the lead.

She eventually did, but not in the way Jamie had hoped. She contacted me for couples therapy. This was a surprise for Jamie, who had figured she would fix things between them. But Clarice was very concerned that they were heading for divorce.

Remember Shareen's story in the previous chapter? Shareen had to claim her awareness and begin living consciously. This is not unusual in couples who struggle with addiction. They rely on their addiction to avoid waking up to the reality of other dysfunctions in their relationship. In fact, the divorce rate appears to increase among couples who enter recovery as compared to those who are still actively using and drinking. Once they enter recovery and begin to live consciously, the dysfunction becomes noticeable. A new kind of trouble has arrived!

But I also said earlier, trouble doesn't mean something is wrong. It means that something is missing. And this is what the trouble meant for Jamie and Clarice. Something was missing in their marriage, no doubt about it. With recovery underway, their awareness awoke to the trouble in their marriage.

> ## Trouble doesn't mean something is wrong. It means that something is missing.

Their work in couples therapy eventually helped them become aware of the "it" that was missing. But first things first.

Jamie's drinking problem needed to be addressed. Clarice confronted Jamie in our first session. He wasn't ready for this discussion, but he stepped up with my support. He was defensive about his drinking, but that dissipated when I asked if there was any part of him that was also concerned about his drinking. There was!

Jamie broke down and started crying. He was ashamed for wanting Clarice to drink again so they could be closer. He admitted he was dependent on alcohol for feeling connected to her. He was disappointed in himself for being an obstacle to her recovery rather than providing her with genuine support. He felt remorse and regret that he hadn't dealt with his own issues and agreed to go to treatment.

Jamie ended up going to the same treatment program Clarice had graduated from. He spent ninety days there and came home excited about recovery. Now we could begin addressing the underlying issues in their marriage.

The first thing Jamie became aware of in therapy was how emotionally dependent he was on Clarice, which made him reactive to her. He realized that most of their fights occurred when he took personally what Clarice said and did. For example, Jamie came back one night from attending a men's AA meeting. He walked in the door, gave Clarice a hug, and started sharing what came up in the meeting. She immediately interrupted him and asked if they could talk about it later; she had to return a sponsee's urgent phone call.

Jamie took Clarice's response like a hit to the solar plexus. He was angry and hurt, and he let her know about it in no uncertain terms. "I can't believe how selfish you are!" he exclaimed.

When I asked Jamie what it meant to him when Clarice stopped him from sharing and asked him if they could discuss it later, he quickly replied, "I'm not important to her. Isn't that obvious? She really doesn't care about me or my recovery."

So, here's the problem. He had the expectation that Clarice should prioritize his desire to talk to her over responding to her sponsee. Expectations are resentments under construction. He took her request to wait as a rejection. He surmised that he was unimportant to her, that she didn't really care about him. He took what she said personally. For Jamie, Clarice's behavior reflected that she didn't care about him, and that both hurt and threatened him.

As it turned out, Jamie had a lot of rules regarding how Clarice was supposed to behave. If he texted her, he expected a response within fifteen minutes. If he did something nice for her, he expected her to express appreciation. If he got upset with her, he expected that she should accept his apology immediately. If he needed reassurance, she was supposed to reassure him. If he approached her to have sex, he expected her to have sex with him. It was all about Jamie.

As far as Clarice was concerned, she let Jamie hold her hostage. She apologized often for not meeting his needs, and when she wasn't apologizing, she'd say things to Jamie like, "I just don't think I can meet all your needs. Maybe we should get a divorce." Clarice felt responsible for Jamie's happiness. He reinforced this notion. This was the one thing they could agree on because Jamie also felt that Clarice was responsible for his unhappiness. She wasn't, but neither of them knew that. They were dancing a terrible tango that was killing their relationship.

What was causing the troubles between Jamie and Clarice? What was making Jamie take things personally? Where did Jamie's rules come from? What made it okay for Clarice to let Jamie hold her hostage? Why did she apologize instead of standing up for herself?

The answer is emotional dependency. Emotional dependency has a pernicious effect on our self-esteem and on our relationships. It interferes with our ability to have a healthy relationship because we make the other person too important on one hand and not important enough on the other hand. That sounds contradictory, but it's not. I'll explain this later.

For now, let's turn our attention to understanding emotional dependency and its insidious and harmful effects on our relationship with ourselves, with others, and with life itself.

How Emotional Dependency Warps Us

Let's begin our exploration of emotional dependency by looking at Bill Wilson's insights regarding this issue. In his search to understand the roots of his depression, Bill identified a powerful dynamic operating in his life. He realized that his basic flaw was "dependence—almost absolute dependence—on people or circumstances to supply me with prestige, security, and the like" (1988, 237). This was an important discovery for Bill, just like it is for us.

I call this realization "seeing who we aren't" because we recognize that we are not the independent adult we always thought. It's devastating when we realize that our sense of independence is imaginary, when we see that in fact we are overly dependent on the people and circumstances of our environment for emotional support and security. This, as you'll recall from chapter 2, is emotional dependency: making our emotional security dependent on situations outside ourselves. Seeing who we aren't is an important step in achieving emotional sobriety. It's just like admitting we are powerless over alcohol or other drugs. Seeing who we aren't is key to the first step in letting go of our emotional dependency.

The importance of owning this truth, rather than avoiding it, cannot be overemphasized here. Please don't shy away from this step. We need to be rigorously honest with ourselves if we are going to grow up. Dr. Nathaniel Branden, a brilliant psychotherapist, noted, "So long as an individual cannot accept the fact of what he is, cannot permit himself to be fully aware of it, cannot fully admit the truth into his consciousness, he cannot move beyond that point: if he denies the reality of his condition, he cannot proceed to alter it, cannot achieve healthy changes in his personality" (1971, 110).

> Bill Wilson realized that his sense of self was contingent on external events. His personal value was determined by what happened to him, by how others treated him, or by what others thought about him.

To make healthy changes in our personality, we need to recognize our emotional dependency and acknowledge its effects on our self-esteem and on our behavior in relationships. (Later in this chapter, I will discuss a technique I have developed to help promote awareness of how emotional dependency operates in our lives.)

Bill W. realized that his sense of self was contingent on external events. His personal value was determined by what happened to him, by how others treated him, or by what others thought about him. He suffered from what I refer to as other-validated self-esteem. His self-esteem was dependent on the thoughts and behaviors of others. If they liked him and did what he wanted them to do, he was fine. If they didn't, he was knocked off balance. He needed support from his environment to be okay, to feel secure, to feel loved and accepted.

Our emotional dependency causes us to perpetually seek environmental support; therefore, we are always looking for sources for that support. Our relationships, especially loving ones, are often seen as best suited for this role in our lives. But as we will see, emotionally dependent support is the stuff that immature love is made up of: We love someone because we need that person, not because we want him or her. Mature love is very different. It is free. We want someone because we have chosen to love him or her, not because we need the person. The impact of emotional dependence on relationships was described by Branden when he noted, "In my emotional impoverishment, I tend to see other people essentially as sources of approval or disapproval. I do not appreciate them for who they are in their own right. I see only what they can or cannot do for me" (1994, 8).

This is what I meant earlier when I stated that our emotional dependency makes other people too important. We define ourselves by how they feel and think about us. We want their approval and fear their disapproval. This is too much power to give anyone. I don't mean to suggest that we put an impenetrable force field around ourselves, because this is also unhealthy. The healthy option is to remain open to feedback but to reserve for ourselves the final say about what fits or doesn't. If we don't reserve this right, we lose our autonomy, thereby making other people too important.

But there's another side to this coin: Emotional dependency also makes people unimportant because we see them only as sources of approval or disapproval. We don't see them as existing separately from us, having their own needs and desires worthy of our consideration. They become objects that we manipulate to get our needs met. We demand that they meet our needs without us having an appropriate regard for theirs. This is what I meant when I said emotional dependency interferes with our ability to have a healthy relationship because we make the other person too important on one hand and not important enough on the other hand. What a mess we create in our lives when we refuse to grow up!

Before we can gain true independence of spirit, autonomy, authentic self-esteem, and mature love, we have to become aware of how we keep ourselves immature. By believing we need our partner, friend, sibling, colleague, coworker, parent, or circumstance to conform to our expectations, we sell ourselves short.

> Before we can gain true independence of spirit, autonomy, authentic self-esteem, and mature love, we have to become aware of how we keep ourselves immature.

We become confined by the judgment or actions of others, and then try to take them hostage because we need to control them to ensure they will think about us and treat us the way we secretly demand they should.

Can you identify Jamie's emotional dependency on Clarice? He depended on her for his self-esteem and his sense of security. His dependency was manifested when he demanded that Clarice behave the way he thought she should. Of course, he presented his demands to her as though they were "reasonable requests." We tend to camouflage unreasonable claims and demands because we know they are outrageous. We have to, or else we wouldn't feel okay about expecting others to honor them.

In reality, there was nothing reasonable about what Jamie wanted from Clarice. Jamie showed no concern for what Clarice wanted. It was all about what Jamie wanted, with no room for Clarice. Jamie insisted that she live up to his expectations. Jamie was outrageous and self-centered.

We become quite clever in the way we manipulate others for support. Jamie put Clarice in a bind. If she didn't give him what he wanted, it meant (according to Jamie) that she didn't care about him. Essentially, Jamie was saying, "If you love me, you will give me what I want and do what I want." He used an immature concept of love to pressure and manipulate Clarice to satisfy his needs. Love is not about giving others everything they demand or want. But Clarice bought into this lie, hook, line, and sinker. This is where Clarice's own emotional dependency came into play in their relationship.

While Clarice cared about Jamie, she also, secretly, wanted to be her own person. But there was no room for her needs in the relationship, and she reluctantly accepted that her role was to please Jamie. She erased herself because she wanted to please him—and also because she didn't want to get him mad. Clarice gave in to Jamie's demands and tried to satisfy his needs, albeit more and more reluctantly and uncomfortably as she started to mature in recovery.

But Clarice doesn't get let off the hook easy in this story. In her way, she too was manipulating Jamie by erasing herself and creating the illusion that she would meet all his needs. She met Jamie's needs, which in her mind was the only way she could ensure his love for her.

Jamie and Clarice were in what family therapist Dr. Virginia Satir called the clutch. (You'll learn more about the clutch shortly.) They were bringing out the worst in each other. Their marriage was based on a toxic agreement: We can't live without each other. The unconscious contract they signed when they got married was that they would never ask their partner to grow up and become an adult. Jamie and Clarice each used the relationship to avoid taking responsibility for their individual happiness and satisfaction. Together, they also used the relationship as a device that enabled them to remain dependent on each other; that is, the relationship enabled their individual forms of emotional dependency.

According to Dr. Fritz Perls, an immature person "may be defined as a person who is unable to assume the full identity and responsibility of mature behavior. He will do anything to keep himself in the state of immaturity, even to playing the role of an adult—that is, his infantile concept of what an adult is like. [He] cannot conceive of himself as a self-supportive person, able to mobilize his potential in order to cope with the world" (1975b, 11).

Clarice and Jamie reinforced their toxic agreement with highly toxic interactions like I described before. Too much toxic interaction can bring a relationship to the point where one or both partners lose the desire to stay together. Clarice was fast approaching this point. Something needed to change. She already had one foot out the door of their marriage, and Jamie could sense that she was no longer as willing or interested in erasing herself to meet his needs.

Emotional Dependency Generates
Unenforceable Rules

Our emotional dependency automatically generates a set of unenforceable rules. These rules are based on our interpretation of the ways that things should be, the ways our lovers are supposed to act, the ways we are supposed to feel and behave. This is how the should demands manifest themselves in our consciousness.

The rules are actually spelled out in the blueprint we adopted for our basic solution. Remember, the ultimate goal of the solution we adopted was to reverse the experiences of our past. So, the unenforceable rules we adopted were related to the missing experiences in our early development.

For example:

> If I wasn't listened to as a child, my unenforceable rules for someone who cared about me would be always listen to me, even when I say things that may not be worth listening to.
>
> If I wasn't accepted as a child, I would have the unenforceable rule that my partner had to accept me unconditionally, even if some of my behavior was hard to accept.
>
> If I wasn't celebrated, then the unenforceable rule for my partner would be always be my cheerleader, regardless of what might be going on in your life.

Though I call these unenforceable rules, the truth is we do everything in our power to enforce them. We will go to any lengths to get our partners to do what we want them to do, including pleasing them, begging them, and threatening them.

We try to enforce these rules with as many tricks as we can muster, but the reality is this: If the other person doesn't cooperate, then we end up feeling defeated or frustrated. Bill Wilson described his experience with his rules in this way, "Failing to get these things according to my perfectionist dreams and specifications, I had fought for them. And when defeat came, so did my depression" (1988, 237).

Our rules have but one purpose: to manipulate others into doing what we want them to do. We seek to control them, to try to make them our puppets so we can play puppet master and so that we make certain everything will go our way.

You might be thinking, "I am glad I don't do that to the people I love."

Bad news if you think you're immune! It might be more accurate for you to say, "I am not aware that I have rules." Fair enough. But if you are emotionally dependent to any degree (as all of us are!), then you have rules that are designed to manipulate others. We all try to get people to do what we want them to do in order to make ourselves feel okay.

Bill W. was aware of this aspect of his emotional dependency. He realized that "my dependency meant demand—a demand for the possession and control of the people and the conditions surrounding me" (Wilson 1988, 238). How did he control the people and conditions surrounding him? With rules. Unenforceable rules.

Dr. Virginia Satir, in her classic book Peoplemaking, identified some of the rules imposed on love that love can never fulfill: "If you love me, you won't do anything without me. If you love me, you'll do what I say. If you love me, you'll give me what I want. If you love me, you'll know what I want before I ask." She went on to write, "These kind of practices soon make love into a kind of blackmail I call the clutch" (1972, 135).

Can you hear Jamie saying these things to Clarice? Of course you can. These are the things he demanded of Clarice. Jamie was more concerned with his rules and her obedience to them than he was with his relationship with Clarice, which is why their marriage was beginning to wear thin for Clarice. When rules become more important than the people, the relationship is headed for real trouble.

Hopefully you are convinced that becoming aware of your emotional dependency is important to the practice of emotional sobriety. The next section will be devoted to increasing self-awareness of how your emotional dependency works.

The Origins of Emotional Dependency

In chapter 3, I discussed the three basic solutions we use to soothe our anxiety that we weren't going to be loved, be accepted, or belong. Each solution created a blueprint for a false self. The blueprint relocated our emotional center of gravity. Instead of our emotional center of gravity being firmly positioned over our true self, which is where it was when we were born, we relocated it and centered it in our false self. I noted that it is as though we'd built our foundation on someone else's property.

What this meant was that if our false self was loved or accepted according to the perfectionistic specifications of the blueprint, we felt secure. But if our false self was not accepted in the way we expected, then we were thrown for a loop. We were knocked off balance and we panicked until we could find a way to stabilize ourselves by manipulating our environment and getting it to give us what we wanted.

> Instead of our emotional center of gravity being firmly positioned over our true self, which is where it was when we were born, we relocated it and centered it in our false self.

This whole operation was based on the need to control the outcomes in our lives, to ensure we were going to belong, to be loved, and to be accepted. We constructed a false self to control how other people would respond to us.

This is what gives birth to emotional dependency. We change ourselves to manipulate others. Our false self is built on the lie that we need people and circumstances to conform to our expectations—to do what we want—for us to feel secure, happy, and content.

That lie is utter nonsense.

This is an insult to who we really are. It discounts our ability to support ourselves and to adapt. We don't need a situation to be a certain way for us to be okay. We don't need approval or validation from others. We need to be able to support ourselves and learn to deal with reality as it is.

I think it's helpful to envision a bonsai tree when we explore our effort to create the false self. You have probably seen these lovely plants. The Japanese art form takes decades, even a lifetime, to execute, just as our false self takes years or even a lifetime to develop. Small or young trees are selected, planted in small pots, and over time their branches are wrapped with wire to twist them into pleasing shapes. Their leaves are carefully trimmed, they are fed minimal amounts of water and fertilizer, and even their roots are trimmed. All of this is done to force the trees to stay miniature and conform to desired shapes. They are lovely, but they are nothing like what their inner nature demands them to be. An old oak bonsai may be only a foot or two tall. A spruce may be trimmed over time to less than a foot tall, kept in a lovely porcelain planter not much bigger than a catcher's mitt. You get the idea. These trees look perfect, but they are warped into perfection over many years of binding, trimming, and so forth. (I mean no disrespect to bonsai; it is a magnificent art form!)

This is what we do to our true self when we attempt to conform to the rules of the false self. We make bonsai of ourselves to win the admiration and love of others. That works so long as we conform to the rules and our partners meet our expectations. And we love them, so long as they can meet the very strict requirements of our "bonsaied" self and continue to love us to our exacting standards. But tap us the wrong way, and it all comes unwound. Our true self wants out. It wants to grow and spread its limbs! This is what you want too.

Becoming Aware of Our Emotional Dependency

In a moment I will introduce you to a way of unpacking a situation that has upset or bothered you. This is the exercise I told you about earlier in the chapter, and its goal is to help you become aware of your unhealthy emotional dependency and the unenforceable rules or demands or expectations you put on people or circumstances. But before we turn to this important task, I want to talk to you about resistance.

We resist things that are difficult for us to face. Our false self doesn't want us to see that we aren't who we think we are. We delude ourselves in hundreds of different ways. The bottom line is we fear discomfort. We avoid suffering. We avoid looking at our defects of character. We avoid facing our limitations.

I've discussed the importance of facing the reality of who we are if we are to have any chance of becoming what we can be. But this isn't easy. Our false self will resist our best efforts. So, what can we do? Are we stuck with being victims of our false self? The answer to this last question is a definitive no. We don't have to let the worst in us control us any longer.

The way to defeat the saboteur is to own the resistance. Remember the paradoxical theory of change? The moment I say, "I don't want to see my emotional dependency because I am ashamed that I am not my own person," I begin to become my own person. By admitting my willful blindness and my shame, I'm beginning to own what I am doing rather than avoiding it, and this begins the process of change.

Sentence Completion Exercise

Let's return to sentence completion work. Write each sentence stem at the top of a blank page, say it out loud or to yourself, and write down the first thought that comes to mind. Repeat six to ten times for each sentence stem. Have some fun with this, and don't take yourself too seriously.

> I don't dare own that I am emotionally dependent be-
> cause it would mean _____.
> The part of me that doesn't want to face my emotional
> dependency tells me _____.
> Being emotionally dependent means _____.
> I hate myself for being emotionally dependent because
>
> _____.
>
> I justify my unenforceable rules by telling myself
>
> _____.
>
> The way my emotional dependency shows up in my life

is _____.

If I were free of my emotional dependency, I would

_____.

After you do this exercise, share your responses with your sponsor, therapist, or a trusted friend. Try to become aware of any pattern to your answers. If you are painstaking about this exercise, you will become aware of a part of you that is going to struggle with facing your emotional dependency.

You need to name this part of yourself to tame it. I call it the false self. Others call it pride or shame. Use what fits you best. Be aware of this part in you. In fact, put it across from you in an empty chair and disagree with it. It is probably telling you that you will be embarrassed or humiliated or something similar if you face your emotional dependency. You can respond to it by adding some reasonable doubt, as in, "Well, I might lose face, but I might gain some freedom and humility."

The reality is that you will gain something when you face your emotional dependency. You will gain emotional freedom, the ability to choose your response. (This is the opposite of being reactive.) You will gain humility, and you will begin the ongoing journey of achieving emotional sobriety.

Another great insight Bill Wilson had about our emotional reactions was this: "It is a spiritual axiom that every time we are disturbed, no matter what the cause, there is something wrong with us" (Alcoholics Anonymous World Services 1981, 90).

We can use Bill W.'s insight to motivate our practice of emotional sobriety. It's a call to take radical responsibility for what we are feeling. "No matter the cause" is the key phrase here. Emotional sobriety requires that we relinquish the concept of blame. There is no one to blame for what we are experiencing. Our feelings are our feelings. Period.

Emotional sobriety asks us to understand what the matter is, what is disturbed within us. Being aware of what is causing us to get upset is critical if we are going to be able to resolve our grievance. Bill W. offered the following suggestion to help us identify what is wrong with us: "If we examine every disturbance we have, great or small, we will find at the root of it some unhealthy dependency and its consequent unhealthy demand" (Wilson 1988, 238). In the language I've been using in this book, the source of our disturbance is not some circumstance around us or the way someone else is behaving. It is our demand that circumstances or people conform to our expectations.

Emotional sobriety requires that we relinquish the concept of blame.

Just a note — this does not mean you shouldn't react to bullies, inappropriate behavior, an abusive mate, terrifying circumstances, and so forth as though nothing were wrong. Emotional autonomy is not about being a martyr and ignoring our feelings. Though I have stated that trouble means something is right, there are times when trouble means something is wrong. If you are experiencing physical abuse, act to ensure your safety as well as anyone who depends on you for their safety. Get away from the perpetrator and seek help. This is easier said than done, of course, but necessary. In a later chapter, I will help you differentiate between reasonable and unreasonable expectations.

Emotional Dependency Inventory Exercise

Let us apply Bill Wilson's wisdom to identifying the sources of our discomfort. I have created a worksheet to facilitate this process. The worksheet is composed of five columns. (This worksheet is provided in Appendix B and you hereby have permission to copy it.) As you can see, each column has a different task assigned to it. In this exercise, we are going to focus on the first four columns, using the topics discussed in this chapter. Fill in what you can for the final column (self-support solutions) now. You can come back to it as you proceed through the book and learn more about that crucial aspect of emotional sobriety.

Describe What Happened - Column 1: The first step in unpacking an upsetting situation is to write down what happened. Describe the situation in as much detail as possible. Describe the context of what happened, and detail what you said, what the other person or people said, and so on. Record this information in column 1. Let's use Jamie's situation when he came home from the meeting and wanted to talk to Clarice as an example. Here's what he wrote in column 1:

> I went to a men's AA meeting on Wednesday night. I was looking forward to the meeting, as I usually do. I often hear something of value for my recovery in this meeting. One of the guys was sharing how reactive he was to his girlfriend. He often gets mad at her when she doesn't live up to his expectations. This really struck home with me and I immediately wanted to share this with Clarice. I thought that this might help us get closer.

> As I entered the house, I felt excited to share this insight with her. I started to tell her about it. Clarice held up her hand as though she was a traffic cop stopping traffic. She asked if this could wait till later because she had to return a troubled sponsee's phone call. I didn't say another word, turned away from her, and walked into

the other room.

Describe Your Reaction - Column 2: Discuss your emotional reaction and how you responded to the feelings you were experiencing. Identify what it meant to you. Here is Jamie's description of his reaction:

> I immediately felt rejected and disappointed when Clarice held up her hand and didn't want to hear about what I learned at the meeting. It felt like I was punched in the stomach.
>
> I immediately got angry and fell silent. Inside I was thinking, I see how important I am to you. I guess your sponsor hasn't told you that if you love someone, you make time for them. I know I am asking too much from you; you are still so fucking selfish. Go ahead and take care of your sponsee; she probably needs you more than I do anyway.
>
> I was pouting, and I withdrew for the remainder of the evening. When Clarice approached me an hour later and asked me if I still wanted to share with her what I learned in the meeting, I told her it wasn't that important—which really pissed her off.

Identify Your Expectation - Column 3: Identify your claim or demand or unenforceable rule. Tip: Be outrageous.

> I expect Clarice to drop whatever she's doing and make me a priority. This is what you should do if you love someone.

Identify Your Unhealthy Dependence - Column 4: Identify the unhealthy dependency underlying the claim or demand or unenforceable rule.

> I need Clarice to do what I want her to do in order for me to feel loved, validated, and secure in our relationship.

Claim Your Emotional Autonomy - Column 5: List what you can do to support yourself, hold on to yourself, recover your center of emotional gravity, and achieve emotional sobriety.

> I fooled myself into thinking that I need Clarice to pay attention to me to prove to me that I am lovable. I don't need her to think this way about me; I need to think this way about me. I am who I am. Clarice's love or interest in me is great, but I don't need it. What I need is to support myself and stand on my own two feet instead of demanding that Clarice supports me.
>
> I am just new to the idea of emotional sobriety. I think that I need to quit thinking about what Clarice wants and start focusing on figuring out what I really want. Maybe then I will not be so dependent on Clarice. I will come back to this in a few weeks and try again.

In several of the upcoming chapters, I discuss in length different ways we can hold on to ourselves. And in chapter 14, I focus on some of the ways emotional sobriety can help us correct the toxic rules that derail relationships with the people we love. To preview, I suggest that to support ourselves, we need to surrender our crippling expectations. Sounds tough, and it is. Like I said, more about this later. In the next chapter, we look at the tendency we have to take things personally, how this relates to emotional dependency, and what we need to do to stop this bad habit.

Chapter 6: Knowing It's Not Personal

Emotional dependency creates all kinds of perceptual distortions. In this chapter, we examine one of the more common ones—taking things personally.

Stop for a moment and think about all the things that upset you during the day. A friend says you're not being attentive enough. Your partner seems to be ignoring you. The auto repair service implies you're stupid for not knowing it was time to change the oil. A driver swerves in front of you and you have to slow down, causing your coffee to spill. No one brought a cake to the meeting to celebrate your fifth AA birthday. Your sponsor doesn't return your call for two days. All of these may seem like personal attacks. They can make you feel sad or angry or worried or all of the above. But are they really about you at all?

Taking things personally means we assume that things other people say and do (or don't say and don't do) are about us rather than them. We all take things personally. It's a hard habit to break, but a habit that must be broken if we are to achieve emotional sobriety.

Taking things personally is a function of low self-esteem. Our low self-esteem makes us very focused on and concerned with the approval or disapproval of others. If we don't love ourselves, then we will do all kinds of things to make ourselves lovable to other people. This is what creates emotional dependency. We erroneously believe we need the validation or approval of other people to be all right. In essence, this makes our emotional well-being, even our sense of safety, dependent on what other people say and do in relation to us. We crave their pats on the back, encouragement, appreciation, praise, or recognition. We turn everyone around us into judges, doling out approval or disapproval. Ironically, as much as this low self-esteem seems to diminish ourselves, it is also a kind of grandiosity, as if we had the power to fuel all these emotional reactions around us. (In the AA rooms it's common to hear this phenomenon described as "We are egomaniacs with inferiority complexes.")

> Taking things personally is a function of low self-esteem. Our low self-esteem makes us very focused on and concerned with the approval or disapproval of others.

Our concern about what others are thinking or feeling toward us makes us acutely aware of what other people say and do around us or how they treat us. Why? Because if they don't feel the way we want them to feel, we need to do something about it—we need to change their mind or run away. This is the basic fight-or-flight response to a threat.

This creates a state in which we are unconsciously and perpetually afraid. When we see people, we need to know if they are a threat. Are they for us or against us? Are they our enemies or friends? Are they safe or dangerous? Will they soothe our anxiety by making us feel loved, or will they reject us, meaning that we are unlovable? Our existence depends on reading their minds. Of course, that's impossible; the best we can do is try to interpret what their statements or actions mean. What's worse, our natural capacity to understand what they mean has been distorted by our emotional dependency and also by any trauma we might have suffered in our childhood. In other words, our anxiety causes us to filter and distort the information we get from other people's words and actions.

In this way, emotional dependency creates a reflected sense of self, meaning we believe the other person's behavior and attitude toward us is an accurate reflection of who we are rather than an expression of who they are. We see in their actions and statements a reflection of our worth or value. We view their behavior as a mirror in which we see a reflection of our worth or value — their approval or disapproval of us. We lose sight of who we are because of what they say or how they act.

Because of this dynamic, we take personally most of what a person says or does or thinks. So, for example, if my wife gives a snarky response to a question I ask her, I take it personally. I worry that she doesn't respect me. On some deep unconscious level, I fear it means I'm not lovable.

These emotional reactions are another tip-off that we have identified with our false self. As you'll recall from previous chapters, we constructed our false self specifically to please other people—to soothe our anxiety that if people knew our innermost being, they would find us unlovable, unacceptable, or unworthy of belonging. This false self is fragile. It requires constant reinforcement and approval. Thus we look to others for validation.

This habitual way of thinking and feeling is very troublesome. Taking things personally has harmed and destroyed many of our relationships. The problem is a very basic error in the hard-wiring of our human computer. We think our feelings are facts, that they are an infallible guide to the truth. Well, they are not. Our feelings are real, but not always true.

I want you to really hear what I just said: Our feelings are not an infallible guide to the truth!

We take things personally, and in so doing we incorrectly conclude that everything is all about us. In fact, this is the furthest from the truth.

If someone disrespects you, it is not personal. If someone is rude to you, it is not personal. If someone dismisses you, it is not personal. If someone slights you, it is not personal. If someone ignores you, it is not personal. If someone puts you down and wants to hurt you, it is not personal. If someone steals from you, it is not personal. If someone betrays you, it is not personal. If someone spreads lies about you, it is not personal. If someone doesn't do what you want, it is not personal.

> ## What you say to someone else when you are upset is not personal.

What you say to someone else when you are upset is not personal. What someone says to you when he or she is upset is not personal. If someone likes you, it is not personal. If someone dislikes you, it is not personal.

This concept may be hard to wrap your consciousness around at this moment, but nothing anyone says to you is personal. Nothing anyone does to you is personal. This is the important lesson that Damian, in my next illustration, needed to learn to achieve emotional sobriety.

It's Not about the Dishes

Damian's first session with me was quite unusual. When I asked him what he was struggling with, he stated, "Doc, I am embarrassed to tell you what's been bothering me, but I figured I had better get some help because it's ruining my marriage."

I imagined he was going to tell me that he was having an affair or had relapsed or something of this nature. But it was nothing like that. He told me he was terribly upset because his wife wouldn't do the dishes.

She won't do the dishes, I thought, and this is upsetting you?

He saw the incredulous look on my face and quickly said, "It's not about the dishes, Doc; it's that I tell her how important it is to me that there are no dishes in the sink when I get home from work, and typically, when I come home from work, there are dishes in the sink and it really upsets me. Come on, Doc, I am only asking for her to do the dishes. This isn't that big of a deal, is it? It's just one little thing."

I asked how frequently the dishes were in the sink when he came home from work. He shifted around in his seat and became quite agitated.

"It is happening most of the time," he said, and then he immediately corrected himself. "It really happens all of the time. Well, not all the time, but I have to text her before I get home to remind her to do the dishes—so it's all of the time because if I don't text her, she won't do them. Why do I have to remind her? I work all day and all she does is watch our two-year-old child. Can't she just do what I ask her to do? I work twelve hours a day. I pay all the bills. All she has to do is watch our child and I ask one thing from her—just do the dishes."

Damian's anger and contempt for his wife, Lulu, was palpable. I could see what was happening that was causing him concern. He was out of control. He expected Lulu to honor his "no dishes in the sink" request, and when she didn't, there was a price she would pay. He'd either get angry and beat her up verbally, or he'd withdraw and pout.

As we are going to see, this was not about the dishes. For Damian, there was something symbolic about the dishes being in the sink when he came home from work that triggered something upsetting, deep inside.

Here are a few things that are important for us to consider to better understand what Damian was experiencing. When we get anxious, we become even more intent on getting people to meet our expectations. We are convinced this is well within our rights. We justify it this way: If someone loved us, really loved us, that person would comply with our request and do what we wanted.

Please note that when we are placing these kinds of demands on others, we are trying to hook them into doing what we want them to do. In the process of doing this, we lose sight of them as people. We lose touch with them. We don't feel any empathy toward them, and we don't show any consideration or awareness of their existence separate from what we want. We treat them like an object that is in our lives for one purpose: to meet our needs, to make us feel loved or lovable, to give us comfort or security. We don't think about what they need, just what we need from them. It's all about us. And what makes matters even worse, we think we aren't imposing on them—that what we want is "just a little thing."

Damian had even said this when he was discussing what goes on between him and Lulu: "I am only asking for her to do the dishes. This isn't that big of a deal, is it? It's just one little thing." But it was a big deal and I told him so.

He expected Lulu to make what he wanted a priority during her day and to override what she wanted to do or thought was important. He had set a rule that if she loved him, she would always do the dishes before he came home. There wasn't any awareness in Damian's consciousness of whether Lulu wanted to do the dishes or not, nor was there any awareness of what she was tasked with during the day in raising their daughter. Damian could see only what he could see, and he couldn't see Lulu. When Lulu wouldn't do the dishes, Damian took her "lack of cooperation" very personally.

I asked him how he responded when he came home and realized that his wife hadn't done the dishes. He said there were two ways he reacted. He used to yell and scream at her, but this got him thrown out of the house. So he stopped yelling and screaming. I asked what he did now.

He stated that when he came home and saw that the dishes were in the sink, he'd go in the living room and lie on the couch and play with his phone.

"What did you play on your phone?" I inquired.

"Angry Birds," he said. A small, bitter smile spread across his face as the irony of his choice dawned on him.

"Angry Birds," I said. "How appropriate. So what happens when your wife comes by the couch and welcomes you home?"

"I ignore her! I think to myself, If you want to talk to me, you should do the fucking dishes. I pay for the car insurance, the rent for the apartment, the food for the house; I buy clothes for you and the baby; I buy the diapers; and all I ask is for you to do the dishes and YOU WON'T DO THEM! But I don't say a word to her; I just think it."

Damian pressured Lulu to do what he demanded by either yelling at her and making her feel like she was a bad partner for not doing the dishes or by emotionally withdrawing from her.

Unpacking Damian's Emotional Disturbance

Damian was in an emotional storm. He didn't know how to soothe himself. In his mind, the only path available to him to restore his balance was to pressure Lulu to do the dishes. But this wasn't working. He was becoming more and more resentful. He was alienating his wife with criticism and contempt. Damian wanted to find a solution, but he just couldn't let go of the dishes. Damian was at an impasse. Nothing was working to help him release or surrender his demands.

Remember, trouble doesn't always mean something is wrong in a relationship; trouble is an opportunity for growth. The trouble that Damian and Lulu were having was necessary for Damian. It was an invitation for him to take the next step in his emotional maturity.

> Remember, trouble doesn't always mean something is wrong in a relationship; trouble is an opportunity for growth.

The first step in helping Damian grow up was to make him aware of his unenforceable rules and the unhealthy dependency at the root of his rules. (Recall that in the previous chapter's Emotional Dependency Inventory exercise, the third and fourth columns asked you to explore your personal unenforceable rules and their underlying dependencies.)

I asked him what it would mean to him if Lulu did the dishes. He didn't hesitate to say, "It would mean she loves me."

I responded, "So then what you are really saying to me is

that if she does the dishes, it proves that she loves you. You are in effect saying to her, 'If you loved me, you would do the dishes every time before I came home from work. If you loved me, you will do what I want you to do. If you love me, you will give me what I want!'"

"Yes, that is what I am saying to her," he said. "Is something wrong with that?" His inquiry was genuine.

I told him I'd answer that in a moment, but first I wanted to explore the effect of this rule on his marriage. "I want you to know that this has a very damaging effect on your relationship with Lulu," I told him. "As long as she operates within the parameters you have defined, you feel loved. But what if her love falls outside of the framework you've constructed? You won't be able to see her love—and worse, you will criticize her for not loving you. That puts her in a really difficult position. As long as she does it your way, you will be okay, but this leaves no room for Lulu in your relationship."

I let that sit for a moment and then continued, "I want you to ponder this: You're worried about her loving you, but the way you are treating Lulu is not very loving."

Wow, that hit him right between the eyes! He looked stunned at first, then became quite pensive. "Damian," I said, "you are so worried about whether Lulu loves you that you have lost sight that you are not giving her what you are asking from her. You have no consideration for her, and yet you want her to consider your needs. Relationships don't work that way. People mostly respond in kind. They give us what we give them."

Although what we were exploring at this point in the session was important, we were about to uncover what the dishes really meant.

What the Dishes Meant to Damian

The moment was right to invite Damian to look even deeper to identify what the dishes in the sink meant to him. I asked him if they reminded him of something in his childhood.

He dropped his head and let out a painful sigh. "Yes, they do," he said. His voice broke, and he paused to collect himself.

He haltingly told me about his childhood: "When I would come home from school and the dishes were in the sink," he said, then paused and wiped a tear from his eye, "it meant my mother had been drinking. She'd be drunk."

"And then what would happen?" I invited.

"Nothing good!" Damian said in a voice both angry and incredibly sad.

It was clear that Damian was in terrible pain. I asked, "What does 'nothing good' mean, Damian?"

Now he really started to cry. "She'd yell at me, call me names, and sometimes she'd hit me. She was mean and cruel. I was always afraid of finding her drunk. Sometimes she'd have guys over, and they'd come in my bedroom and do bad shit to me—they'd molest me. I fucking hated her for not protecting me and not caring how I felt!"

When Damian described what happened in his childhood, I realized what it meant when he saw the dishes in the sink. The dishes evoked all the unresolved pain and traumas from his childhood. He felt unsafe and anxious when he came home and saw dishes in the sink.

I pointed out to Damian that when he walks into his house and he sees dishes in the sink, it triggers all of these unresolved feelings. I wanted him to see that trying to get his wife to do the dishes so he wouldn't feel his pain would not solve the problem. It would only help him keep his pain buried and unresolved. What he really needed to do was to go back and work through the feelings he harbored toward his mother and the men who molested and abused him. He needed to resolve his past so he could set himself free from it. When he set himself free, he could also release his wife from his unconscious demand that she reverse the experiences from his past.[3] I pointed out that Lulu could not heal what happened to him, but he could. He discovered a new possibility in that moment in our therapy session.

After that session and in the months that followed, Damian focused his energy on healing rather than on manipulating Lulu. Following this initial session, we did a lot of work on resolving the unfinished business he had from his childhood. One day he shared something very special with me. He said, "When I walked in the house yesterday and saw the dishes in the sink, I went up to my wife and thanked her for not caving in to my unreasonable expectations. I told her, 'You gave me a gift by frustrating me. I am now happier than I have ever been in my recovery.'" After he said that to her, he walked in the kitchen and did the dishes.

Damian had learned to quit taking things personally. He had embarked on the practice of emotional sobriety.

Why We Take Things Personally

Of course, sometimes it really is just about the dishes. Couples disagree about who should do what chore when and how often all the time; that's normal, and there's nothing wrong with it. So how do we know when a disagreement is just about the dishes and when it's really about something else?

Damian's case, involving severe childhood neglect and abuse, is extreme, but the lesson from it applies to everyone: When we make a request for something and our partner or friend doesn't

---

3   Recall that in chapter 3 we discussed Dr. Alexander Lowen's theory that we expect the future to reverse the traumas of our past.

comply, we will be disappointed, but then we'll simply seek another resolution. We will suffer what isn't and appreciate what is. We'll get up and do the dishes ourselves or talk about ways to better coordinate to solve the problem.

But if instead of simple disappointment we have a catastrophic response, then the issue isn't about the request; it is about us wanting to make the other person do something that resolves our inner anxiety. So, it's about getting someone to do what we want, not the dishes! Our response is disproportionate to the situation. In fact, it's outrageous.

And this is how we know that our issue is not at all about the dishes. It's something else, and our job, if we want to overcome our emotional dependency, is to figure out what that "something else" is.

A simple way to remember: If your response is disproportionate to the actual situation, you are taking it personally. If your response is to try to manipulate the other individual, you are taking it personally. You are being emotionally dependent.

Have you ever thought about the reason you take things personally? Some of us who are still asleep haven't even noticed we react this way. Those of us who are living consciously are aware that this happens quite frequently. This issue is so prevalent and crippling that it was chosen to be one of the four agreements that Don Miguel Ruiz discusses in his book aptly titled The Four Agreements (1997).

The second of the four agreements is "Don't take anything personally." Ruiz identified the reason we take things personally. Simply stated, it is because we agree with them. For example, if someone calls you stupid and you have never thought of yourself as stupid, you wouldn't take that personally. You'd wonder what the person's problem was, but you wouldn't give that insult a second thought.

But if you held any doubt about your intelligence because

you struggled in school or because you were called stupid by your father or mother or an older sibling when you were a child, then you'd take the person's words very personally. Why? Because a part of you agrees with them.

No one hurts us. We hurt ourselves.

Here's another way to say this: No one hurts us. We hurt ourselves. Meaning we connect what the person is saying to a wound we already have. According to Ruiz, when we agree with whatever the person says, we become trapped in the dream of hell.

Ruiz goes on to say that what causes us to be trapped in the dream of hell is "personal importance." He writes, "Personal importance, or taking things personally, is the maximum expression of selfishness because we make the assumption that everything is about 'me'" (1997, 48).

Ruiz believes that we learn to take everything personally because of how we were raised. "We think we are responsible for everything. Me, me, me, always me," he writes. "Nothing other people do is because of you. It is because of themselves" (1997, 48).

Ruiz is describing a person with low differentiation. Differentiation is a concept introduced to clinical psychology and psychiatry in the 1950s by Dr. Murray Bowen. Our level of differentiation determines our ability or inability to function in a healthy way in our relationships. It refers to our capacity to act on our own behalf without impinging on the welfare of others. The higher our level of differentiation, the more autonomy we experience in our relationships. Drs. Michael Kerr and Bowen noted that people with a high level of differentiation are attracted and interested in one another but are not dependent on each other's acceptance and approval. They seek to cooperate with one another rather than manipulate each other. As a result, the relationship does not cause an excessive amount of anxiety in the partners (1988, 74). This means we honor our integrity, because when our differentiation is high, it is not negotiable. We hold on to ourselves (keep our integrity) and don't get lost in the relationship.

People who hold on to themselves are not overly influenced by what the other person does or does not do. Therefore, people who are well-differentiated will not take things personally. They do not see their reflection in the other person; they see only the other person. Kerr and Bowen note, "The individuality of well-differentiated people is developed to the point that they can be responsible for themselves and not fault others for their own discontent" (1988, 74). This also means that when our differentiation is high, we will not blame our partner for how we feel. Our feelings are our feelings. We are responsible for how we feel and how we act.

If we apply this concept to what Damian was experiencing in his marriage, we can clearly see that he did not possess the capacity to be responsible for himself. He blamed his discontent on Lulu. He made Lulu responsible for his emotional storm. Damian and Lulu were fused. He demanded that she adhere to his rules, and when she didn't, he faulted her for his discontent. We can deduce from Damian's behavior that his ability to differentiate was low.

The lower our differentiation, the more fused we are in our relationships. We accommodate the other person's needs because of our emotional dependency and not from a thoughtful recognition of the need to improve cooperation. We make our partners a hostage to our unreasonable demands and unenforceable rules, or we decide to let ourselves become a hostage to their demands and rules. Either way, we do so to soothe our own anxiety.

If we have low differentiation, then our individuality or sense of self is less well developed. This creates a strong need for togetherness. It also means that our emotional reactivity is more intense, we are more easily triggered, and we are more likely to take things personally.

Can you see Damian in this description? He took Lulu's unwillingness to do the dishes as a reflection of her lack of love for him. Damian was unconsciously hoping that Lulu would finally repair the pain he had experienced from a mother who never showed consideration or love for him.

How to Stop Taking Things Personally

What can we do to raise our level of differentiation so we stop taking things personally? The suggestion I have for you is to listen to your second voice. What do I mean by that? Your first voice is the part of you that speaks first—the part that speaks from fear, anxiety, and emotional dependence. It represents the part of you that takes things personally, the part that is stuck in its personal importance. This is the part of you that says, "What they are saying (or doing) is about me." This first voice is a reactive voice, and it speaks from the part of you that takes what others say as a personal slight, something cruel, condescending, hurtful, mean-spirited, or humiliating.

Your second voice comes from a different place, a place that is typically more mature than the first. The second voice comes from your wise self. It will remind you that what other people said or what they did wasn't personal. It will help you see that their statement or action was about what they thought and believed, not who you are or what you deserve. It will remind you to stop taking things personally.

Depending on the situation and your personality, you may have to listen closely to hear your second voice. You may even have to practice speaking it silently to yourself until it starts to emerge.

But there is another crucial ingredient in this antidote.

The next step in this process is to empathize with the other person. That's right. No matter what the person says, put yourself in his or her shoes. My mentor Dr. Walter Kempler, a pioneer in family therapy, would say, "To be more personal with someone, you have to stop taking what they are saying or doing personally."

> Instead of taking what others are saying personally, we need to ask ourselves, "What am I learning about this person?"

Instead of taking what others are saying personally, we need to ask ourselves, "What am I learning about this person?" If they are calling us stupid, it might mean this is how they were treated in their childhood when someone didn't know a better way to deal with or express frustration. If they are saying things in an attempt to hurt us, it might mean they took something we said personally. Remember, they do what they do because of who they are, not because of who you are.

Empathizing with the other person this way will help you stop taking things personally. It will also help you have a healthier relationship. It will help you hold on to yourself and raise your differentiation. Not taking anything personally will help you achieve emotional sobriety.

In The Four Agreements, Ruiz states,

As you make a habit of not taking anything personally, you won't need to place your trust in what others say or do. You will only need to trust yourself to make responsible choices [differentiating yourself from others]. You are never responsible for the actions of others; you are only responsible for you. When you truly understand this, and refuse to take things personally, you can hardly be hurt by the careless comments or actions of others. (1997, 60)

What I've just told you is a lot to digest. We are so used to taking our emotional reactions as facts that it's hard to realize they are only clues about the way our brains are processing events about us.

Waking up to your emotional dependence is hard work. Extracting yourself from its clutches is even harder! You may have buried your "second voice" so deep that at first you can't hear it. You may be so used to blaming your personal reactions on what others say and do that you can't claim your reactions as your own. You may be so used to manipulating other people or yourself to soothe your own fears that you simply can't see that what was said or done is not about you. It's not personal.

The act of "not taking things personally" is not a one-and-done event. We have moments where we achieve real emotional sobriety and other moments where we slip and have to remind ourselves that "it's not all about me." Emotional sobriety is a practice, a way of approaching ourselves, the people in our lives, and the situations we encounter.

Fortunately, we have many opportunities to practice it throughout the day. If we don't get it right, we can think about our failed attempt and plan for the next opportunity, which may be only moments away. Just as with living consciously, we get better at this practice only a bit at a time. The more we practice, the more accustomed we become to taking stock of our first voice of emotional response, listening for our second voice of wisdom, and combining that with empathy for the other person to break our habit of emotional dependence. As our practice gradually becomes a new habit, our differentiation increases, we stop taking things personally, and we gain emotional independence.

Just so you know, it's a lot easier to write about than it is to do! I've been at it for years, and I still have to check my reactions. But I'm much more emotionally independent now than I was years ago. The practice works.

Sentence Completion Exercise

Here are some incomplete sentences for you to work with to further explore this issue in your life. Take each sentence stem and write it at the top of a piece of paper. Next, repeat it silently (or aloud) to yourself, and then complete the sentence stem with the first thought that comes to mind. Do six to ten completions for each.

> I expect people to _____.
>
> When someone doesn't do something I want that person to do, I feel _____.
>
> I take things personally when someone _____.
>
> A painful experience I had that I took personally was _____.
>
> To stop taking things personally I need to remind myself _____.
>
> If I had 5 percent more awareness about how I take things personally, I would _____.

A lot of what happens when we take things personally is about our expectations for how life should be. We all have something in common with Damian, who expected that his wife would resolve his past trauma. In the next chapter, we see the importance of knowing that no one is coming.

**Chapter 7:
Realizing That
No One Is Coming**

In the past five decades of working with people, I can state without doubt that I have never met anyone quite like Philip. What made Philip unique was his relentless pursuit of a solution to his suffering. He was a seeker on a heroic scale, not unlike author Hermann Hesse's character Siddhartha. But as with Siddhartha, Philip was also discouraged about what he discovered on his journey.

Philip's commitment to understanding himself and to healing his deep wounds caused by childhood traumas was inspiring. He went to AA meetings on a regular basis and attended five AA retreats every year. He spent time helping others and got regular guidance from his sponsor. He was proud to say he had worked through all of the Steps at least four times with his sponsor in the past fifteen years of his recovery.

But that's just the beginning with Philip! He had graduated from the Landmark Forum (a personal development program). He attended four of Tony Robbins's weekend workshops. For a time, he became a saved evangelical Christian. After that, he lived in a Christian commune for five years. Most recently he had become a Buddhist

What stood out in the first meeting with Philip was that he didn't feel like he profited from the journey he had been on. He saw himself as a failure. He blamed himself. He concluded that there was something unfixable about him and his true nature. He was disillusioned and upset because all of his seeking and searching hadn't led him to the so-called promised land.

The bottom line was that Philip still suffered from a deep emotional pain. This was clear even though his speech was peppered with various platitudes he'd picked up from all of his workshops. His demeanor revealed a strong underlying current of nihilism. Even as he had tried so hard to find meaning and purpose, he doubted the value of his own life and of life in general. On some level he felt betrayed by all his seeking and was nearing the end of a long, hard road. He had resigned himself to failure.

In our first session he made this point very clear: "I would have hoped that I'd be further along in healing my pain than I am. I'm discouraged."

Philip paused for a moment, then took a breath. "No, it's even deeper than that. I am beginning to lose hope that I can ever feel okay."

I asked Philip what he meant about losing hope. Here's how he responded: "All the effort and time I've invested in seeking a solution hasn't paid off. I am still in a lot of pain over things that happened to me in my childhood. I've tried to forgive those who have hurt me, but I just can't. I've been given some outstanding direction by some very spiritual teachers, but that hasn't made a bit of difference. The pain is still there. I must be defective because nothing has helped. I've seen several miracles along my journey, but I am not one of them, and I've come to believe that I'll never be one of them. I can't be fixed."

I thought to myself that Philip was very harsh in his conclusion that he was defective and unfixable. I commented on this, and he immediately responded, "Yes. I am hopeless. But I've good reason to be. I've been working on this stuff for over twenty-five years. I've gotten nowhere in dealing with my childhood traumas."

The Wrong Diagnosis

Sometimes we diagnose ourselves as hopeless rather than thinking that we just haven't found the right path to healing. But the conclusion that Philip made was also based on all the effort he put into his self-improvement. He had, he believed, solid evidence for his despair.

In one sense, Philip was right. He had taken a twenty-five-year journey through a variety of self-improvement methods, and none of them had worked. That's sound evidence, except that Philip couldn't see that the thread running through his journey was a toxic idea that was blocking him from feeling better. We'll get to that toxic idea in a bit.

As a therapist and a man who has been in recovery for many years, I've witnessed time and again a powerful force that moves people to seek peace within themselves. What Philip couldn't see in himself was the force within him that moved him toward wholeness. This force was relentless in finding an answer to his suffering. It was this very force that had kept him seeking for twenty-five years.

We cannot fault him for this focus; he was in a lot of emotional pain and longed for peace of mind. He was tired of feeling torn to pieces. But Philip was caught up by the toxic idea that the "right" program or healer would somehow fix him. His absorption with the idea of seeking the right cure meant that he missed out on the remarkable fact that he possessed the balm he sought all along. If he recognized this, it might have given him some peace of mind. But he couldn't see it because he was focused on seeking the program that would yield the results he desired.

There is an inner force that is always moving us toward wholeness, toward what we can be. This is not some hollow platitude. It's something you can observe in yourself. Even though he couldn't see it, Philip had it in droves: He stuck with the effort for twenty-five years! This force creates a biological and psychological imperative. It is always moving us toward what is next. It is always trying to restore our wholeness. It is this force that makes babies learn to walk. It is this force that makes our recovery from addiction possible. It is this force that makes it possible to achieve emotional sobriety.

> There is an inner force that is always moving us toward wholeness, toward what we can be.

Philip had diagnosed himself as unfixable. His misdiagnosis was based on a mistaken assumption that some outside power was going to rescue him. Whether it was AA, self-improvement, Jesus, or Buddha, it was always something outside him. He failed to see that his own drive to seek solutions was a great resource and asset. He missed the answer because, like so many of us, he thought it would be found through some magical outside force. Like Cinderella who desperately wanted to attend the palace ball, he was expecting a fairy godmother of sorts to tap him on the head with a wand and solve all his problems. He was expecting that someone would come to rescue him.

The trajectory of Philip's life was, as you will soon see, based on the desire to have his future reverse the experiences he had in his past.

Philip's Childhood Experiences

Philip's father was severely depressed and alcoholic, drinking a fifth of vodka a day for the first twelve years of Philip's life. During this time, his father, Joseph, was in and out of the household.

Philip was six years old when his father told his wife, Evelyn, that he couldn't cope with the daily pressures of life, including the family, and needed a break. He moved up to the family's mountain cabin, essentially abandoning them for four years. Every now and again, Evelyn would take the children up to the mountain cabin to visit Joseph. But Philip said these visits were always marred with terrible fights between his mother and father. Even at this early age, Philip recalled "being their marriage counselor." He remembered sitting and talking to them about the fight they just had, encouraging them to make up. "I was very good at it, but there was something wrong when a child has to parent his parents," he told me.

Unfortunately, this is an all-too-common experience for children from families suffering from alcoholism and other drug addictions. Children need to be cared for. They lack the experience and emotional dexterity to understand the complexity of adult problems. But worst of all, their internal sense of safety and security is ruptured when the adults around them can't be effective adults, let alone parents. They suffer when they are thrust into the role of being caretakers for their parents.

Joseph eventually moved back home, but he became verbally and physically abusive toward Philip. His mother never addressed any of the abuse, blaming his father's inappropriate behavior on his "depression." She neglected Philip's needs and unintentionally dismissed him and his feelings. She'd encourage Philip to be more understanding and tolerant of his father. Philip recalled her making excuses for his dad, saying, "He can't help himself. He really loves you; he's just depressed." She never mentioned his alcoholism. She was in denial.

Though the family members were all excited about their father coming home, Philip said it was soon apparent that things weren't getting better. His mom seemed overwhelmed and angry.

"You know," he said, "now, as an adult, I can see that for all intents and purposes she was a single parent—except she also had to deal with the craziness my dad inserted into our lives." The fights between his mom and dad escalated, and Philip continued to act as their marriage counselor, despite the physical and verbal abuse he experienced.

When I asked Philip when he first remembered feeling bad about himself, like he was defective or didn't belong, he paused and stated that it was around the age of six or seven. "I never fit in with the other kids. I was a bit of a nerd," he said. "I was awkward, shy, self-conscious, sensitive, and lonely. I basically felt uncomfortable in my own skin."

No wonder he never fit in. He lived in a constant state of fear that his family would fall apart if he wasn't around to save it. He suffered terribly under his father's abusive words and angry fists. He hid all this. So while most children were playing, he only pretended to play. He was absorbed in the very difficult job of rescuing his parents from themselves. Philip had burdens he could share with no one, especially not his peers, and even if he tried to play in order to fit in, it's likely the other children could see that he wasn't really in the game.

Philip's upbringing was a classic example of how to rear an addict. His parents were inconsistently loving and abusive, especially his father. They dismissed his own emotional experience (especially his fears) and gave him praise only when he served as a sort of go-between counselor for them. He lived on a razor's edge, constantly worried that he'd lose them if he didn't do a good job of keeping them together.

What made matters even worse for Philip was that as a preteen, he was molested by a neighbor for three years. An older, married man groomed him to become his sexual object. He recognized Philip's awkward outsider manner, befriended him, and took full advantage of his emotional vulnerability. Philip needed a parent, friend, and confidant, and this predator knew how to play the part.

As he became a young adult, Philip realized how he had been exploited and betrayed. He was ashamed of this experience and never told his friends or teachers, only rarely talking about it as he entered his early adulthood. No surprise: Philip started drinking and using drugs when he turned twenty-four years old. It quickly became a problem for him, and at the age of thirty, he attended his first AA meeting.

He loved it.

The Search for Wholeness

Physical maturity is inevitable. We seem to flow with the biological imperative that moves us toward what we can be. We develop the ability to walk, to feed ourselves, to use the toilet, to put ourselves to sleep, and so forth, all due to this inner drive.

The development of intellectual, emotional, and spiritual maturity follows a path similar to physical development, with one significant difference. Dr. Nathaniel Branden noted that the difference was the vulnerability of intellectual, emotional, and spiritual maturity. He observed the following:

> At any step the process can be interrupted, frustrated, blocked, or sidetracked, either by an environment that obstructs rather than supports our growth, such as a home life that subjects us to gross irrationality, unpredictability, violence, and fear, or by choices and

decisions that we make that are intended to be adaptive but turn out to be self-destructive. Such a choice, for instance, would be to deny and disown perceptions and feelings so that, short-term, life is made more acceptable, although in the process we give up pieces of ourself. Then growth is thwarted, intelligence is subverted, and many of the self's riches are left deep in the psyche, unmined. (1996, 18)

Branden could have been writing about Philip. His childhood was marked by irrationality, fear, and violence. The molestation he experienced as a preteen only furthered his insecurity and vulnerability. His decision to turn to alcohol and drugs as a way to soothe his pained spirit in essence constitutes an adaptive choice that subverted more of his growth but ensured his survival.

Philip knew he was struggling. The Catholic church was the first institution he turned to for help. He went to church on a regular basis, loved attending his catechism classes, and became very close to a young priest at the church.

The priest was very supportive of Philip, but the one thing that bothered Philip was that the church seemed to reinforce the idea that there was something defective about Philip. He was, after all was said and done, a sinner first—someone who could be made whole only by Jesus. This was the message he received from catechism, from the church, and from the priest. Philip told me, "The message was that Jesus Christ died for my sins so that I could be free. But I never felt free from pain or rage, no matter how hard I believed."

When Philip discussed the family dysfunction and the alcoholism that occurred at his home, the priest told Philip he needed to pray for his family. Prayer was also the remedy for the neighbor's betrayal and molestation. But no amount of prayer seemed to help Philip heal the wounds of growing up in a dysfunctional family or resolve his rage toward his neighbor.

He next joined a Christian commune, hoping to become whole. It was more of the same philosophy. He was told his anger was a sign that he was living by his will rather than by God's will. If he would surrender to God, he'd forgive his neighbor and his parents. But once again, this reinforced the notion that he was the problem. This just didn't feel right to him, but he couldn't explain why.

This same pattern repeated itself. Every place he turned for help he was told that he was the problem. This unintentionally reinforced his self-hate and self-contempt. Despite the frustration, he kept searching.

Philip's Realization That No One Is Coming

After Philip shared his story with me, I looked at him and said, "It looks like no one is coming, Philip."

By the look on his face you'd have thought I shot his best friend. "What do you mean, no one is coming? I've spent my entire life searching, and you are telling me that no one is coming?"

I answered him directly, "I want to tell you what I mean. I can see it upsets you. I think this is a critical piece of information that no one has talked to you about—until now." I went on to explain that I believed he was looking in all the wrong places for the answer to his pain. He seemed to believe that the answer would be found out there, in the world, rather than within his own psyche.

Philip started to get defensive and responded by saying, "My best thinking got me to this awful place, and you're telling me that the answer lies within?"

This was a very interesting response; he now sounded like everyone else who told him that he ("his best thinking") was defective in some way and that therefore he needed someone to tell him what to do.

I pointed out that he sounded like all the other people who suggested that he was the problem, that he was broken. I told him that was nonsense, that I disagreed with all of them, and I especially disagreed with him. His best thinking brought him to therapy, and that was all the evidence I needed to show him that he had bought the lie. The big lie. That he was defective. His best thinking had brought him to therapy, to church, to workshops, and finally to AA. This was a resourceful self part, not a defective one.

The look on his face said it all. He didn't know how to process what I was telling him. He seemed dumbfounded but a bit curious. I asked Philip what he was experiencing.

He said, "I am having trouble thinking that I haven't seen myself in the way that you are seeing me. It's like I've been looking in the wrong place for all these years. I am curious to learn more. You mean I might be able to heal some of my wounds?"

"Yes," I said. "I believe you can discover some new possibilities in coping with your pain."

I invited him to do some chair work. He eagerly agreed. I gave him the choice to start with his mother or father, or the neighbor who molested him. I knew his choice would reflect the most urgent issue that needed to be resolved. He told me he wanted to speak to the man who molested him. He paused and stated that he had never confronted him. I told him there was no time like the present.

We imagined that his neighbor was in the office, sitting in the open chair. Philip began to recover the integrity and dignity that this man had stolen from him.

Over the next forty-five minutes Philip unloaded years of pain from being exploited and betrayed, rage over being taken advantage of, and sadness because he had really thought the neighbor cared for him, only to find out that he'd been manipulating Philip to get him comfortable doing sexual favors. There were several times during this encounter where I cried with Philip. His loss of innocence was poignant.

At the end of this piece of work, I asked Philip what this experience meant to him.

He immediately responded, "You are right, Dr. Berger; no one is coming."

Philip paused a moment, took a breath, and then said something profound: "I am the one I have been searching for."

Toxic Ideas and Nourishing Ideas

The idea that someone is coming to solve our problems is a variation on the emotional dependency theme. We mistakenly believe that the right environmental support will solve our problems. Well, it won't. This idea diminishes our role in our well-being. It says that we can be fixed only when someone else gives us the answer.

This idea is toxic because it contradicts our true nature. We, each of us, have the answer to our dilemmas deep inside, waiting to be discovered. Because we have somehow and somewhere lost faith in our ability to grow and heal, we don't even realize we possess this wisdom. It's like we have forgotten that we learned to walk.

No one taught us to walk. We had the innate desire and motivation to learn to walk. We wanted to actualize our potential to walk. So, we figured it out. We put one foot in front of the other. But it took time. We didn't just jump up on our two feet and walk. We started where we were at, on our back or on our stomach, and grew from there. We never had the thought that we should be starting from somewhere else. Nor did we have an expectation of how long it should take. We just accepted that we were where we were. We experimented and learned from our experience. How many times did we fall and pick ourselves up and try again? As many times as we needed to learn. We didn't have an expectation about how many mistakes we could make before figuring things out.

Please don't confuse what I am saying as meaning that we don't need environmental support or that we can be self-sufficient. Because that is nonsense—another toxic idea.

We all need environmental support and will continue to need it for our entire lives. I need the oxygen around me to support my life, but it is my responsibility to inhale and exhale. I need the support of my friends and family as I move through life, but it is my responsibility to do the work that helps me progress in my recovery. Those people outside don't "cure" me. They support me.

In other words: No one is coming. We need to show up for ourselves.

In recovery, our sponsors can give us guidance and make suggestions. But we have to try those suggestions on and see if they fit for us, if they are in fact helpful. We need to play an active role in our recovery, especially if we want to achieve emotional sobriety.

•••

I have said that our drive to be whole is innate. Instinctual. But if that is the case, why didn't Philip arrive at his place of healing after twenty-five years of searching? What holds each of us back as we seek to become whole? What makes us lose sight of our true nature?

I believe that a toxic idea holds us back. A toxic idea is an idea that diminishes who we are. It obstructs our development and interferes with self-actualization. It reinforces stereotypes and reinforces the idea that we need to be someone we are not to be okay. It reinforces the idea that I am OK only if conditions, people or life itself lives up to my expectations.

In his constant seeking, Philip sought someone or something that would give him the solution to his pain. He had bought into a toxic idea. In Philip's case, his perpetual seeking is quite understandable. He was set up for it! Remember, we expect our future to reverse the traumas of our past. Philip had an expectation that his future would somehow undo the damage done to him by his parents and his predatory neighbor.

Deep in his heart, Philip believed that something or someone would magically make right the betrayals of his childhood. He had been abandoned, so he thought his future would reverse that by providing him with the person or program who would step in and cure him, show interest in him, act in his best interests, and care for him. He then tried out an astonishing variety of systems, believing each might hold the magic key that would open the doors to peace.

This was Philip's toxic idea: that there was something out there that would rescue him from his pain. Philip hitched his life to the idea that someone was coming to the rescue. This idea is toxic because it diminished the role Philip needed to play in his own healing. Only Philip could unearth the events buried inside him that caused his pain and suffering. He alone needed to find the words that would surface his pain, allow him to share it with another person, and begin to heal his wounds. No one else could give these words to him. He needed to rescue himself.

Of course, Philip, like most of us, needed support to help him find the words. We all need others to hear and understand our pain, to let us know we're lovable and safe despite the wounds we've hidden from public view. I felt fortunate to be in the room with Philip as he found the words and began to regain control of his life. But ultimately, it was his job to do the work.

> Nourishing ideas support our true nature. They enhance our growth and encourage us to honor our integrity. They foster self-esteem and self-confidence.

Nourishing ideas support our true nature. They enhance our growth and encourage us to honor our integrity. They foster self-esteem and self-confidence.

Believe it or not, the statement "No one is coming" is a nourishing idea. It may feel like abandonment, but it is not; it is a statement of your innate access to wholeness. We need to cultivate this idea to support our recovery and help us achieve emotional sobriety.

Sentence Completion Exercise

What does the insight that "no one is coming" mean to you? Complete the following exercise to explore your attitudes toward this news. A warning: This idea is heretical. I think if you are honest, you'll find that on some level, you've been trained to expect someone or something to save you.

Take each sentence stem below and write it at the top of a

piece of paper. Next, repeat it silently (or aloud) to yourself, and then complete the sentence stem with the first thought that comes to mind. Do six to ten completions for each.

> If I took more responsibility for what I want, I'd _____.
>
> A toxic attitude I have that interferes with me showing up for myself is _____.
>
> When I hear the phrase "No one is coming," it means _____.
>
> A nourishing attitude I can integrate into my consciousness that would help me achieve emotional sobriety is _____.
>
> If I had more faith in myself, I would_____.
>
> I interfere with my maturity when I _____.
>
> To have more faith in my internal wisdom, I need to remind myself _____.

Acceptance is the key to emotional sobriety. We explore the importance of accepting what is and its role in achieving emotional sobriety in the next chapter.

Chapter 8: Accepting What Is

Charlene was divorced and shared custody of a beautiful little girl, Emily. Charlene had a solid six years of sobriety and had come to me for therapy at various points when she felt her recovery was threatened. One thing that stood out with Charlene was the incredible relationship she had developed with Emily.

Charlene was a wonderful parent and worked hard at it. One of the pleasures of working with Charlene was the stories she told about Emily, and over the years I began to develop a sense of this lovely girl. Emily brought Charlene so much joy. The two of them made a tight-knit family. Charlene loved to sing and had thought of becoming a professional vocalist. Emily already seemed prepared to follow her mom, by dancing and playing guitar. Together the two spent many evenings after work and school learning new songs, working out harmonies, and recording themselves.

Sure, Emily and her mom fought, the way all mothers and adolescent daughters fight. But they were as close a team as could be. Their relationship was strong. Their bond was impressive.

Then Emily started complaining of a pain in her back. Testing revealed a tumor on her right kidney. It was biopsied and found to be malignant. The doctors removed the tumor and the kidney and started aggressive radiation treatment to prevent the cancer from growing in Emily's remaining kidney.

Emily did great for some months. It was during this time that Charlene began seeing me regularly again. She told me her recovery program felt shaky, and she needed emotional support. Within a month, she had secured a better footing. Her daughter's steady improvement helped solidify Charlene's ground. It looked like things would be okay.

Then the earthquake struck. Emily's cancer was back, a malignant tumor on her remaining kidney. She was not a candidate for a transplant. There was nothing the doctors could do, and nothing Charlene could do to save her daughter's life.

By this time, I was meeting with Charlene several times a week to provide her with emotional support. She was devastated. The cruelty of this situation was unfathomable. I wept alongside Charlene multiple times.

Emily was a gift to her mother and the world, and now she was losing her.

Charlene was reeling. She wanted to drink but didn't. It wasn't easy. Nights were the worst. She had slept at the hospital next to her daughter almost every night and cried herself to sleep most of the time. The conversations with her daughter had been powerful and poignant. This was one of those times in every alcoholic's recovery when they'd like to drink—if only to numb the pain. Sometimes sobriety is about not drinking when it makes more sense to pick up a drink.

In addition to her regular meetings with me to process the pain she was experiencing, Charlene was also attending three AA meetings a week. Still, she struggled. And the main question she came back to again and again was: How could I possibly live in a world that is so cruel and unfair? What is the point of sobriety?

What is the point of life, in a world like this? Is there any path out of this dismal desert?

Indeed, Charlene's question is one we all face. There are times when it seems there is no sense in this world. As a former patient of mine used to say, "Life sucks, and then you die."

The difficulty, unfairness, cruelty, and harshness of life can crush any of us. It was crushing Charlene. She was in a full-blown existential crisis. The foundation of her life was shattered. Her purpose in life was being ripped out of her heart. She wondered why she should keep living if there is no hope. "This isn't the way life should be," she'd tell me. "I shouldn't be dealing with my daughter's death. She should have to deal with mine. How can life be worth living if it doesn't meet any of these expectations?" She was losing hope as fast as her daughter was losing her life. There was an answer to the questions that were emerging from the grief, pain, and trauma she was experiencing, but it would take some effort to discover it.

One of the most frequently cited pages from the Big Book of Alcoholics Anonymous is on page 417. The phrase that is used when quoting this page is "Acceptance is the key to our recovery." Let's explore its content:

> Acceptance is the answer to all my problems today. When I am disturbed, it is because I find some person, place, thing, or situation—some fact of my life—unacceptable to me, and I can find no serenity until I accept that person, place, thing, or situation as being exactly the way it is supposed to be at this moment. Nothing, absolutely nothing, happens in God's world by mistake. Until I could accept my alcoholism, I could not stay sober; unless I accept life completely on life's terms, I cannot be happy. I need to concentrate not so much on what needs to be changed in the world as on what needs

to be changed in me and in my attitudes. (2001)

There's a lot of wisdom in this passage from the Big Book, which explains why it is so widely cited in Twelve Step meetings. This passage has helped many people in recovery come to grips with life, thus beginning the journey of emotional sobriety. But the passage is not perfect—indeed, it did not help Charlene and not because she wasn't working a good program. She was! She attended at least three meetings a week, checked in with her sponsor, and was in therapy. We're going to explore the "page 417" problem in this chapter, but first, let's look at the notion of acceptance.

Acceptance and Self-Acceptance

Acceptance comes in two types: acceptance of the world as it is and, more specifically, acceptance of who we are as individuals.

Acceptance is one of the "big ideas" in recovery. This is one of the great challenges we face: accepting that life is what it is. When we struggle with addiction, we struggle with the idea that we are powerless not just over our capacity to use or not use some substance; we struggle with our powerlessness over everything around us too. Much of our work in recovery, and in achieving emotional sobriety, involves letting go of our crazy-making desire to control things. We have to accept the world on its own terms. We will discuss this big idea later in the chapter, as it is crucial to Charlene's crisis. For now, I want to focus on self-acceptance.

Self-acceptance is a special flavor of acceptance. It is about understanding who we are at our truest moments, accepting all that we are—the good, the bad, and the ugly. It is about understanding our strengths and weaknesses and acting in accord with both. This is a tough job! Admitting our powerlessness is the start of self-acceptance because it forces us to accept that we can't control our addictive behaviors and that our lives have become unmanageable.

Accepting that our lives have become unmanageable reaches far beyond the impact of our addiction. It speaks to the fact that we have created a foundation for our lives that doesn't work. A foundation that is fragile and creates an unmanageable life. A foundation built upon emotional dependence.

When we accept that our problems are of our own making and that we have built our lives upon a shaky foundation we can begin the process of real change.

So, self-acceptance is the foundation for solid recovery. Without self-acceptance there can be no change, no honesty, no physical sobriety, and no emotional sobriety. Self-acceptance is the basis for having a nourishing relationship with ourselves. When we accept ourselves, we become our own ally! We are on "our side" of the struggle because we accept ourselves as we are, not as our false self tells us we should be. Self-acceptance means we can shed the extra pressures of the shoulds that constitute our false self. If we lack self-acceptance — if we are not on "our side," then it will be hard to support our recovery. It will be easy to give in to the addict self when it pressures us to drink again. But when we are on our own side, we protect ourselves, and we honor our integrity.

> Without self-acceptance there can be no change, no honesty, no physical sobriety, and no emotional sobriety.

Dr. Nathaniel Branden, to whom I've referred many times in

this book, thought of self-acceptance as simply "being for ourselves." He went on to define self-acceptance as the "refusal to be in an adversarial relationship to myself" (1994, 91).

If we refuse to be in an adversarial relationship with ourselves, then it becomes quite evident that self-acceptance requires self-support. We support ourselves, our growth, and our maturity. We support ourselves so we can learn from our mistakes rather than judge, criticize or shame ourselves for not being perfect. We ultimately support ourselves by having faith in our ability to grow, to become what we can be, to become whole.

Self-acceptance gradually wears down the prison of our false self. It erodes the shoulds from which we build our own prison walls. Self-acceptance is rooted in authenticity, integrity, and honesty. These elements combine to form a sort of "kryptonite" that weakens the control of our false self. Remember, our false self is built of expectations we swallowed whole, thinking that if we met them, we would keep ourselves lovable. We cannot be authentic and honest and still fulfill the demands of our false self; fulfilling those demands is essentially dishonest and requires that we be manipulative.

In many ways, self-acceptance is outrageous. It challenges the rules imposed by the tyranny of the shoulds. It creates a revolution. It is the means by which we dethrone the false self and recover our lost, true self. It is a step towards our emotional freedom.

I like to think that self-acceptance operates like a calibrating mechanism. It brings us into alignment with who we really are. Dr. Fritz Perls understood the importance of acceptance in addressing a personal problem. He spelled it out this way: "As long as you fight a symptom it will become worse. If you take responsibility for what you are doing to yourself, how you produce your symptoms, how you produce your illness, how you produce your existence—the very moment you get in touch with yourself—

growth begins, integration begins" (1969, 178).

In many ways, self-acceptance is outrageous.

When Perls says, "take responsibility for what you are doing to yourself," he is referring to a kind of acceptance. He invites us to accept that we have been the builders of our own prison. This is radical self-acceptance.

Recall that in Stage I Recovery, we achieve sobriety. Stage I required us to admit our powerlessness over alcohol, over our addiction (or if you like, over our addict self) so we could achieve physical sobriety. Self-acceptance is born at the moment we truly admit that we are powerless and that our lives have become unmanageable. It was at this moment that we began, even slowly, to embrace who we truly are! The admission of powerlessness in turn helped us find a healthier source of power to achieve physical sobriety. The admission that our lives have become unmanageable created an experience of humility which is necessary if we are going to do the psychological work we need to do to achieve emotional sobriety.

Please don't think of self-acceptance as something that just happens. It is something we do. We won't admit or own a problem if we don't first accept we have it. Self-acceptance helps us begin to align ourselves with reality, with recovery.

Being aligned with the reality of our fatal condition (addiction) is a critical step in all recovery. As Bill Wilson stated, "Little good can come to any alcoholic who joins A.A. unless he has first accepted his devastating weakness [alcoholism or addiction] and all its consequences" (Alcoholics Anonymous World Services 1981,

21). But this isn't as easy as it sounds. We don't like to admit we are powerless.

There are many forces at work that make it hard for us to accept ourselves as we are. As Bill W. stated, our natural instincts cry out against the admission of powerlessness. We developed our false self to gain power over our environment so we wouldn't be rejected, be unacceptable, or be unloved. We wanted to control and manipulate people to get them to respond to us as we want them to. Admitting powerlessness threatens the very nature or construct of the false self. It means we don't have the power to control. That's a crisis for us!

If you're reading this book, you are likely either an addict or someone who loves an addict. That is, you're already in recovery, and you have struggled with powerlessness and self-acceptance. There's a reason we resist self-acceptance; it threatens who we think we should be. "Who we think we should be" is our false self, and we mistakenly believe that our false self will make us feel safe in the world. Let's see how one young addict overcame her resistance to self-acceptance.

Backing into Self-Acceptance

Kimetha received a DUI when she was twenty-three years old. She was a single recent college grad who loved her job scouting locations for a company in Hollywood that filmed commercials.

The job required a valid driver's license and a car. The DUI threatened her job. I met her shortly after she was arrested. Her father had worked with me ten years earlier when he finally addressed his alcoholism, and he thought I might be able to help his daughter too.

When Kimetha and I first met, she was quite upset—really put out with all the issues she had to deal with for being arrested for driving under the influence. I asked, "What brings you here to see me?"

"I got a DUI," she said in a surly tone. "Like you didn't know."

"You sound very upset," I said. "What is upsetting you?"

"Of course I'm pissed off. I've got to jump through all of these hoops. Go to court, get an attorney, borrow money from my dad—I really hate doing that—pay fines. I'll lose my job if I can't drive. Everything was going great until this, and now I have to deal with this mess."

Clearly, Kimetha was more concerned with the trouble the DUI was causing in her life than the fact that she'd gotten a DUI. I pointed this out. "I hear how much this is bothering you, Kimetha, but there's something important missing. You are very concerned about the trouble this DUI has caused you—but not the cause of the trouble."

"I don't get it," she said. She gave me a defiant look.

"Well, you're upset about all the issues that you have to deal with because you received a DUI, but what's missing is that you aren't at least equally concerned about what is causing the trouble—your DUI, which means you were driving while intoxicated."

"Are you saying that you think I have an alcohol problem?" Kimetha sounded like I was accusing her of something preposterous, like hiding an elephant in her glove compartment.

"It seems like you might have a problem with alcohol, but right now I'm more concerned with how you're responding to what is happening. I am concerned with your thought process. Instead of focusing on the cause of this trouble, you are acting like a victim of the system," I told her. "When you focus your energy on the hassle from the DUI, you are not able to learn from this experience. You miss important information that may help you prevent being in this situation in the future. After all, one of your chief concerns is that you don't want to lose your job, which would happen if you couldn't drive yourself around to scout locations."

Our conversation continued. Kimetha admitted this wasn't the first time she'd driven while intoxicated, just the first time she'd been caught. We explored other ways in which, since the beginning of college, her drinking had caused problems in her life. As she opened up, she revealed her biggest fear was that she'd be like her dad (who, as you recall, was an alcoholic). Kimetha resented him for his drinking during her childhood and swore to herself that she would never be like him.

She started to cry. "I hate that I am anything like my dad. I despised him when I was a child for his drinking, and now I am drinking too. It's disgusting." Making this admission was an important step for Kimetha to begin to accept her reality.

As we started this session, it was clear that she was unprepared to admit she had a problem with alcohol. Confronting her directly about her denial would likely make her more resistant to seeing the truth. Instead it was necessary to make her aware of her thinking process. Kimetha backed into self-acceptance as she began to understand her thought process. This helped her see the reality about herself: She was drinking like her father—something she'd vowed not to do.

Resistance to self-acceptance must be addressed if we are to achieve any permanent change in our lives—especially if we are ever to achieve emotional sobriety. What a paradox! We need to accept our resistance to self-acceptance in order to begin the process of accepting ourselves as we really are! This is what Kimetha did when she identified her resistance—that she didn't want to be like her father. This declaration set a process in motion that would move her toward acceptance.

Kimetha's process and progress is an excellent example of movement in Stage I Recovery: the recognition of powerlessness and the self-acceptance required to admit we are powerless. Stage II Recovery, as I noted in chapter 2, is really where we begin our journey of emotional sobriety. In this stage of recovery, our first step is to admit that our lives have become unmanageable because of our emotional dependence.

In Stage II, we need to accept that our emotional dependency has caused serious problems in how we function in relationships. We need to accept that we are immature and need to grow up. This is where our false pride can enter and object to such an admission. We must learn that "our ego is not our amigo," as I heard in a meeting. Our false pride is not acting on our behalf—it is protecting the false self.

Bill Wilson recognized the importance of self-acceptance in the letter he wrote on emotional sobriety. In it, he discussed his failure to grow up, emotionally and spiritually. He realized that he had the cart before the horse, that he expected life to conform to his expectations. The turning point for Bill in achieving emotional sobriety occurred when he accepted that "my basic flaw had always been dependence—almost absolute dependence—on people or circumstances to supply me with prestige, security, and the like" (Wilson 1988, 237).

Bill W. accepted that he needed to grow up. He accepted what he was doing that produced his immaturity. He accepted that he was emotionally reactive. He accepted his basic flaw of dependency on people or circumstances for his security.

Bill W. also accepted the responsibility to grow up. He realized that he needed to surrender the hobbling idea that people should behave according to his "perfectionist dreams and specifications" (Wilson 1988, 237). He needed to unhook people and things from his perfectionistic specifications. Another way of saying this is that Bill needed to surrender his crippling expectations.

Self-acceptance is grounded in humility. We realize that no one is here on earth to live up to our expectations. Neither are we here to live up to the expectations of others or to the expectations of our false self. We see ourselves as we are, not according to the specifications of our false self. We are free to own who we are because we are no longer being controlled by false pride. When we accept ourselves, our life will no longer be dictated by should demands. We begin to experience true emotional freedom.

Growing toward Acceptance

Earlier I said that acceptance was one of the "big ideas" in recovery. There is a natural connection between self-acceptance—learning to accept our true self as we are — and learning to accept the world as it is. And the world as it is never fits our expectations. That's a tough lesson, because a part of us always clings to the idea that the world will magically solve our problems. That is, a part of us refuses to grapple with reality. However, our wise self knows the world does not belong to us. It knows that our expectations do not fit reality.

When we are not aligned with reality, we will experience internal conflict. We will be in a civil war with ourselves. We will try to control something that is not in our power to control.

> When we are not aligned with reality, we will experience internal conflict. We will be in a civil war with ourselves.

We cannot alter reality to meet our expectations, but this doesn't stop us from trying. We cannot negotiate with reality, but this doesn't stop us from negotiating. We cannot force reality to bend to our will, but this doesn't stop us from trying to force it.

But at some point, reality forces our hand. We are forced into acceptance.

Acceptance aligns us with the reality of the situation we are facing. When we are aligned with reality, we can discover new possibilities and paths (something we'll cover in an upcoming chapter). Branden acknowledged the key role acceptance plays in making any change: "I cannot overcome a fear whose reality I deny. I cannot correct a problem in the way I deal with my associates if I will not admit it exists. I cannot change traits I insist I do not have. I cannot forgive myself for an action I will not acknowledge having taken" (1994, 93).

If we accept the situation we are in and we let the situation inform our actions, then we learn to cope with life. This is where we left Charlene. She had found herself in an untenable situation with her daughter's medical condition. Her reality had suffered an earthquake. More than shaken, the very ground had fallen from beneath her feet. And her AA group wasn't helping. If anything, it was making things worse.

Remember, when we left Charlene, she was struggling with a horrible dilemma: How could I possibly live in a world that is so cruel and unfair? What is the point of sobriety? What is the point of life, in a world like this? Is there any path out of this dismal desert?

Charlene brought these questions forward as we met over the period that her daughter was dying. Week after week we met. She was struggling to find any sort of hope in her life. Her grief sat in the room like a third person, heavy, dark, immovable. And she was incredibly angry. One session I asked her how her AA meetings were going. It was then that she really exploded.

"They keep throwing page 417 in my face. I can't buy it. I'm not going back."

"Acceptance?" I asked.

"Yes," she said. "Fucking acceptance."

"That's a well-marked passage in my copy of Big Book," I said. "What upsets you about it at the meetings?"

Charlene sighed, closed her eyes, and tilted her head up, reciting the section from memory:

"'Nothing, absolutely nothing, happens in God's world by mistake.'

"I'm sure," Charlene snarled, "that they mean well. They deliver it in the most soothing tones, as though they understand. But they don't understand. Not at all."

"What do you mean?" I asked.

She exploded. "How in the HELL is it soothing to say that 'nothing happens in God's world by mistake'? How is THAT going to help me cope with this nightmare? Are they out of their fucking minds?"

I often ask clients who ask questions to convert their questions into statements. When I asked this of Charlene, here's what she said:

"They are out of their fucking minds. They have no idea of what I am experiencing or what it is like to sit with your twelve-year-old daughter who asks what is going to happen to her body after she dies. They are ignorant, and I don't buy this concept that nothing happens in God's world by mistake. This is a big fucking mistake, and it is happening in their God's world."

If I were a minister delivering a homily, this might be the point where I could provide some sort of helpful, comforting answer to Charlene's dilemma. But I am not. I am a therapist who has lived his own tragedies and been present for the tragedies of many others. And I knew there was nothing I could say that would soothe Charlene. Charlene needed to grieve. She needed to give full expression to all of her feelings, including her rage. She needed to repair herself, and the mechanism to do that resided deep inside of her, buried under mountains of pain and unreasonable expectations. We set out on an excavation to help her unearth the parts of her that could help her integrate this traumatic experience.

I invited her to put the AA group in an empty chair and give the group members a piece of her mind. She jumped at the opportunity. She gave them much more than a piece of her mind that late afternoon.

She started out saying that she recognized they were trying to help her, but then she let them have it. "How can you tell me that God doesn't make a mistake when my daughter is in the hospital dying? She's an innocent child who is being ravaged by cancer. She didn't do anything to deserve this pain and suffering, and you tell me that this is God's will? Fuck your God that would do this to my daughter! And for you to even present me with this cruel idea—you are not helping me; you are making me feel even more alone."

With that last statement she collapsed into tears. They poured forth from some place deep inside of her suffering. Inexpressible pain was voiced only in sobs. This was Charlene's brutal path to acceptance. She needed to discover or uncover the words and sounds that reflected the outrage and horror of the experience both she and her daughter were going through.

This is what her therapy consisted of while her daughter was in the hospital and after she passed away. Charlene needed to feel and express her pain, her outrage, her loss, and her objection to "the whole motherfucking thing," as she called it.

In one of our sessions, I encouraged her to have it out with God. The dialogue was quite powerful. After raging about what she felt was God's betrayal, she came to an important realization. For Charlene the bottom line was that she had the idea that God was supposed to be someone who would protect her and her family, especially from the kind of experiences she was currently having. She smiled after she made this claim out loud, "What a ridiculous expectation. I really set myself up with that one, didn't

I?"

I smiled in agreement.

One day Charlene came into our session with her own idea of who needed to go in the chair. She wanted to dialogue with the cancer that was killing her daughter. I immediately commented on what a wonderful idea this was. So, she did it.

She tore into the cancer like an angry mother bear defending its cub: "I hate you. I hate what you are doing to my daughter. How dare you invade my precious little girl! You are a fucking monster."

But this wasn't enough. She needed to use her whole self to express these feelings. I handed her a rolled-up towel to wallop the cancer. She attacked the chair. With every swat, she yelled, "I hate you. Leave my daughter alone!" Over and over again she hit and shouted. This must have gone on for a good half an hour. Finally, she collapsed in a state of exhaustion. But I sensed that with each swing of the towel, she had inched closer to acceptance.

I want to remind you that acceptance is something we do. What Charlene was doing was actually helping her move closer to accepting the unacceptable, the unimaginable. How was she moving closer to acceptance? By owning her truth. By experiencing her rage, her outrage, her pain, her fears, and by declaring her truth.

Sometimes acceptance is born out of a paradox: We declare we won't accept the situation as it is. As we declare our lack of acceptance, we are actually moving closer to acceptance. This was Charlene's path.

At certain times, I would present her with a sentence completion task—like, "I will not accept what is happening," or "It's impossible to accept this because it means _____"—and then she would fill in the blank. Here are some of the completions:

- ☐ "My life will never be the same."
- ☐ "I will never be certain of anything ever again."
- ☐ "Life is fragile."
- ☐ "I am not in control."
- ☐ "I will no longer be able to hold my precious Emily."
- ☐ "Life isn't fair."
- ☐ "God sucks."
- ☐ "I will be alone."
- ☐ "There is danger lurking everywhere."

We can get a sense of the effect this was having on Charlene's worldview; it was shattered. As Perls stated, suffering our death is not easy. But until Charlene let her beliefs or worldview be totally shattered, there wouldn't be room for a better and stronger foundation in her life. This is what Charlene was building, a new healthier foundation for her life—one that was better aligned with reality. She was doing this without being aware of it.

Dr. Viktor E. Frankl, author of the popular and important book *Man's Search for Meaning*, understood the powerful transformation that takes place when we accept the reality of the situation we are in. He pointed out, "The way in which a man accepts his fate and all the suffering it entails, the way in which he takes up his cross, gives him ample opportunity—even under the most difficult circumstances—to add a deeper meaning to his life" (1984, 76). He drew this conclusion from the experiences he had as a Nazi concentration camp prisoner and from observations he made of other prisoners and their reaction to the abhorrent reality they all faced on a daily basis.

If men and women in a Nazi death camp could face the reality of situations as difficult and demanding as they experienced on a daily basis, then it seems possible for you and I and Kimetha and even Charlene to accept whatever challenging and painful situations we are facing and learn to cope with it.

In therapy, Charlene realized she had an unconscious expectation that God was supposed to protect her. This is what made her so outraged by the idea that in God's world there are no mistakes. Remember what Bill Wilson suggested: Every time we are upset, regardless of the cause, there is something wrong with us. In this case, Charlene had the expectation that God should protect her daughter, Emily, and God was not. Her reality did not conform to her expectations. Remember, when we fight reality, we lose.

Once she realized her unconscious expectation and faced it, she was able to surrender it. This helped her grow toward acceptance. It was a slow process, a very complicated and traumatic bereavement. Loss associated with trauma is much more difficult to process and accept than other types of loss. But it is possible, with help.

It is here where I would like to discuss a major problem with the oft-quoted "page 417." The problem lies in the following two sentences: "I can find no serenity until I accept that person, place, thing, or situation as being exactly the way it is supposed to be at this moment. Nothing, absolutely nothing, happens in God's world by mistake."

Remember that the prison of our false self is constructed from shoulds—expectations about the way we are supposed to feel, think, and behave in order to be loved, to be safe, and to belong. Did you recognize the "should" in this quote? This passage has replaced our personal shoulds with a new should, one for God: God's world should be perfect; that is, nothing in it happens "by mistake." How does this match reality? Somehow, some way, this concept is supposed to make things okay.

Well, there are situations where this rationale just won't work! Charlene's case is one of them. There are others too. Let's take an instance where a child is molested by a stepparent. Can we say to this child that nothing happens in God's world by mistake? What kind of a God would allow this kind of abomination? Clearly this way of thinking has many limitations. There's nothing okay about trauma, and trying to comfort a person who has experienced a trauma by saying "It was meant to be" will not help that person deal with his or her feelings. In fact, this is encouraging the person to take what Dr. John Welwood called a "spiritual bypass." Welwood, a clinical psychologist and author known for integrating psychotherapy and spirituality, described it as "a tendency to use spiritual practices to try to rise above our emotional and personal issues—all those messy, unresolved matters that weigh us down. I call this tendency to avoid or prematurely transcend basic human needs, feelings, and developmental tasks spiritual bypassing" (2000, 12). The road to acceptance is traveled by honestly stating, confronting, and acting upon what we are feeling, not by avoiding or dismissing our feelings.

You see, Charlene's tragedy placed her directly in conflict with the passage on page 417 of the Big Book. The idea that "nothing . . . happens in God's world by mistake" actually interfered with her grief and her own struggle to accept and incorporate into her life the unfair and tragic loss of her child. Charlene's questions about her expectations were honest, and the path she would follow would help her add meaning to her own life in her own way. The important and brave characteristic of Charlene was her willingness to explore why she reacted so strongly to the shoulds presented to her by her friends and peers in AA. She was angry about the unfairness of her tragedy, and her path would involve deepening her understanding of the difference between unfair and unfortunate.

Allow me to sum this up for you: The expectation of fairness is a major way we resist acceptance.

Overcoming Resistance

Resistance to acceptance generally comes from the idea that what is happening is not supposed to be happening. This means we have an expectation that life should conform to what we think it should be. We idealize what life should be like, and when it doesn't live up to our expectations, we object.

The should is very strong in every person's idealized life or idealized reality. It is at the heart of the problem of acceptance. This expectation was generated by our deep unconscious desire to have life reverse the experiences of our past, as discussed in chapter 3. Every human seems to have a built-in expectation of fairness; in fact, research studies on primates and other animals have shown that we are not the only creatures on the planet who get upset when things don't seem fair.

On a fundamental level, we all are exposed to and terrified of the unfairness of life. This sets us up to try to create an adult life that reverses the unfairnesses we experienced during childhood, whether those unfairnesses were naturally occurring or caused by others around us. Kimetha, for example, fantasized that her future wouldn't include problems with alcohol. She believed that because she hated what happened to her life because of her father's alcoholism, she would never have a problem with alcohol herself. The formula we have is simple: UNFAIR PAST = FAIR FUTURE. That's one big should. Unfortunately, life doesn't work that way.

Charlene had to rage against the reality of her situation; she needed to object until she came out on the other side. The other side is acceptance. When we achieve acceptance, we unleash an incredible force within us. We are hardwired to integrate experiences so they become contributors to our integrity, our wholeness. This force is known as self-actualization. It automatically operates outside of our awareness.

When we achieve acceptance, we unleash an incredible force within us.

Earlier, I described this force as having a biological and psychological imperative that moves us toward "what's next." If I say one, two, three—you automatically think four. This is a small example of how this force is always present and how it operates. It wants closure. It wants to create what has been called a gestalten—a satisfying experience of a reality that is greater than the sum of its parts. This is the same sense we get when we find that missing piece of a puzzle, plop it in place, and suddenly see the whole work of art come together.

Once Charlene reached acceptance, she integrated the terrible experience of losing her daughter into her person. Believing her experience could be of value to others who were forced to experience an unthinkable traumatic event, she decided to go back to school and become a therapist. She converted her deep wound into a sacred wound. The way she carried her cross brought deeper meaning to her life. Charlene found emotional freedom. She achieved emotional sobriety.

The Serenity Prayer is one of our most powerful tools in coping with the seemingly unfair events of life: God, grant me the serenity to accept the things I cannot change, courage to change the things I can, and wisdom to know the difference. The prayer, which can easily be secularized, reminds us to differentiate between those very few things that we can control and the many things in life that we cannot. Among the few things we can control are our expectations—our shoulds. When we recognize and then surrender our shoulds, we clear the way for acceptance. We clear the way for emotional sobriety.

We can also create a different context around our shoulds. Many people have found success reframing the word unfair as unfortunate. In a sense, this is what the Serenity Prayer invites us to do. We cannot control unfortunate events. When we cling to the idea that our life should be fair,[4] we set ourselves up to determine what is fair and what is unfair according to our own expectations. When we reframe events as unfortunate, we release ourselves from the expectation that events should conform to our wishes. We can back into acceptance of the world.

Sentence Completion Exercise

Any endeavor to change must include looking at the forces within us that would sabotage our best efforts. We need to become aware of how we interfere with the process of acceptance. The following exercise can help. Take each sentence stem and write it at the top of a piece of paper. Next, repeat the sentence stem silently (or aloud) to yourself, and then complete it with the first thought that comes to mind. Do six to ten completions for each.

Something that I have trouble accepting about myself is _____.

Something that I have trouble accepting about life is _____.

Something I can't control that I try to control is _____.

One way that I can better support my true self is _____.

The most powerful should in my life is _____.

One way that I can overcome my resistance to accepting

4   There is an important difference between what is just and what is fair. I believe we need to always seek justice in life, for ourselves and others, but that discussion is outside the scope of this book. Here, I am limiting the idea of "fair" to those things that agree with our expectations in life, whether those expectations are reasonable or not.

a reality I am having difficulty with is _____.

If I could undo one unfair thing from my past, it would be _____.

If I could reframe that experience from my past as unfortunate, it would mean _____.

To make acceptance a daily practice, I need to _____.

If I can increase my level of acceptance by 5 percent it would _____.

Acceptance is not passive. It is something we do, and when we do it, it can actually change us and our life's trajectory. It is a daily practice of learning to live life on life's terms. We look at ways to do that in the next chapter.

**Chapter 9:
Living Life on
Life's Terms**

The concept of living life on life's terms sounds so simple. That's because it is, but don't confuse simple with easy. Living life on life's terms takes a major and difficult shift in our consciousness. We have to surrender our expectations. All of our expectations. Simple concept, arduous execution.

Our expectations are deeply woven into the fabric of our consciousness. Some of our expectations are obvious to us and we can easily state them: We expect to be treated fairly, we expect others to be honest with us, we expect to gather on a holiday, and we expect that a contract will be honored.

Other expectations are hidden and unconscious. They surface spontaneously when we hit a bump in life: We expect that our mate will automatically know and do what's best for us, we expect that our work colleagues will notice and appreciate our performance, we expect a fellow member in recovery to have empathy, we expect a sponsor to make our time together a priority, and we expect that our holiday gathering will leave us with a sense of being loved and being a part of something greater than ourselves. We expect life will unfold a certain way.

For most of us, letting go of our expectations—both the obvious and the hidden—will be the greatest challenge in our quest for emotional sobriety.

> For most of us, letting go of our expectations—both the obvious and the hidden—will be the greatest challenge in our quest for emotional sobriety.

Surrendering our expectations and living life on life's terms takes humility and the ability to "roll with the punches." These two traits are necessary to achieve emotional sobriety.

What makes these two traits important to emotional sobriety? The answer is important. Humility is defined as "the quality of being humble, characterized by a low focus on the self, an accurate (not over- or underestimated) sense of one's accomplishments and worth, and an acknowledgment of one's limitations, imperfections, mistakes, gaps in knowledge, and so on" (American Psychological Association 2015).

Humility creates an experience of being right-sized. The important part of this definition for our purposes here is that we have a "low" (a reduced and more realistic) focus on self and acknowledge our limitations, which means we surrender the idea that we have the right to impose our expectations on people, on circumstances, or even on life itself.

Having the flexibility to roll with the punches is also important in achieving emotional sobriety. We need to be able to adapt to the demands of whatever situation we are facing. If I am rigid, I am going to be unable to roll with the punches. That means that when I take a punch, I will complain about it and get caught up in my should demands: Life shouldn't be like this, people shouldn't act this way, people should just see it my way, etc.

When I let go of my expectations, I am not up against should demands or supposed-tos. I can roll with the punches. The more flexible I can be, the better I can take care of myself. I can respond in a healthy way to whatever a situation demands from me—meaning in a way that keeps me balanced and whole.

Let me start by sharing a personal experience. I've shared this story before, in other contexts, and because it remains a relevant and powerful illustration of the need for this insight, I'll offer it here. This particular event illustrates the incredible power of humility and flexibility to help cope with a very challenging situation.

Facing the Unexpected

My wife and I became pregnant with our first child in July 2012. We were super excited to become parents together. We could hardly wait the nine months to meet this new member of our family who was growing inside my wife's belly. We walked around beaming with joy and love.

This pregnancy had quite a bit of meaning for both of us. For me, it was a matter of wanting to enlarge our family. I wanted to share the experience of parenting with Jess, and I also wanted her to experience being a mother; I knew how important this experience would be to her.

I have two children from a previous marriage and have cherished the experience of being their father. Being a dad has been one of the most rewarding experiences in my life. I love and respect Danielle and Nick, my two older children, very much. The gift of being their father ranks right up there in importance with my recovery, which is saying an awful lot.

My wife was also excited with the pregnancy for her own reasons. Jess seemed to catch "baby fever" shortly after her older sister gave birth to her niece. Baby fever is real, and it seemed to possess her. Her eyes lit up whenever she saw a newborn child. Sometimes I even thought she would start speaking in tongues.

At the time, neither of us realized that deep within the recesses of our minds slept expectations about how the pregnancy was supposed to unfold. We didn't know we had these expectations, but circumstances would soon thrust them into the foreground of our consciousness.

In 2012 my wife was working on her postdoc at a laboratory at UCLA, studying B-cells, an important component of our immune system. She is a cancer biologist. Because she worked at UCLA, we decided to use the services of a group of nurse-midwives who had a clinic at the university. Their reputation was outstanding. My wife preferred a natural birth, and she thought that working with a midwife would best fit that plan. I agreed. My older children were both born at home with the help of a midwife. It was an amazing, personal, and meaningful experience. I even got to boil water! Very cool, from my perspective.

After having an initial meeting to familiarize ourselves with their practice, we decided to have them help us bring our child into the world. "Well-baby" visits were scheduled about three weeks apart, increasing in frequency as the due date approached.

Because we were part of the UCLA hospital, we were also enrolled in genetic counseling. UCLA's genetic counseling program is designed to help parents anticipate the birth of a child with genetic abnormalities so they are better prepared to cope and gather necessary social and community resources. Genetic counseling involves testing the mother's blood and DNA, accompanied by an extensive interview with a specialist who does a very detailed family tree to identify genetic problems in the family lineage. Results are compiled and then given to the midwife to discuss with the parents.

I was attending most of the well-baby visits with Jess. To our delight, they were routine. Baby and mother were healthy. (Daddy was okay too—not that I mattered much!) The pregnancy was progressing without any apparent problems.

One day when I was driving to my office in Hermosa Beach after another routine well-baby visit, I received a phone call from my wife. She was crying hysterically. Between sobs, she told me that as she was walking back to the laboratory after her midwife appointment, the receptionist called. She said the midwife wanted her to return to the office to follow up on the results of the genetic testing. When Jess was brought into the examining room, the midwife turned to her and said, "We have the results back from the genetic testing, and it's not good." Then she explained, "You have a gene that causes spinal muscular atrophy, a very serious medical condition in newborns. If your husband also tests positive for this gene, then your child will have a 25 percent chance of being born with this condition. If he tests negative, the probability of your child being born with this condition changes dramatically in your favor. In such cases, only one out of a thousand children are born with this condition."

My wife's heart leapt into her throat. No expecting mom wants to hear there is a threat looming over her unborn child.

The midwife went on to tell her, "If your child has the worst case of this illness, she will only live a year and a half. Best-case scenario, if she is born with this condition, is that she will live to around the age of fourteen. But she will always be dependent on a ventilator and therefore will not have a normal life."

My wife was in shock. The midwife asked her if she had any questions. Jess was speechless. The midwife ended the genetic counseling session by urging my wife to get me to go to the lab to have my blood drawn so they could determine if I also carried the gene.

Here's the next punch in the gut: It takes six weeks to get the results. Six weeks! You can imagine what that meant to us. We were going to be living on pins and needles for six weeks, at a time when we had expected to be planning for and enjoying the excitement of our growing family.

I rushed back to UCLA, canceled all my sessions for the day, and met Jess at the laboratory for the blood draw. When I saw her, she collapsed into my arms, sobbing uncontrollably. I started sobbing too. We found a corner in the waiting room where we sat and held each other. Although we tried to find comfort in each other's embrace, there was none to be found. We were both flooded with fear and anxiety.

Fear and anxiety are very different emotions. Fear is based on an objective threat, which we had. My wife had the gene. The risk was real. We had something to be afraid of. That would have been difficult enough to deal with, if it had been the only thing on our plate. But it wasn't. We served ourselves a heaping portion of anxiety to go with the fear.

> # Anxiety is impossible to deal with when you treat it like it is fear.

Anxiety differs from fear because it is created by an active imagination rather than some threat we really face. We imagine some terrible thing happening in the future and project catastrophic outcomes. We call this awfulizing. This function of imagination creates a lot of anxiety.

Anxiety is impossible to deal with when you treat it like it is fear. Anxiety is a bit like shadow boxing. There is no one there — and the opponent, who you can never hit, gets to strike back with new and previously unheard-of blows. With Jess's background in medical science and mine in psychology, our imaginations went wild. Our capacity to envision tragic and horrid futures blossomed in the shadows between what we knew and what we didn't know.

I fantasized that we would be spending the next several years of our lives sitting next to our daughter, who was lying in a hospital bed on a ventilator. The picture I painted in my mind was so bleak and depressing. My daughter would never be able to leave the hospital, never be able to enjoy her life, never have friends, never laugh, never run and play, and never dream about a future. I would never be able to push her on a swing, teach her how to ride a bicycle, or show her how to hit a tennis ball. These and other shadowy opponents of my plans for happiness assaulted my consciousness over the next several hours.

I was torturing myself. It would be more accurate to say I was terrorizing myself. I was torn to pieces and couldn't find any respite. Sometimes recovery is about not drinking and using when it makes more sense to drink or use. This was one of those times in my life. But I knew drinking or using would just make matters worse. It would be like throwing gasoline on a fire.

My thinking got quite bizarre. I started imagining that I was in some way responsible for creating this situation, like I was being punished by God for some terrible thing I had done. I found myself in a nightmare, being punished for some unknown reason. Yes, I had done some terrible things in my past, but was there a God up above who was keeping a tally of right and wrong and who suddenly decided it was time for me to pay the price? I hoped not.

I know I sound crazy, but this is where I let my fantasies lead me. Jess was battling similarly wild, once-unthinkable futures. We were out of touch with reality. We were letting our anxiety spin us out of control, and to make it worse, our anxiety was spinning us in separate directions — each into our own private future hells.

I couldn't accept that this sort of thing—a major, unexpected health crisis due to my wife's unknown deadly gene — would happen in the course of life. Captivated by my anxiety, I never considered that it was up to us to figure out how to cope with the potential threat to our unborn child. There is a reason for my failure to cope, and we'll get to that in a moment.

After I had my blood drawn at UCLA, we went home. We received a lot of support from our friends and family that night, but their calls, well wishes, and prayers didn't really help. Don't get me wrong; it mattered to us that we were loved and had a network of friends and family who cared about us. But we were fixated on the worst-case scenario, and no amount of love or support could comfort us.

That evening, on a scale of 1 to 10 with 10 indicating the highest level of anxiety, mine was cranked up to an 11. I wanted to jump out of my skin. I felt terrified, restless, agitated, sweaty, fidgety, defeated, and depressed. My thoughts raced and I cried uncontrollably — classic signs of anxiety. With my training, I should have seen it immediately. But the truth is, I was knocked off balance; I had been hit by a shadow Mike Tyson.

My wife was at least as anxious as I was, maybe even more. The night dragged on. What was there to do? Nothing. The only thing we could do, we concluded, was to wait six L O N G weeks for the results of my blood test. We let ourselves be claimed by the experience we were having. We were collapsing under the blows of our opponent shadow boxers. Positive responses evaded us, and it looked like our only option was to cave in to terror. Our anxiety caused us to maximize the risks we faced and minimize our internal coping resources. This is how anxiety feeds on itself: It catastrophizes the future and discounts our capacity to fight.

Sleep that night was nearly impossible. We tossed and turned, praying for some respite from the anxiety and fear. But we weren't that lucky. How could we sleep when we were so agitated? Our bodies were in a flight-or-fight response. We may have dozed off for a few moments at best, but there was no restful sleep to be found that night.

Understanding Our Shadowy Opponents

Jess and I faced shadow boxers who knocked us off our emotional center of gravity. Now here's what you, as an outsider — say, a coach watching us box — should think about. Were we justifiably upset or was there something else going on that would account for the intensity of our reactions to what the midwife told us?

I believe that anyone would be concerned and upset about being told there was a likelihood that your unborn child would be born with a debilitating genetic disease. There was a portion of our reaction that was appropriate to the situation we were facing. No doubt about it. But there was another aspect of our reactions that wasn't at all in line with the reality of our situation. Let's explore this.

What lurked in the shadows of our consciousness was an expectation. There it hunched, a hidden and slumbering opponent, a giant of a boxer who was roused by the results of the genetic testing. Awoken, our expectation hammered us to pieces. We were flooded with fear and anxiety.

We unconsciously believed that life should conform to our expectations. To be more specific, we expected that we should have a "normal" child. Yes, all expecting parents endure moments when they fear that their child will not be born healthy, but most of us repress this thought and typically don't give it much energy. But Jess and I weren't able to repress what we were experiencing. It was now a real possibility that our daughter would be born with spinal muscular atrophy. We didn't have a clue as to how to soothe ourselves or how to quiet our minds and calm our hearts.

The expectation that we should have a normally healthy child was strong. This is how life was supposed to be. We unconsciously expected life to be as we hoped it would be, that it would satisfy our expectations, that it was supposed to make us happy. This was the heart of the problem. We believed that life should be what we thought and wanted it to be. This way of thinking seemed right. Wasn't it?

No, it wasn't! We had it all wrong. Life unfolds and brings us many surprises, good and bad. Life is what it is. Period. Reality is reality 100 percent of the time.

As I look back at what happened, I realize that we both had placed our emotional center of gravity in our expectations about how life should be. We were being consumed by the experience we were having because we were knocked off balance. Our emotional center of gravity was placed in something beyond our control. As long as we were stuck in this place, nothing would change. We would remain at an impasse, riddled with anxiety and pummeled by fear. We needed to find a way to recover our balance, to find a new perspective that could help us claim this experience. We needed a heavy dose of emotional sobriety.

Defeating Our Shadowy Opponents

We struggled to find sleep throughout the night, flooded with anxiety and fear. The shadow boxers we faced seemed to have won. How could we find a way to quiet our minds and calm our hearts?

I have often found that getting some distance from what I am experiencing can help me discover a novel solution. I kept telling myself that I needed to recover my emotional balance. I reminded myself several times of the advice I've often given to others: The problem is not the problem; it is how we cope with the issue that counts.

I also had page 417 of the Big Book (see chapter 8) rattling around in my head. I believe that acceptance is the key to solving any problem. It also seems true to me that when I am disturbed, it is because I find some person, place, thing, or situation in my life unacceptable to me and I can find no serenity until I accept that person, place, thing, or situation as it is. (That's my version of page 417, edited to fit my perspective on life.)

Reviewing our situation in light of the wisdom of page 417 enabled me to step back and ask myself, "What does it mean to accept the possibility that our daughter could be born with a genetic illness?" The answer to this question would be critical for me to recover my sense of inner stability and balance.

I knew a solution could be found in the concept of acceptance, but I couldn't see it. As I noted earlier, anxiety causes us to maximize the risks we are facing and minimize our awareness of the resources we have to cope with the situation at hand. My anxiety prevented me from seeing any way out of the pain and anxiety. I was at an impasse.

I have experienced many times when my unconscious mind, left alone, uncovers a solution that I could not otherwise find. This is why sleep is so important to me and so very important in this situation. Though it seemed that neither of us were sleeping, Jess and I both must have finally dozed off. I awoke at dawn with an epiphany: I was letting the situation determine my response because I didn't want to accept reality. This is why my shadow boxer was winning.

When I brought my authentic self — the self that accepts reality as it is — to the situation, my course of action became clear: I resolved then and there that regardless of the circumstances, I would love my daughter.

I wanted to be her father, and nothing was going to change that. If she were born with a severe case of spinal muscular atrophy and she lived for only a year and a half, I would love her a lifetime in that year and a half. If we were lucky enough to have her in our lives until she was fourteen, then I would be grateful for the time we had, and I would love her a lifetime in fourteen years. As soon as I made this declaration, my anxiety and fear vanished. They were totally gone. My acceptance of reality shone a light on my shadowy opponent, dissolving it immediately. I was at peace. When I shared this with my wife, she had the same reaction.

We found emotional freedom that morning. After I sat with this newfound peace of mind, a second thought popped into my mind. I realized that my daughter would only know the reality she lived, not the one I fantasized that she would experience. She would experience her life through her eyes and heart, not mine. This meant to me that her life could be rich and fulfilling if we did what we could to make it so. Our emotional maturity was the key.

Our epiphany was not unique. This was also the answer that Dr. Viktor Frankl had discovered decades before our crisis, in the Nazi concentration camps when he was trying to help himself and his fellow prisoners cope with the atrocity they were living. Here is what he wrote about his discovery:

> What was really needed was a fundamental change in our attitude toward life. We had to learn ourselves and, furthermore, we had to teach the despairing men, that it did not really matter what we expected from life, but rather what life expected from us. We needed to stop asking about the meaning of life, and instead to think of ourselves as those who were being questioned by life—daily and hourly. Our answer must consist, not in talk and meditation, but in right action and in right conduct. Life ultimately means taking the responsibility to find

the right answer to its problems and to fulfill the tasks which it constantly sets for each individual. (1984, 85)

Life on Life's Terms

Frankl's insights validate the discovery my wife and I made as we struggled to cope with the potential reality of our unborn daughter's medical condition. What Frankl taught us is that we must have a fundamental change in our attitude if we are going to live life on life's terms. If we are going to achieve emotional sobriety, we must learn to let go of our expectations. This means we have to surrender our expectations of what life is supposed to be and how things should be. Why? Because it does not matter what we expect from life. In fact, our expectations interfere with accepting life as it is. Our expectations interrupt and interfere with our ability to cope.

Physical sobriety began with an admission that our lives had become unmanageable, and this admission opened up a new future for us. In the same way, accepting that we need to live life on life's terms opens the door to emotional sobriety. We discover the possibility of a new way of living that will lead us to right action and right conduct.

> Physical sobriety began with an admission that our lives had become unmanageable, and this admission opened up a new future for us. In the same way, accepting that we need to live life on life's terms opens the door to emotional sobriety.

Taking responsibility for finding the right answer to the problems that life sets before us helps us mature and achieve emotional sobriety. Dr. Fritz Perls described the benefits in this way: "There is always something to be integrated; always something to be learned. There's always a possibility of richer maturation—of taking more and more responsibility for yourself and for your life" (1969, 64–65).

We grow ourselves when we take this kind of responsibility. We stunt our growth, or sabotage it, when we become a victim of the circumstances we find ourselves in.

Please don't misinterpret what I am saying as being insensitive to people who are truly victims; there are many such unfortunates. Suffering is real. Injustices abound. Bad things happen. But as you are learning, it is how we deal with what has happened to us that makes the difference in our lives. Our attitude, which means the position and orientation of our emotional center of gravity, will either facilitate our growth after trauma, or it will reinforce being a victim and therefore disempower us.

To achieve emotional sobriety, we must operate with an attitude that says, "Life is what it is, and our job is to find the best way to cope with whatever challenges life sets before us." When we focus on finding a solution to the issue at hand rather than getting lost in the "this shouldn't be happening" response, we unleash a powerful force that moves us toward a solution.

This is the force I tapped into when I slept on the challenge that my wife and I were facing. The wisdom that came to me that night lives inside all of us — you, me, your loved ones, your neighbors, everyone! I've said it before and I will say it again: One of the major problems we will face in achieving emotional sobriety is having faith in ourselves and our ability to cope.

We've discussed the importance of balance in achieving emotional sobriety. This refers to a balance between our awareness of reality and our self-awareness of our inner experience.

Dr. Nathaniel Branden provided us with a powerful insight into the importance of this balance. "Psychological well-being and effective functioning entails the ability to be aware of the facts and requirements of external reality without sacrificing awareness of inner experience—and to be aware of our inner experience without sacrificing awareness of the facts and requirements of experiential reality" (1971, 128).

When we operate with what I'd call this 360-degree awareness, then we are best able to cope with whatever challenges life presents. As we practice coping with life on life's terms, we will eventually begin to intuitively handle situations that used to baffle and defeat us.

I would be remiss if I did not tell you the end of Jess's and my story. Our daughter Maddy was born without the disorder! She is a happy and delightful person. I believe she would have been just as happy and delightful had she been born with spinal muscular atrophy. The flavor and shape of her happiness and our happiness would have been different, to be sure, but I am certain it would have been just as rich as the happiness we share today. We would be living life on life's terms, and we would be bringing our inner strengths to cope with those terms, whatever they were. Jess and I share the goal of helping our children, and each other, find a happy and rewarding path in life. I know now that, regardless of the terms we were dealt, we would be traveling that path together.

Sentence Completion Exercise

Here are some incomplete sentences for you to work with to explore this topic further. Take each sentence stem and write it at the top of a piece of paper. Next, repeat it silently (or aloud) to yourself, and then complete the sentence stem with the first thought that comes to mind. Do six to ten completions for each.

Life should or is supposed to _____.

I expect that _____.

One expectation about life in general that I am willing to surrender is _____.

One current problem has revealed my expectation that _____.

The expectation I need to surrender to better cope with a current problem is _____.

The hardest expectation for me to surrender is _____.

When I am struggling with a situation because I want it to be different, I need to remind myself _____.

So far, each chapter of this book has set out to help you see what underpins your emotional dependency and come to grips with your particular version of emotional dependency. In this chapter, we've begun to pivot. We are now building a solid foundation to better cope with life by releasing our emotional dependency. In the next chapter, we continue to lay this foundation through the importance of making creative adjustments, or adaptations, to whatever challenges we face, and we learn to discover novel solutions.

Chapter 10: Discovering Novel Solutions

I often repeat the adage "The problem is never the problem." This concept helps us understand ourselves and understand the nature of emotional sobriety. Of course, the statement sounds strange, almost like nonsense. That's what I thought when I first heard it. How could the problem not be "the problem"?

Most often, when we identify a problem, the problem we are describing really revolves more around the way we are coping with an issue rather than the actual issue at hand. Let's take a simple example. Our vehicle has broken down while we're on vacation. We're midway between here and there. It's horrible! What can we do? What if it rains? What if no one will come get us? What if we can't find a service station? What if the car is too expensive to repair? What if the hotel cancels our reservation since we can't show up? On and on. The real problem here is NOT that the car is broken; that happens all the time. The problem is how we're coping.

How we cope with the issue that we are struggling with determines if it continues to be a problem or not. Our coping skills can be effective or ineffective. When we cope well, we achieve peace of mind, serenity and self-respect. We quiet our mind and calm our heart. We find closure. We feel resolved. We feel satisfied. Later, we will not have residual thoughts or feelings regarding what we should have done or said beyond those that help us prepare to handle the next problem.

Coping well allows us to let things go. We can let go because we are finished with it. We are done; there's no reason to hold on. When we are unable to let something go, it means there is still some unfinished business.

> Coping well allows us to let things go. We can let go because we are finished with it. We are done; there's no reason to hold on.

In the previous chapter, we learned that life is what it is. It's how we cope with it that determines our happiness and serenity.

Think about what that second sentence says: "how we cope." We all have a set of coping skills. In early recovery, we have fewer coping skills than later on in recovery. Many of us reading this book once improperly used alcohol or other drugs to cope. In recovery, we may still have unhelpful coping skills, such as manipulating other people. As we've learned, this is the heart of our emotional dependency.

Emotional sobriety adds a lot of new tools to our repertoire, like increasing our awareness, taking responsibility for our feelings, unhooking our expectations, and coping with life on life's terms. These are some of the coping skills we have discussed so far. One of the most important coping skills, I believe, and the subject of this chapter, is to look for and find novel (new) solutions to problems we are facing. As well as being a skill in itself, this is a strategy to improve our way of coping with life. As a strategy, it can help us avoid the trap of emotional dependency — of looking to others or our life situation to "fix" us.

If we look back at the situation that my wife and I faced regarding our daughter Maddy's birth, we can gain some insight into what I am discussing in this chapter. Recall that Jess and I were locked in a vicious cycle of anxiety. Over the course of that long and painful night, I found a path to peace of mind with the prospect of our daughter being born with a genetic abnormality. I had an epiphany, an "aha moment," that helped me regain my equilibrium.

At first, I was lost in the situation I was facing. I responded to the stimulus (the discouraging information about Maddy's genetic risk) by catastrophizing the future. I believe that if I had taken time and slowed my response to the negative stimulus, I could have avoided the catastrophic response. It was only after I finally slept that my unconscious was able to show me the space between the stimulus (the news we received from the midwife) and the response (my catastrophic projection into the future). I was then able to quiet my mind and find myself. In that space I found my truth. I became grounded in the love I felt for my unborn daughter. I chose love over fear. When I recovered my equilibrium, I was able to let the situation go. I was resolved. The situation was completed or finished.

The problem was not the potential health issues of my un-born daughter. The problem was my catastrophic projection of all I imagined losing. You see? The problem is never the problem.

And beyond that, once I quieted myself, I found a novel way back to peace of mind. I recognized a truth that was waiting to be found: Of course we would love our daughter, and the life she would experience — however brief or troubled, from our perspective — would be the only life she'd know. I found a novel solution to our problem, an answer that came from beyond our fears and anxieties.

I hope it is clear that if we are going to achieve emotional sobriety, we need to align ourselves with reality. As we accept reality as it is, we will be ready and able to take the next step. Acceptance automatically moves us to what is next. Because we are aligned with reality, the action we take will be appropriate to the reality of the situation.

Life has movement to it. We feel compelled to move toward wholeness. We automatically move toward what comes next as long as we don't interrupt our natural movement toward wholeness. When we encounter a challenging situation that either we have created or that life has placed on our path and we accept it as it is, then we will get on with the business of coping. But if we get lost in objecting to what it is — refusing reality and telling ourselves "This shouldn't be happening" or "I should have known better"—then we lose any chance of discovering how to effectively cope with the situation at hand. We are too busy objecting to reality or beating ourselves up to find a solution. Blaming ourselves never leads to effective functioning. To the contrary, blame leads to feeling shame or self-hate because we have judged ourselves as defective. It undermines self-confidence. On the other hand, taking responsibility for finding the best and most appropriate solution to whatever we face leads to empowerment and self-confidence. I want to share another personal experience that is relevant to this discussion.

The Miracle on Hollywood and Vine

You have already met our daughter Maddy in the previous chapter. She's a wonderful little girl who loves life. She also loves to watch live plays.

We live in Southern California, near Hollywood, and we are

fortunate to have a lot of live theater available. When she was little, we loved going to the Pasadena Playhouse to see its plays, such as holiday season adaptations of Disney classic children's movies—productions such as A Cinderella's Christmas or A Peter Pan's Christmas. These wonderful shows included a twist of humor for the adults and lots of audience participation, like booing the villain and cheering for the hero. I think I enjoyed them as much as Maddy.

We had so much fun attending these Sunday matinee events that I thought Maddy might enjoy an even bigger production, one at the famous Pantages Theatre in Hollywood. I kept my eye out for a show that I thought might be fun and appropriate for us to see.

When Wicked came to town, it seemed to fit the bill. I purchased three tickets for the day after Christmas in 2016. Maddy was just three months shy of four years old at the time. We were so excited that Sunday as we left our home in Westlake Village. We were all dressed up in our holiday best for our big outing to the Pantages Theatre. Watch out Hollywood and Vine, here we come! Maddy was wearing a beautiful red velour Ralph Lauren Christmas dress. She was so cute.

We parked the car and walked up to the entrance of this grand theater, and I handed the young usher the three expensive tickets I had purchased through StubHub. She took the tickets and then looked at Maddy, whom I was holding in my arms. I was expecting her to say how beautiful she looked or something like that. But instead the usher said, "Sir, how old is your daughter?"

I told her she was three years and nine months old, without thinking twice about it. I imagined she was just inquisitive. Clearly my intuition was off that day.

She looked me square in the eye and said, "I have some bad news for you, sir." I naively asked her what the bad news was, thinking the lead character was replaced or something like that. I was wrong. She said, "I am unable to let you in to see the play. You see, each company that puts on a production here at the Pantages sets their own age limit for the audience they are entertaining. The Wicked Production Company requires that all attendees be five or older for this particular show."

I was shocked. This was the last thing I had expected to hear. This wasn't a part of the wonderful day-after-Christmas extravaganza I had planned for the family.

I asked the usher where this information existed on the website, hoping there might be some loophole I could use to gain entrance to the show. There wasn't one. She explained that the information was provided in the body of the description of the show. My acceptance was setting in. We weren't going to see Wicked; that was becoming clear. I was aligning myself to the reality of the situation.

She handed the tickets back to me and I turned to her and said, "Can I at least get a refund?"

She gave me a sad frown and said, "No. Unfortunately I have more bad news for you, you purchased these tickets through a third-party vendor, StubHub, and we do not give refunds under these conditions."

Now what was there to do? Here I was, standing in the lobby of the Pantages Theatre holding Maddy and $800 worth of tickets we were unable to use. I thought of standing in front of the theater to scalp these tickets but then thought twice, as a police officer was positioned strategically out front to discourage such activity. Noticing there was a Starbucks across the street, I looked over at my wife apologetically and said, "How about we go get a cup of coffee and decide what to do?" She agreed.

Now the good news, and I mean really good news, is that I didn't start "shoulding" on myself. I accepted that I made a mistake and I wasn't beating myself up over it or berating myself. I was just disappointed, which was appropriate for the situation.

We crossed the street and entered the Starbucks, which was moderately crowded. I kept asking myself, What can we do with these tickets? I' d hate to see them go to waste. As we stood in the queue to order drinks, I noticed a young man at the condiments bar fixing up his drink. He seemed to be accompanied by his wife and teenage daughter. I turned to my wife and said, "I think I know what we can do with these tickets."

As I approached this young man and his family, I told him I had three tickets for Wicked and I was wondering if he would like them. I repeated what happened and reassured him that the tickets were a gift and it wasn't a scam — I didn't expect to be compensated for them. He graciously accepted the tickets and looked a bit stunned by the experience.

I rejoined my wife and daughter in line. A moment later he approached me and my family. He was joined by his daughter and his girlfriend. He had tears in his eyes. He asked if he could tell me why he was at Starbucks.

"Of course," I said.

This is what he shared with us:

"I work on the oil drilling platforms out at sea, and next week I will be leaving town for a six-month assignment. I was just notified about this job on Christmas Day, so I haven't had a lot of time to get things in order. But because I am leaving so soon, I wanted to do something special for my daughter before I left for Texas.

"I am divorced and I share custody with my ex-wife. This will be the longest period of separation from my daughter I've ever had, so I wanted to do something special with her before I left. She has wanted me to take her to see Wicked for some time now. So, after I accepted this assignment, I immediately called the box office at the Pantages Theatre and asked if I could purchase three tickets. They told me that all remaining shows were sold out, but that if I came down for the matinee there might be a chance that some seats would open up last minute. The line for these last-call tickets was ridiculous, so we decided to come and get a cup of coffee to decide what to do with the remainder of the afternoon.

"It was like a miracle," he said. "You walked up shortly after we picked up our drinks and offered me these tickets." He started crying. "I can't tell you how much this means to me, to my daughter [she was nodding her head in agreement with tears running down her cheeks too], and my girlfriend. We are very grateful to you and your family. Can we give you guys a hug?"

"Of course you can give us a hug," I said. We hugged and cried together for a short period of time, and then they left to go see Wicked.

I turned to my wife. We looked at each other and said almost simultaneously, "This was the best money we have spent this Christmas." We were so happy that our disappointment became a reason for another family's celebration.

What Went Right

You know by now that many of the stories in this book are about painful and tragic events. But sometimes we can learn just as much by examining what is right in a situation. Several things in the story above stand out.

First, I didn't get lost in beating myself up or getting mad at the Pantages Theatre. If I had become focused on what an idiot I was for not reading the small print on the Pantages website, or if I had focused on how unfair it was that the production company had an age limit for the viewing audience, I would have narrowed my awareness and limited the possibilities of discovering a solution. It is not hard for me to imagine that I might have been so upset that I would have just left the Pantages Theatre in a huff, driven home, and complained about the entire experience. In this scenario, I would have turned myself into a victim of the circum-stances— and in turn victimized my wife and daughter with my self-reproach and self-pity. This would have been unfortunate and unnecessary. I would have been so focused on beating myself up or objecting to the rules that I wouldn't have wanted to go get a cup of coffee, and then I wouldn't have become aware of the opportunity to give these tickets away.

Acceptance of the situation as it was positioned me psycho-logically to discover new possibilities—novel solutions. Accep-tance of the situation as it was allowed me to stay balanced and maintain an awareness of myself and others.

Second, I did not immediately react to the usher's disap-pointing news. Instead, I paused. Had I been reactive and not taken the time to pause, I would have also missed the opportu-nity to discover a solution to the problem I was facing. When I paused, I entered into the space between the stimulus and a re-action. In that space I found a solution to the dilemma we faced. I was able to use my awareness to identify someone who might be interested in using the tickets.

So, I coped with the situation by accepting it for what it was, identifying the real issue to be resolved, and then discovering a novel solution. I avoided getting hooked into an emotionally dependent response. And the result was a Christmas gift that benefited two families — ours and a perfect stranger's.

Viktor Frankl pointed out that when we live in the space between the stimulus and the response, we have the power to choose, and in that choice lies our emotional freedom and our emotional maturity. I would go so far as to say that in that same space, between the stimulus and our reaction, lies our emotional sobriety.

Bill Wilson recognized the importance of learning how to pause before jumping into action. He said, "Our first objective will be the development of self-restraint. This carries a top priority rating . . . . Nothing pays off like restraint of tongue and pen . . . . We should train ourselves to step back and think. For we can neither think nor act to good purpose until the habit of self-restraint has become automatic" (Alcoholics Anonymous World Services 1981, 91).

Living in the space between the stimulus and our reaction allows the best of us to take charge of the rest of us. When we enter into this zone of possibility, we can discover a solution that is based on an integration of both our right- and left-hemisphere thinking. We can define this as the best in us. Let's explore what this means.

> ## Living in the space between the stimulus and our reaction allows the best of us to take charge of the rest of us.

Two Modes of Thinking

Researchers have learned that the two sides of our brain—left hemisphere and right hemisphere—have different approaches to processing information. Each hemisphere has a very specific mode of operation or function. These different modes of thinking can uncover novel solutions to problems.

Our left hemisphere is quite linear and conceptual in its function. It processes information in an orderly and sequential way. It houses our language. It thinks logically and literally. It labels things. It specializes in deductive reasoning, it analyzes particulars, and it asks lots of why questions. It likes to identify cause-and-effect relationships. The left hemisphere of the brain categorizes things into good and bad. It is concerned with the letter of the law.

When we use our left hemisphere to deal with an issue, we see a world divided. This mode of thinking creates an "OR" orientation to the world, meaning that only one view of reality is right. This is true OR that is true; one OR the other is true, not both (Siegel 2011).

Our right hemisphere functions very differently. It is holistic and nonlinear. It is the part of the brain we use to sense emotion and to process information from the body. It operates with sensations, and it sends and receives signals that allow us to communicate, such as facial expressions, eye contact, tone of voice, posture, and gestures.

The right hemisphere cares about the big picture and the meaning of an experience. It specializes in images, emotions, and personal memories. Our sensory experience comes from our right hemisphere. This is where our intuition resides. It is this part of the brain that has a greater role in coping with stress and in regulating our emotions. The right hemisphere is concerned with the spirit or intent of the law.

When we look at an issue with the right hemisphere of our brain, we see a world full of interconnecting possibilities. This AND that can be true at the same time (Siegel 2011).

Dr. Daniel Siegel, a neuroscientist who has conducted extensive research into brain functioning, describes the dynamics between the right and left hemisphere in this way:

> The left hemisphere . . . lives in a kind of "ivory tower" of ideas and rational thought compared with its more visceral and emotional right-hemisphere counterpart. But the two spheres do communicate. These right-left cortical neighbors are linked by the corpus callosum, a

band of neurons deep in the brain that enables ener-gy and information to be sent back and forth between them. Considered in isolation, these differing patterns of energy and information flow enable us to have something like "two minds" that can cooperate and compete. We'll call these the right and left "modes." When the two hemispheres collaborate, we achieve "bilateral" or "horizontal" integration. (2011, 108)

Remember that old saying that two heads are better than one? Well, we have discovered that two minds are better than one. If we can allow ourselves to move freely between these two modes of thinking, our ability to solve problems improves dramatically. Why? Because these two modes of thinking focus on very different information and, therefore, they can identify new possibilities or solutions. We see a much wider range of possibilities because our hemispheres are focusing on and integrating very different data and information. What we might miss if we are being purely logical or literal can be picked up by seeing the whole picture and thinking emotionally, and vice versa.

Let's look at how we can use these two modes of thinking to discover novel solutions to problems—which is an essential skill if we are going to achieve emotional sobriety.

Integrated Thinking Reveals New Solutions

I want you to think of these two modes of thinking as different ways of being in the world. They are two very different modes of consciousness and, as I just mentioned, they both have a role in finding novel solutions to problems.

Remember, the problem is never the problem. The problem is our limited capacity to cope. We have set our own limits, and most of us have a few fixed responses to problems. These responses are dictated by the rules of our false self, which, over time, set artificial limits on our ability to respond. Early in our life we experimented with responses to problems. If a response fit the blueprint of the false self, it was considered appropriate and acceptable. If it didn't, it wasn't an option. This created a pattern to our behavior: We needed to be right all the time or we apologized all the time or we acted helpless or like a know-it-all. Each of these is a fixed response. Like the broken clock that displays the correct time twice a day, our fixed responses work now and then. But most of the time they don't serve us well.

This is what makes it so important to increase our capacity to cope—to enhance our ability to find novel solutions to our problems. We need to develop flexibility and creativity. Awareness of how the two thinking modes operate within us helps us gain control of their capabilities so that we can be flexible and creative. In order to be more effective and to increase our capacity to cope, we need to learn to shift between these two modes of perceiving the world. Moving from one mode to another, almost seamlessly, comes with practice. But we also need to recognize the difference.

> Remember, the problem is never the problem. The problem is our limited capacity to cope.

Following is a list of integrated modes of being that we can use as a frame of reference to begin to experiment with this important ability. All of these integrated modes of being are paradoxical. We need to learn how to hold a paradox in our consciousness or live in a paradox if we want to discover novel and creative solutions to challenging situations.

Grabbing hold while hanging loose: Our left hemisphere grabs hold of an issue and tinkers with it. This can be important in solving a problem. But it is also important to hang loose and not continually focus on the issue your left hemisphere has taken hold of. For example, when my wife and I were envisioning what it would mean to have a child with spinal muscular atrophy, we were clutching the issue and wrestling with it, trying to make some sense of it. When I hung loose and went to sleep, I discovered a novel response to the situation, one that I couldn't find when I was only grabbing hold of it tightly. My right hemisphere saw the bigger picture, which I couldn't see when I was trapped in my left hemisphere mode of thinking.

Being active while living in passive, receptive wonderment: The left hemisphere is looking to get into action to solve the problem. It thinks sequentially and looks at what caused the problem and therefore what can be done to solve it. When I was notified by the usher at the Pantages Theatre that we were going to be denied entrance, my logistical left hemisphere quickly got into action to figure out what to do—find a loophole, get a refund, scalp the tickets, or accept that we weren't going and suggest we grab a cup of coffee. The right hemisphere is more passive and receptive. It takes in the experience and processes it by looking at the big picture. The right hemisphere has a sense of wonderment. When I stepped back to pause, gather my thoughts, go get a cup of coffee, and see if I could gain a new perspective about what to do when we were in Hollywood, I was listening to my right hemisphere.

Analyzing particulars while seeing the whole picture: We know that the whole is greater than the sum of its parts, but there are times when analyzing particulars is valuable. We can find novel solutions when we break problems down, look at the parts, and then allow our right brain to assemble a new whole.

We can also apply the reverse, looking at the whole picture and then the particulars. For example, when struggling with emotional sobriety, I may analyze what upset me, and this can help me identify my unenforceable rules and my unhealthy dependency; I've looked at the parts and then worked my way back to the whole. But I can also look at the whole problem by getting honest with myself about how I am responding to my emotional dependency. Am I still demanding that things go my way, or am I surrendering my inappropriate expectations? Am I committed to growing my emotional maturity and willing to let go of environmental support to learn how to support myself? These are bigger-picture questions and the realm of the right brain.

Being in control while letting go of control: Control is a left-brain activity, while letting go of control is right-brain. We can use both at the same time. This is the essence of the Serenity Prayer. We seek the serenity (a form of right-brain activity, releasing control) to accept the things we cannot change (a left-brain recognition that life is what it is), the courage to change the things we can (a form of control, or left-brain action), and the wisdom to know the difference (an analytical or left-brain activity). This hemisphere switching requires us to be very flexible in our thinking, taking control when necessary and releasing control when it is clear that our attempts at control are blocking our search for serenity. For example, I took control when I explored my options with the Pantages Theatre usher. I also took control when I accepted that the situation was what it was, and we were not going to see the play. But I also let go of control when we meandered over to the Starbucks to explore what we might want to do with our change of fortune. Moving between these two modes of thinking leads us to finding the best solution available to us at any particular moment.

Being certain while allowing for confusion or uncertainty: The left mode of thinking is about certainty. Remember, the left hemisphere deals in binaries and absolute truths—this or that is right, not both of them. There are times when this kind of certainty can be extremely valuable in solving a problem. Other times, it is more beneficial to remain in a place of confusion and uncertainty while we wait for more information. For example, if someone is pressuring me to pick up a drink or get high, being certain about my recovery is critical. But if I am having a difference of opinion with my partner, it is helpful to be open to seeing my partner's side of the situation and to allowing myself to let go of what my left hemisphere is fixed on. Being certain of my position without a willingness to understand the other person's position is demanding that things be my way. This behavior is going to alienate people, not bring them closer to me. It only reinforces our belief in our often-unreasonable expectations, and thus promotes our emotional dependency.

Being serious while having a sense of humor: To achieve emotional sobriety, we need to make a commitment to improve our emotional autonomy. This is serious left-brain business, no question about it, because our emotional dependency is toxic. It destroys even the best relationships. But we must also learn to laugh (right brain) at ourselves as we see how outrageous we are when we expect everything to go our way. How ridiculous, expecting people or life to conform to our expectations! As William Blake once said, "If the fool would persist in his folly he would become wise." The only caveat I'd add to this is that the fool will become wiser even quicker if the fool can laugh at how foolish he or she is. I tell everyone that I became a lot wiser when I realized how stupid I am.

Being curious while being with "what is": They say curiosity killed the cat, but it wasn't the cat's curiosity that killed it—it was the cat's behavior. Curiosity can be very helpful when facing a problem. If we can become curious about what is happening, instead of taking things personally, we can look with a clear head at what we need to change or accept. Emotional sobriety involves seeing patterns in our behavior and habitual ways we have of thinking and responding to situations that bother us. Recognizing patterns and habits is essentially a left-brain activity. Being curious about this is a good thing and can lead to identifying the patterns and habits that are spawned by our emotional dependency. But we also need to be with what is. To sit with what is and let it really speak to us. This "sitting with" is essentially a right-brain activity. Staying with what is can be a very powerful experience and leads to many unexpected discoveries and solutions.

Naming things while experiencing things: Siegel has a saying, "We need to name it to tame it" (Siegel and Bryson 2012, 27). If I can identify and label my emotional dependency and the unenforceable rules it generates, then I can surrender my expectations. This can be a very logical (left-brain) way of achieving emotional sobriety. But we also learn about our emotional dependency through experiencing it, by sitting with the pain or frustration of the experience we are having (a right-brain way of thinking). Both sources of information help us become more aware of ourselves and the issues we need to address to achieve emotional sobriety.

Being intellectual while being intuitive: A lot of times we are going to see the right path for us to take before we are going to be able to take that path. This is okay because it seems to be a step along the arc of learning. Learning is a process that uses both the left brain (intellectual) and the right brain (intuitive). We seem to follow an arc that begins with unconscious incompetence, progresses to conscious incompetence, continues to conscious competence, and if we stick at it long enough, our conscious competence becomes unconscious competence. I believe this is what is meant in the Ninth Step Promise that "we will intuitively know how to handle situations which used to baffle us" (Alcoholics Anonymous World Services 2001, 84). This Promise is that after much conscious practice, our competence becomes unconscious competence. We will intuitively know what to do. Our left-brain work has been integrated into right-brain solutions.

Remember, we use our whole brain all the time. But we can learn how to dip into our intuitive, image-filled right hemisphere to see the whole picture while integrating and harnessing the illuminating experience of our right mode with our left mode. Shuttling back and forth between these two modes gives us a greater range of possibilities for coping. The more degrees of freedom we have, the more likely we are to discover novel solutions, like I did in that Hollywood Starbucks.

Sentence Completion Exercise

Here are a few sentence completions that will help increase your awareness of your ability to cope. Take each sentence stem below and write it at the top of a piece of paper. Next, repeat it silently (or aloud) to yourself, and then complete the sentence stem with the first thought that comes to mind. Do six to ten completions for each.

> I become rigid when addressing a problem when I
> _____.
>
> To stay more flexible when I am confronting a problem, I need to remind myself that _____.
>
> Shifting between my right hemisphere and my left hemisphere when I confront a problem means
> _____.
>
> Hanging loose means _____.
> Seeing the big picture means _____.
> I stop myself from being more flexible because

_____.

If I could laugh at myself more rather than taking everything so seriously, I would _____.

The hard thing about letting go of control is _____.

If I had more faith in my ability to cope, I would feel
_____.

In order to achieve emotional sobriety, we have to surrender our special status. What does that mean? It means we have to surrender the idea that we can be perfect. In the next chapter, we address ways of breaking the bonds of perfectionism, a critical issue if we are going to achieve emotional sobriety.

Chapter 11: Breaking the Bonds of Perfectionism

I want you to meet Maria, who was struggling in her marriage and was sabotaging her own attempts to achieve emotional sobriety. As you will see, her unrelenting pressure to achieve perfection was making it impossible to achieve emotional sobriety. I would even say that for Maria, as for all of us, perfectionism is as much of a threat to our emotional sobriety as emotional dependency.

Maria scheduled an appointment to see me because she was having a lot of conflict with her wife, Judy. She knew their relationship was in a bad place, and she was very concerned that Judy was close to leaving.

Maria told me she didn't know how to address Judy's concerns. She found herself being extremely defensive and dismissive whenever they would try to discuss the matter. She realized that these responses were pushing Judy out the door. She told me she believed her defensive and dismissive responses were really a function of her emotional dependency. She wanted to work on her emotional sobriety and learn how to have a better relationship with Judy.

Maria had been working on her recovery for almost eight

years but relapsed about three years ago, for an entire month. Maria was very proud of the years she had in recovery, which made the relapse even more devastating. She felt humiliated and became suicidal during the relapse, which resulted in her being hospitalized in a locked psychiatric ward for two days. Upon release, her shame was crippling. She had never imagined that she would drink again. She was still perplexed as to what happened that led to her relapse.

Maria said that during her relapse, her alcoholism was "stronger than ever." This is not an unusual phenomenon for many of us in recovery. Addiction seems to progress whether someone is actively drinking or not, and relapse means we pick up where we'd be if we'd never stopped using at all. "It was like I'd just continued to drink for five years," she said. "My behavior and drinking were crazy, out of control on a level I'd never imagined. It was humiliating."

This time around, Maria doubled down on her commitment to recovery. She knew she needed to start growing up. She knew she needed emotional sobriety. Maria wasn't exactly certain how her immaturity contributed to her relapse, but she had some sense that it must have and that it was also contributing to her marital problems.

She was right on both accounts. Because this was a complex situation, one involving Maria's partner, with Maria's consent, I invited Judy to see me in preparation for couples therapy. Judy's story filled out my understanding of Maria.

Judy had been in recovery for twelve years. She was a very active member in Al-Anon. When things went to hell three years ago during Maria's relapse, Judy doubled her Al-Anon meetings and met more frequently with her sponsor. She tried to hold on to herself, but, she said, "It was really hard. I was flooded with anxiety for the entire month Maria was in relapse."

In truth, Judy explained, she had become quite unhappy in

the relationship before the relapse. When they first met, Maria had been committed to making their life partnership "perfect." This seemed to be a good thing at the time. Judy loved Maria's devotion to their marriage and commitment to making her happy. But Judy soon learned that Maria demanded Judy's happiness and satisfaction in return. There wasn't room for how Judy really felt. "If I tried to tell Maria that something she was doing wasn't right or that she was doing too much or that I needed something different from her, she either ignored me or yelled at me or went to pieces. It seemed like she really wasn't doing things to make me feel better or to make our marriage better based on what I had to say—it was only about what she felt was right. I felt pressured all the time to be happy and satisfied, even when the things Maria did were meaningless to me or even went against my wishes and made me angry!"

It was clear that Maria felt threatened whenever she didn't please Judy. Maria couldn't tolerate Judy's response if it didn't exactly align with the way she wanted it.

Maria wanted her life to be perfect, their marriage to be perfect, and, yes, even her recovery to be perfect. Her definition of perfect was very limited and self-centered. Her perfectionism was wreaking havoc in every area of her life.

This dynamic was obvious in the first couples session I had with Maria and Judy. When I asked them what they wanted from each other that they were not getting, Judy spoke up immediately and said, "I want to be able to tell Maria how I really feel about some of the things she does in our relationship that bother me or upset me without her blowing up and putting me down. I'm sick and tired of the fighting."

I turned to Judy and invited her to say that directly to Maria, which she did.

As if on cue, Maria's response proved Judy's statement to be true. Maria launched into blaming Judy instead of responding to her concerns. She dismissed Judy's feelings and started aggressively defending herself. "You never have anything positive to say about me. You are always complaining about me. I am always trying to please you and you don't seem to appreciate it. You are never pleased with anything I do. You are just like my mother!"

My mentor, the late Dr. Walter Kempler, a psychiatrist and pioneer in the field of family therapy, would say that in the first five minutes a couple will show you what is wrong and what is missing. It only took two minutes for Maria and Judy to show me both of these things.

Problems in relationships are caused bilaterally, meaning that both parties in a relationship contribute to the difficulty. The problem between two people is not "the problem"; it's how they are coping with what is happening between them that is causing the real problem. (See chapters 9 and 10 if you need to revisit why the problem is not "the problem.") This means that neither party in a relationship had learned a better way to cope with what was happening.

> The problem between two people is not "the problem;" it's how they are coping with what is happening between them that is causing the real problem.

I could go into depth on the complex problems Maria, Judy, and I discussed, but we're going to focus on healthy relationships in a future chapter. For now, I just want to focus on Maria. Her attempts to craft the perfect marriage were, in fact, destroying the marriage. Maria's relentless drive for perfection was also destroying her own life.

Maria's Curse of Perfectionism

Let's look at how Maria's perfectionism was making a mess of things. Maria couldn't tolerate displeasing Judy. She became highly threatened whenever Judy was unhappy with her. Instead of sharing her vulnerability with Judy, she attacked her. She made Judy be in the wrong and therefore she, Maria, wouldn't have to feel bad about not pleasing her.

She demanded that Judy be happy with everything she did to please her, no matter how Judy really felt about her actions. Maria claimed she wanted to please Judy because she loved her. But her behavior was not very loving.

Maria had a strange definition of love. She believed that love was contingent on the degree to which you made the other person's life perfect. This was one of her core beliefs. If Judy wasn't happy with her, then Maria feared that Judy would no longer love her. Judy's love, in Maria's mind and heart, was conditional. This meant that Maria had to be the perfect partner. She should never displease Judy, never screw up, never be imperfect. But this was also a projection of what Maria wanted. Maria's love was conditional too. Judy had to appreciate everything Maria did to please her.

Maria's expectations of perfection were relentless. She was willing to manipulate and control the woman she loved in order to prove that she was perfect. She was driven to be perfect because of her fear and anxiety that if she wasn't perfect, she wouldn't be loved, she wouldn't belong, and she wouldn't be accepted.

We can see that Maria didn't want to please Judy as much

as she demanded that Judy be pleased with her. That difference meant everything for Maria's troubles. It affected the spirit behind what Maria did for Judy and what and how she gave to her.

Psychologist and author Dr. Jerry Greenwald observed that not all giving is truly generous. Sometimes we give to take. This kind of giving is a manipulation. He explains: "Relating with an expectation that others should respond to our giving in some positive fashion is a prime example of how we create a pattern of self-induced loneliness. Such expectations hamper our ability to become aware of how others actually do respond to us. A phony relationship of mutual manipulation is usually the consequence when two people relate to each other primarily on the basis of each other's expectations" (1980, 52).

Maria was driven by perfectionism, which created a deep sense of loneliness. It also set up a deadly situation where she had to be perfect and Judy had to be perfect. Their marriage had to be perfect, which in Maria's mind meant they were always pleased and happy with each other. There was no room, in Maria's mind, for the kind of imperfection that is normal in relationships. In other words, there was no room in Maria's consciousness for Judy. She didn't show a concern for what Judy wanted or experienced—unless, of course, Judy's response met Maria's expectation.

For Judy, some of Maria's "helpful" actions amounted to a "thank you for nothing, darling." Maria did only what she thought should make Judy happy—not what Judy told her about what she wanted. It's impossible to make someone happy without coordinating your efforts with the other person's desires. But there wasn't room for Judy to say what she wanted in the relationship; Maria took any feedback as criticism if it differed from what she believed Judy should want or feel. She'd say things like, "You never like anything I do for you," and "I work hard day and night to make this marriage good and all you do is tear it down—do you want a divorce?" She just shut Judy down and silenced her, making her wrong for not being pleased with what Maria had done. This created quite a dilemma and was driving Judy out the door.

In truth, there was a part of Maria that genuinely wanted to please Judy, but there was another part of Maria that prioritized doing things perfectly. Maria was in conflict with the side of her that expected perfection. We are going to refer to this perfectionist side of Maria as her top dog bully.

Maria had the idea that she was responsible for Judy's happiness, and therefore the burden was on her to make Judy happy. Why? Because her top dog bully told her so. It is common to take responsibility for your partner's feelings when you are emotionally immature, but when you add perfectionism to this mix, you've really got a serious problem because you are then required to do a perfect job of managing your partner's feelings.

Maria summed up her struggle when she said to me, "If you don't do something perfectly, it's not worth doing." What a terrible curse she suffered from! And it was affecting more than her relationship with Judy. The curse of perfection was infecting every area of Maria's life.

The Spawning of the Top Dog Bully

Perfectionism spawns a self-part called the top dog bully. This part of us is righteous, absolute in its thinking, authoritarian, and punitive. The top dog bully believes it is always right. It tells us, "You should" and "You should not" and "Why don't you?" If these admonishments don't work, the top dog bully becomes verbally abusive and sometimes even physically abusive. I've had patients slam fists into their face or even burn themselves with a lighter because they weren't perfect. Although the top dog bully controls us like a puppet master, it has an impact on the outside world too, as it manipulates others to get what it needs in the same way it manipulates us.

The top dog bully manipulates us with demands of perfection and threats of a future catastrophe, such as "If you don't please your partner or if you aren't perfect, you won't be loved. You'll be left all alone in the world. No one will want you." This is what Maria's top dog was telling her when Judy wasn't pleased with her. It was driving Maria mad with fear that she was unworthy of Judy's love.

Maria's top dog bully was running and ruining her life. Maria was treating Judy in the same way she treated herself. She bullied her with her top dog just like she bullied herself. Her top dog bully made it impossible to have a good relationship with Judy. It also limited her capacity to achieve emotional sobriety because the top dog bully required that she control people and events around her. Her top dog bully, her perfectionism, demanded that life conform to her expectations. As you know by now, this is the very definition of emotional dependency.

Dr. Fritz Perls saw perfectionism as the basis for the famous self-torture game we play with ourselves:

> We usually take for granted the top dog is right. In many cases the top dog makes impossible perfectionistic demands. So if you are cursed with perfectionism, you are sunk. This ideal is a yardstick which always gives you the opportunity to browbeat yourself, to berate yourself and others. Since the ideal is an impossibility, you can never live up to it. The perfectionist is not in love with his wife. He is in love with his ideal, and he demands from his wife that she should fit in with this [Greek mythological] Procrustes bed of his expectations, and he blames her if she does not fit. (1969, 18)

I'd like to paraphrase those last two sentences, since they sum up the problem for Maria and Judy: The perfectionist in Maria was not in love with Judy but with her ideal; she demanded that Judy measure up to her expectations and blamed Judy when she didn't. Just imagine for a moment what it was like for both Judy and Maria to live under those rules.

> Perfectionism is not doing things perfectly; it is expecting ourselves to do things perfectly. It is the relentless drive toward an unrealistic, inhuman, and unattainable goal.

Perfectionism is an expectation of rigid precision: We should do things perfectly, others should do things perfectly, life should be perfect—which means life has to conform to our expectations. Some people assume that perfectionism means they actually do things perfectly. This is a misunderstanding of perfectionism. Perfectionism is not doing things perfectly; it is expecting ourselves to do things perfectly. It is the relentless drive toward an unrealistic, inhuman, and unattainable goal.

The Origins of Perfectionism

What is the origin of the curse of perfectionism? How did our natural instinct to move toward wholeness, toward mastery, become hijacked by perfectionism? While it is beyond the scope of this book to delve into a thorough undertaking of the origins of perfectionism, we must discuss one aspect of its genesis that relates to the concept of the idealized self.

I have previously discussed how we develop a sense of self in relationship to our childhood anxiety that we aren't going to be loved, be accepted, or belong to the group (Dr. Michael McGee, a brilliant psychiatrist, calls this a love wound). This anxiety drives us to search for a solution that will ensure our emotional security. Our "search for glory" results in adopting a persona that we believe will ensure love and acceptance. This becomes our false self or idealized self—the person who will be loved. You can trace the origins of Maria's anxiety in her statements to Judy, "You are never pleased with anything I do. You are just like my mother." Of course, we don't know anything about Maria's mother. But we hear Maria projecting onto Judy her deep anxiety about not being lovable—that is, not pleasing her own mother. In this we hear the origins of Maria's idealized self, the persona that would please her mother and be lovable. We hoped this idealized self would be our salvation. But it wasn't. Because it is false, we can't really live up to it. Our true self always agitates and expands against the prison of this ideal.

Perls noted that the critical point in our development is when we attempt to actualize (make real) a concept of who we should be (the ideal self) rather than actualizing our real self. Expectations are the by-product of actualizing a concept of who we should be. We expect that we should live up to the ideals of the false self. This mandate is absolute. We have to perfect the persona of the idealized self or else we won't feel emotionally secure. Our "should demands" become the driving forces to actualize this ideal concept of who we should be.

Like magma expanding against the earth's crust, the true self is in constant struggle with the idealized or false self. The discrepancy between our true self and the superimposed, idealized self generates massive stress and strain in our lives, and as we face the possibility of failure, we experience ever-greater conflict and unhappiness. Our pursuit of perfection — of some-how aligning our fallible, human authentic self with the unblink-ing image of our idealized self—sabotages any chance for a happy and fulfilling life.

Perls gave a ridiculously exaggerated example to make this point. "An elephant wants to be a rose bush; a rose bush wants to be an elephant. Until each resigns to being what they are, both will lead unhappy lives of inferiority" (1975a, 3).

Perls is telling us that the person who attempts to actualize his or her real self expects the possible, whereas the person who wants to actualize a concept of who he or she should be attempts and expects the impossible. Maria's demands for perfection lim-ited her ability to function well within herself, within her recov-ery, within her marriage, and within other social situations. Maria was attempting the impossible. She was tearing herself and her relationship to pieces in order to live up to her unrealistic ideals. Her perfectionism was creating an impossible way of life.

Coping with Perfectionism

There's a reason why Bill Wilson included the following passage in the Big Book: "No one among us has been able to maintain anything like perfect adherence to these principles. . . . The point is, that we are willing to grow along spiritual lines. . . . We claim spiritual progress rather than spiritual perfection" (Alcoholics Anonymous World Services 2001, 60).

Bill W. warned us that striving for perfect adherence to the principles of recovery would interfere with emotional sobriety. He anticipated that many of us had a streak of perfectionism that would threaten our recovery if it went unchecked. Maria needed to check this part of her.

In a couples session with Judy and Maria, I challenged Maria,

"You're not in love with Judy. You think you are, but you are not. You're in love with your idea of who she should be. You are in love with an ideal."

Maria turned and glared at me. She crossed her arms and demanded, "What are you talking about?"

I held my ground. "I am talking about how you treat Judy. You say you love her and I believe you do, but the part of you that is running your life right now doesn't know what it means to really love someone," I told her. "There's a bully inside you who is running your show. It's the top dog, and the only thing your top dog knows to do is to put demands on Judy to do its bidding. Your top dog bully doesn't care about Judy—it cares about Judy's obedience to its rules. It wants Judy to be a puppet, not a wife, and Judy is tired of it."

Judy began to cry. Her sobs, soft at first, grew louder and louder.

I sensed Maria was starting to become aware of her outrageousness. I pressed on, "This is what Judy has been trying to tell you. It's gotten lost in some of her demands, which we will talk about later.[5] Judy loves you and wants to have a life with you, but there is no room for her with all of the rules your top dog bully puts on her," I explained. "She hates that part of you, and all you do is defend your top dog as if it is the best of you. It is not! There's another part of you that knows that what your top dog bully is doing to Judy, and even to you, is wrong."

At that, the magma force of Maria's true self surged forth. Now Maria started crying. Soon heavy, heartfelt sobs surged from her core. At length she said, "I do know that I'm wrong, but it's so hard for me to admit it."

I told Maria that I'd like for her to think about it in a different

5   A reminder: Both parties in a relationship participate in creating the relationship troubles. I have left Judy's role in the problem out of this story for the sake of simplicity, since this chapter is focusing on perfectionism. Perfectionism shows up in myriad ways whether you're single or partnered. The dynamic we see here—where Maria wants her partner to conform to some ideal—is a feature in many relationships but was especially pronounced in this one and is an example of the destructive force of perfectionism.

way. "It's not hard for you to admit you are wrong—you just did it. It's hard for your top dog bully to admit it's wrong. When it is in charge, it won't admit that it is wrong. I think you need to learn how to deal with your top dog bully before you can learn to have a better relationship with Judy. What do you think?" She agreed.

I asked Maria to confront her top dog. She put it in the empty chair across from her. Frowning, Maria said, "This is long overdue. You've been ruining my life with all your demands and rules!" As she continued, her words slowed, coming between tears. "You're just like my mother. Nothing I did was ever good enough for her. You're doing that same thing to me, and now you're hounding Judy too. And if anyone knows how much that hurts, I do! Leave Judy alone. Leave me alone. Enough is enough." She turned to Judy and sincerely said, "I am so sorry." She sobbed for about five minutes.

Next, I asked Maria to be her top dog and respond to Maria. Maria's top dog said, "You don't want me to leave you alone. You need me. I make certain that everything you do is right. You'd be even more of a fuckup if you didn't have me. You'd never stay sober and you'd never find someone stupid enough to love you."

"Okay, Maria," I said, "now switch and respond to your top dog."

Speaking as herself, Maria said, "I know this is what you've been telling me for a long time and I've believed you before, but I'm beginning to see that you are the real problem. I thought I needed you to be okay, and what I'm realizing is that I've given you unlimited power." She continued, "I can see that you are the reason I relapsed. I couldn't stand your pressure. I let you put it on me to have a perfect program of recovery. The only way I've known to deal with you is to shut you up by getting drunk. No more. I don't want to hurt myself anymore. I don't want to hurt Judy anymore. You work for me now. I am no longer working for you!"

Striving to do things perfectly is destructive only if we let it become so.

Maria was recovering her lost, true self. She was on her way to achieving emotional sobriety. Emotional sobriety is realized when there is an appropriate balance and coordination of all that we are. Maria had been out of balance, and her top dog had begun running the show. In individual therapy, she reorganized her personality and put a much healthier part of herself in charge. This part of her was humble, willing to learn. This part of Maria disagreed with the top dog and the rules it had for Maria, and she brought that dog to heel. This part of her accepted the imperfections that are a part of life.

Things were starting to get better for Maria and Judy. Their relationship was on a new and healthier trajectory.

Bill W. understood that emotional sobriety is contagious. In the beginning of his discussion of Step Twelve in Twelve Steps and Twelve Traditions, he noted, "Here we begin to practice all Twelve Steps of the program in our daily lives so that we and those about us may find emotional sobriety" (Alcoholics Anonymous World Services 1981, 106, emphasis added). As we transform our emotional immaturity into emotional sobriety, others respond. They become more honest with themselves. When we lead by example, honesty is contagious. Emotional sobriety thrives.

I am reminded that it takes just one emotionally mature person to have a better relationship. Maria's clarity and work inspired Judy's clarity and hope.

The drive for perfection can destroy us and our relationships, but it is not all bad. This is what Maria revealed when she said to her top dog bully—her perfectionist self—"You work for me now." Doing things to please our partner (when our partner actually will be pleased by them) can be a good and generous activity that helps make our lives better. Striving to do things perfectly (or very well) is destructive only if we let it become so. My mentor, psychiatrist Dr. Walter Kempler, had some words of wisdom for me on a day when I was struggling with my own perfectionism: "Listen Allen, there is nothing wrong with you striving to do things perfectly, as long as you don't fool yourself into thinking you can achieve perfection. Being perfect is impossible. Your problem is that you expect to do the impossible."

He was right on that day, and his words have helped me find freedom from my own top dog bully. I hope his words help you too.

Sentence Completion Exercise

Here are some sentence stems for you to work with. Take each one and write it at the top of a piece of paper. Next, repeat the sentence stem silently (or aloud) to yourself, and then complete it with the first thought that comes to mind. Do six to ten completions for each.

> The messages that my top dog bully gives me about being perfect are _____.
> The effect that my perfectionism has had on my relationship with myself is _____.
> The effect that my perfectionism has had on my most intimate relationships is _____.
> The effect that my perfectionism has had on my career is _____.
> The effect that my perfectionism has had on my recovery is _____.

My perfectionism demands that I _____.

My perfectionism demands that you _____.

My perfectionism demands that life _____.

I can surrender the demands that my perfectionism
makes on myself or others by _____.

If I were to be free from my top dog I'd feel _____.

As we come to peace with ourselves, it is important to also find peace with those people who have hurt us. In the next chapter, we explore healing through forgiveness and its role in achieving emotional sobriety.

Chapter 12: Healing through Forgiveness

To err is human, to forgive divine.

—Alexander Pope

Forgive and forget? I'm neither Jesus, nor do I have Alzheimer's.

—Anonymous

We hear a lot about forgiveness in our culture, through religion, our AA groups, and elsewhere. The concept seems to split people into two camps. As in the quotes above, one camp makes a virtue of forgiveness and pushes us toward it, while the other camp discounts forgiveness as an unreachable ideal.

Where do you stand? I think both these quotes have merit, but they do a disservice to the genuine usefulness of forgiveness. As a therapist, I can tell you that forgiveness improves mental well-being in profound ways. As a recovering person, I can tell you that forgiveness is essential to emotional sobriety.

Forgiveness is a skill. It is something that requires practice. The skill of forgiveness can be difficult to learn and apply, and moreover, if we tackle it or are pushed into it before we've accomplished other important psychological tasks, it can be disingenuous and prevent us from actualizing our true self.

So there's a reason this chapter on forgiveness comes so late in this book. I wanted to be sure you understood certain things before grappling with the role of forgiveness in your own emotional sobriety. Before we delve further into forgiveness, let's review the journey we've been on so far.

We saw that to achieve emotional sobriety, we must learn to take care of ourselves. There is a process involved in this kind of self-care. Whenever we feel emotionally disturbed, it is because something is disrupting our emotional balance. Achieving emotional sobriety requires that we figure out what is knocking us off balance and take steps to regain it. This is referred to as self-regulation. We need to learn how to restore our emotional equilibrium, regardless of what disrupted it.

Becoming aware that we were sleepwalking is the first step toward emotional sobriety. Our emotional dependency prevents us from real awareness, and as we regain emotional sobriety, we begin to live consciously. As we heighten our self-awareness, we gain insight into our emotional dependency and how it is controlling our lives. We become aware of the expectations that grow out of our emotional dependency and how our expectations create conflict and suffering in our lives. We saw that when people upset us, their actions are about them, not us—that whatever is going on that upsets us, it isn't personal.

To achieve emotional sobriety, we learned that we need to surrender our expectations. We discovered that no one is coming to rescue us and that we need to accept the events of our lives. We need to learn how to live and let live. We need to unhook people from our assumptions that they should think, feel, or behave the way we expect them to.

Releasing people and life from our expectations (our should

demands) helps us regain our emotional center of gravity. We no longer need people, places, or things to "be the way they are supposed to be" for us to be all right. What we need for our growth and maturity is to find a path to serenity even when we don't like the way things turn out. We evolve from an "I am okay if" attitude toward life to the more mature "I am okay even if" attitude.

We learned that sometimes unhooking our expectations means we have to resolve past pain, unhappiness, and trauma — often the unfinished business of our childhood. We survive this pain by imagining a future that would be better than our past. This adaptation to our childhood pain creates an unconscious expectation that we are owed something — that our future experiences and relationships should reverse the pain from our traumatic past. Unfortunately, expectations put us back in the same dependent position that we were in when we were traumatized. We discovered that expecting someone else to resolve our pain is magical thinking and in fact is re-traumatizing.

When we let ourselves say what wasn't said, feel what wasn't felt, cry the tears that weren't shed, and shout the rage that was silenced, we begin to recover the parts of ourselves that were lost. This work is tough and takes a lot of courage and support. But integrating traumatic experiences into our lives results in post-traumatic growth.

There are times when we need to take another step in healing a hurt or betrayal from our past if we are going to find the place in bright sunshine that Bill Wilson referred to in his Grapevine letter on emotional sobriety. This next step is forgiveness. The psychotherapist Thom Rutledge, my dear friend and colleague, describes forgiveness as the natural emotional state we are in when we are not holding on to old pain.

Forgiving those who have hurt or betrayed us is key to addressing our unfinished business with them. We forgive these people so we may release them from our expectations. We do this for us, not for them.

> Forgiving those who have hurt or betrayed us is key to addressing our unfinished business with them. We forgive these people so we may release them from our expectations. We do this for us, not for them.

Forgiving others does not mean that we rise above the hurt we feel, nor that we are no longer upset at what they have done to us because we are now living a more spiritual life. It means that we work through our feelings. How do we do that? That's the skill in this chapter. To see it in action, consider this story from a Saturday evening at one of my Emotional Sobriety Workshops.

The Unforgiven and Unforgivable

I met Victoria at one of the Emotional Sobriety Workshops I lead. Typically, I start the workshops on Friday night with introductions to each other and to emotional sobriety. We have educational sessions during the day on Saturday, exploring emotional dependency, unenforceable rules, our emotional center of gravity, and knowing it's not personal. On Sunday morning we adjourn.

Saturday evening is a special session because it is devoted to personal work. On this particular weekend, there were twenty-eight people attending the workshop. We arranged the chairs in a semicircle and left space at the front of the circle for me to meet with volunteers who wanted to work on their emotional sobriety. Sign-ups are done on Saturday afternoon. Victoria was first on the list.

She eagerly joined me in front of the group. Victoria started the session by telling me, "Even though I have been in recovery for three years, my emotions are frozen."

I asked her what she meant by that statement.

"Ten years ago I was driving a Ford Pinto. My husband was in the passenger seat and my three-year-old daughter was in the back in a child's car seat. We were stopped at a traffic light when a drunk driver in a truck slammed into the rear of our car going about forty-five miles an hour. Our car instantly burst into flames."

A few readers may recall that Pintos had a design flaw. Their gas tanks would often catch fire when they were struck from behind.

"My three-year-old daughter burned to death in the back seat. My husband had burns over three-quarters of his body. He's been in physical and emotional pain ever since the accident. He can only walk with a cane.

"I didn't have a scratch on me. But a part of me wishes I died that afternoon too."

You could feel the mood in the room darkening as Victoria told her story. Even though she didn't answer my question directly, her delivery of this horrific story demonstrated what she meant when she stated she was frozen. Her voice and affect were flat, as though she were in front of an eighth-grade class reading an excerpt from the local newspaper. It was obvious that she was emotionally shut down and disconnected or dissociated from her feelings.

I imagined she had no choice but to shut herself down. It's like we possess an emotional fuse that shorts out when we experience or witness an event that overwhelms our psyche.

I told Victoria that I now understood what she meant when she told me she was frozen. She responded, "I know it's bad for me to not feel my feelings about what happened. But I don't know how to do it. Can you help me?"

I told her yes, there is way. "We get unfrozen when we speak the words that most accurately reflect our experience. When we find the right words, our emotions will flow freely." I then explained the protocol for the empty chair work I wanted to do with her. She consented to trying this exercise during the workshop. Very brave! Her unbearable pain no doubt pushed her to confront her past in front of the group.

The first encounter I asked Victoria to have was to talk to the drunk driver who killed her daughter and injured her husband. "Do you know his name?" I asked.

"Yes," she said, "it's Chad."

"Put Chad in the empty chair in front of you and see what surfaces for you."

Victoria looked over at me and said, "I don't know what to say to him."

I told her to tell him that.

Turning to the imaginary Chad and telling him that she didn't know what to say seemed to unlock a sealed chamber for Victoria. "I don't know," she said, "if there are words to tell you how much I hate you and what you have done to our family. You killed my little girl." Her tears welled up, but she continued. "She burned to death in the back seat of the car, and there was nothing I could do to save her. I don't get to hold her in my arms anymore. I don't get to brush her beautiful brown hair. I don't get to dress her in the morning."

Victoria stopped to wipe her tears, but this only seemed to make room for more. She began sobbing, and her cries of sadness gradually turned to shouts of rage. "I don't get to hear her call out my name, see her reach for me with her tiny arms, hold her as she looks to me for comfort. You killed her. YOU MOTH-ERFUCKER!!!!!! You had no right to be drinking and driving. You were reckless. You crippled my husband too. You took so much from my life. I will never be able to forgive you."

Victoria dropped her head. She cried and cried and cried.

Victoria had touched the entire group. At least half were in tears. I invited those group participants to share what they were experiencing. Several who were in recovery for their alcoholism or addiction related how guilty they felt for driving under the influence. "There I sit in Chad's chair but for the grace of God," one member noted.

When Victoria had recuperated enough, I asked her to have a conversation with her daughter. Things got much heavier. Crying heavily, she told her daughter how much she missed her. She talked about how painful it was to not be able to pull her out of the burning car. She told her daughter that her screams from the back seat still pierced her heart whenever she closed her eyes. Each of these statements were accompanied by tears and deep cries of pain.

No longer frozen, Victoria was alive again. She was grieving her daughter's death and reliving the trauma of that experience. She was still feeling resentful and angry toward Chad, but these emotions were beginning to transform as we talked. She was beginning to finish some unfinished business.

When we interfere with experiencing what we need to feel, we create unfinished business. This interrupts an instinct that moves us toward completion, resolution, and wholeness. Dr. Nathaniel Branden understood this process well. He wrote:

> The emotions that are most frequently repressed are pain, rage and fear. Healthy growth, development and change are thereby prevented from taking place or

significantly obstructed. A person who does not permit himself to know what hurts him, cannot permit himself to know what he wants — cannot permit himself to know and/or experience the importance of the desires and needs that are frustrated, and therefore cannot take effective steps toward their fulfillment . . . . Healthy change necessarily begins with self-awareness — which in turn requires an attitude of self-acceptance. (1971, 121–122)

When we cut ourselves off from what we are feeling, we cut ourselves off from our potential. We cut ourselves off from our humanity. We cut ourselves off from peace.

Victoria was recovering her humanity in the group on that Saturday night. But as you will soon find out, she was also able to liberate herself from the resentment and anger she felt toward Chad and toward herself too.

This is the real significance of forgiveness. Later we tune back in to the group to take a deeper look at how Victoria forgave herself and the man whose decisions had so horribly altered her life.

The Benefits and Nature of Forgiveness

Forgiveness has been shown to be good for our emotional and physical health. Studies have proven that forgiveness is associated with lower blood pressure, less muscular tension, a decrease in anger and rage, and a lower risk for cardiovascular problems. How does forgiveness have such strong effects on our physical and psychological well-being? It creates peace of mind and serenity, emotional states that accompany emotional sobriety. That's one reason why the skill of forgiveness is essential in our quest for emotional sobriety.

The American Psychological Association defines forgiveness as

> … putting aside feelings of resentment toward an individual who has committed a wrong, been unfair or hurtful, or otherwise harmed one in some way. Forgiveness is not equated with reconciliation or excusing another, and it is not merely accepting what happened or ceasing to be angry. Rather, it involves a voluntary transformation of one's feelings, attitudes, and behavior toward the individual [achieved by working through a forgiveness processs or ritual], so that one is no longer dominated by resentment and can express compassion, generosity, or the like toward the individual. (2015, 432)

Forgiveness is at the core of a powerful transformative healing process. The process that leads to forgiveness transforms resentment and pain into peace and serenity. Forgiveness helps us achieve freedom from an emotionally painful experience. By forgiving we recover our ability to claim the experience we have had, rather than letting the experience overwhelm or claim us. Forgiveness helps us take back our power and recover our emotional balance. It helps us regain our emotional center of gravity.

> Forgiveness helps us take back our power and recover our emotional balance. It helps us regain our emotional center of gravity.

When we forgive, we cease blaming people, places, and

things for what we feel. We take responsibility for our feelings. This is something we discussed in chapter 6, Knowing It's Not Personal. We stop taking personally the events that locked us into an unforgiving stance.

The heart of forgiveness is surrendering our unenforceable rules of how people should act or how life is supposed to be. Sounds familiar, doesn't it? Of course it does. Our expectations play a significant role in developing a grievance. A grievance is a serious complaint about some issue we've dealt with, one that feels grounded in principle and thus has a sense of righteousness about it. Yet it really is a shell, housing deep hurt in the form of resentment. The act of forgiveness involves unbinding the resentment and releasing the grievance. How does this happen?

Hurt and betrayal create anger and rage, along with a narrative of what happened that justifies our anger and rage. As we forgive, we temper the anger and rage with compassion, empathy, humility, and a new narrative about what happened. This new story and the emotions that manifest, with deeper understanding of what happened, help transform all of that locked emotion into the powerful act of forgiveness. But this transformation doesn't just happen. It takes courage, an open mind, and action.

The transformative process that creates forgiveness was discovered by the foremost authority on forgiveness, Dr. Fred Luskin, author of Forgive for Good.

Luskin began his inquiry into forgiveness by studying the conditions that caused a grievance. He found that a grievance was the result of four experiences.

First, we took an offense too personally. All offenses have a subjective and an objective component to them. If a man robs me at gunpoint, the subjective component of this is that he chose to rob me. I was held at gunpoint. It happened to me. The objective part of the offense is that he did this because of who he is, not because of who I am. Though it affected me, it wasn't about me. It wasn't personal. This difference becomes very important in the process of forgiveness. In order to forgive someone, it is necessary to not take what the person did personally.

Second, we blamed the offender for how we felt. Taking the example above, I'd blame the robber for scaring me. Yes, he did hold me at gunpoint, but I was scared because I valued my life. Well, our feelings are our feelings. We own them. No one makes me feel this way or that way. I feel what I feel. But when we develop a grievance, we blame the other person for how we feel.

Third, we created a "grievance story." Luskin noted that our minds store memories in categories. We have many files, but we all include a "life is unfair" file, an "I am unlovable" file, and a "this isn't what is supposed to happen" file. The most harmful memories are those in which we felt helpless and angry. When we experience helplessness in response to some current tragedy, we quickly categorize it and create a narrative around that emotion. The narrative we generate turns us into a victim. This undermines our ability to cope because we have disempowered ourselves with the narrative we have generated.

Finally, the tragic event violated one of our unenforceable rules, leaving us with a sense of being betrayed on a fundamental level.

Luskin defined the nature of unenforceable rules in this way: "An unenforceable rule is one where you do not have control over whether your rule is enforced or not. An unenforceable rule is one where you do not have the power to make things come out the way you want. When you try to enforce one of your unenforceable rules you become angry, bitter, despondent, and helpless. Trying to force something you cannot control is an exercise in frustration" (2002, 51).

The most harmful memories are those in which we felt helpless and angry.

Let's take a look at how unenforceable rules interfered with a client of mine who, in sobriety, was having trouble managing his diabetes.

Reframing a Lifelong Grievance

Billy had a challenging childhood. His father struggled with alcoholism, and his mother was a raging codependent. Despite the family dysfunction, Billy tried to make the best of things. He was quite resilient and resourceful. But in adolescence an unforeseen medical problem knocked him off balance for the next fifteen years of his life.

Shortly after he turned fourteen, Billy started to feel extremely fatigued and weak. He was thirsty all of the time and frequently urinated. The family doctor was baffled. But as soon as Billy was sent to see an endocrinologist, he was diagnosed with type 1 diabetes.

Billy was devastated. It was unfair. He was the only one in a family of eight siblings who had this problem. "Why me?" he would cry at night, alone in his room. He felt frightened and anxious about what this medical condition would do to him and how it would affect the rest of his life. He didn't know how to accept it. He was engrossed in the unfairness of his situation.

Type 1 diabetes requires a lot of medical management, much of which must be done by the individual with the disease. Because Billy concluded that his diabetes was unfair (it violated his unenforceable rule), he was in conflict. He resisted accepting his diabetes and the onerous tasks required to manage it successfully. At best, he was partially compliant with his daily management routine.

Poor compliance caused his physical and emotional health to fail. He continued to struggle with how unfair it all seemed. Despite the pleas of his doctor, Billy refused to take better care of himself.

Within a year after he was diagnosed, Billy turned to alcohol and other drugs. Drinking and drug use enabled Billy to smother his anger about having diabetes for a time but ultimately amounted to dousing a fire with gasoline. For the next fifteen years, Billy's alcoholism and drug addiction burned out of control. Like a thief, addiction stole Billy's life, family, friends, integrity, and health—everything of value. For the better part of each day, he stayed locked up in his room drinking or getting high while playing online video games.

Billy's parents decided to organize an intervention. They contacted me, and after a week of preparation, we met with Billy. He was ready. He was concerned about himself too. The intervention was successful, and Billy entered recovery.

Billy and I developed a very strong therapeutic alliance. He did well in therapy, worked hard at his recovery, attended AA meetings, and really embraced the concept of emotional sobriety. After five years of solid recovery, he decided to go back to school to become a therapist. Eventually he joined my two-year training program in Gestalt Experiential Therapy.

This training program has two requirements for students during their second year. First, the students must each conduct a therapy session in the round so that they can be given feedback about how they functioned as a therapist. Second, they must volunteer to be a client.

Billy did very well in the program. He was well on the way to becoming a very good clinician. During his second year, Billy volunteered to work on a personal issue to satisfy the second part of his second-year requirements.

When asked what he wanted to change about himself, he said he wanted to work on his attitude toward his diagnosis. Despite his excellent recovery, he was still struggling with accepting his diabetes because the lifetime "sentence" felt so unfair. Diabetes would likely shorten his life. Worse, he was still only partially compliant with the diabetes management regime his doctor had prescribed. He attributed this to his lack of acceptance of his "unfair state." In his mind, his condition was unforgivable.

Billy was out of balance and poorly coordinated within himself. In therapy, I asked him to talk to his diabetes.

Billy started the dialogue by playing the self-part that was angry about how unfair it was for him to have diabetes. This part raged and railed about this atrocity. Next, Billy shifted to play the healthy self-part. It was informative that even Billy's healthy self found the situation unfair, untenable, unforgivable. That told the story: There wasn't a part of Billy that could help him accept the unfairness of his state.

We tried another angle. This time I had Billy talk as the diabetes. This was the trick. Billy's diabetes said, "It doesn't matter if you think that it is unfair that I am in your life, because it won't change things. I am here to stay. I will be with you the rest of your life." Something seemed to soften about Billy when he said that out loud. It seemed to open the door to some sort of acceptance.

As I listened to Billy, it came to me: He had developed a grievance about his diabetes, supported by the narrative that his diabetes was unfair. This was creating his resistance to accepting his disease; he could not find it in himself to forgive life for afflicting him this way. The word unfair was too much for Billy to accept. Immediately, I thought of a better description. I turned to Billy and suggested he say to his diabetes, "It isn't unfair that you are in my life; it is unfortunate. It's some bad luck for me, but it's my job to play the hand I've been dealt."

It's impossible to know the transformation that took place in Billy's consciousness, but as he described it, it was close to a spiritual experience. Billy loved the word unfortunate. It gave him the seed for a new story about his diabetes, and there was no place in this story for his long-held grievance that his diabetes was unfair. This freed him up to quit fighting his diagnosis and accept it for what it was. After fifteen years, Billy found the internal resources to reframe his battle and, most important, to accept that "it's my job to play the hand I've been dealt." He reframed an unenforceable rule ("Life must be fair") and turned it into something he could act on ("I must deal with my misfortune.") Billy had more work to do, but he was now on the path to playing the hand he was dealt rather than fighting the dealer.

Life happened, and Billy objected. His unenforceable rule about fairness prevented Billy from effectively coping with his diabetes. Our unenforceable rules also make it hard for us to cope with personal offenses. They help us create the grievance narratives that Luskin wrote about.

Billy had stumbled upon a formula developed by Luskin. Luskin designed a protocol for forgiveness, which he said is a learnable skill. Here is his formula for forgiveness: Forgiveness takes place by undoing each of the steps of the grievance process. We learn to balance the impersonal aspect of hurt with the personal, which most of the time means taking something painful less personally. We take responsibility for how we feel when someone hurts us. Finally, we change our grievance story to a forgiveness story, where we become the hero instead of the victim (2002).

During his therapy, Billy saw that the personal aspects of diabetes and its management—all the impacts he had to deal with, from daily injections to potentially a shorter life—were not, in fact, personal. He took responsibility for his feelings of anger as he reframed his experience of diabetes. Finally, he created a new story about his experience, one in which he was no longer the victim of the disease but instead someone who was doing his best (a kind of hero) to deal with an unfortunate life event.

Billy's experience was painful but manageable. Let's now return to Victoria and the truly horrific loss she experienced. Could she practice the skill of forgiveness? Does it apply in such circumstances?

Forgiving the Unforgivable

Victoria had worked hard in the group during the weekend workshop. Using the chair exercises, she had confronted Chad about killing her daughter and maiming her husband. She had grieved and made her poignant good-byes to her daughter. But I sensed there was more work to be done. Victoria seemed ready to take the next step, in the direction of forgiveness. It was late Saturday, but we forged ahead.

I asked Victoria if she'd be willing to continue to work with me to see if we could find her even more peace of mind. She agreed. I asked her to put her alcoholism in the empty chair. "I think you have a lot to say to that part of you," I suggested. She agreed.

This turned out to be a very important step in Victoria's journey toward forgiving Chad. She started out being very harsh toward her alcoholism. "We were already in a crisis, and then you came along and made the situation worse. You told me that the only way I could get through the death of my daughter was to drink my way through it," she said. "That was bullshit. It didn't help me grieve my daughter's death. It didn't resolve anything. And what made matters worse is I abandoned my husband because of you. He really needed me, and I was rarely there for him. I even drank and drove. Do you believe that? I drove drunk full knowing what I might do to someone. That was insanity."

Victoria had a lot to say during that interaction with her alcoholism. What stood out to me was that she was stuck blaming her alcoholism for all of her trouble—which meant she wasn't taking responsibility for listening to that part of her. I made a mental note that this might need to be addressed.

"Okay," I said after she finished speaking to her alcoholism. "Now change and be your alcoholism and respond to Victoria." When she became her alcoholism, she was quite matter-of-fact. "You are blaming me for your drinking, but you picked up the bottle. All I did was to tell you to drink. You chose to drink because you needed to, but you blame everyone for what you do. You even blamed your husband for your drinking, yelling at him that he was not supportive enough and that's why you drank. You're disgusting. Quit being a victim," she instructed. "You wanted to check out because you couldn't deal with losing your daughter. Don't blame me. Now you're all righteous because you're in recovery."

Her alcoholism showed surprising insight. I asked her to switch back to being Victoria and respond.

"I don't want to take responsibility for anything, if I am really honest about how I feel. I don't want to deal with any of this. My denial of this pain is why I drank and why I still want to drink at times." She started to cry, but it was a very different cry than before. It seemed to come from a wiser place inside of her consciousness. Her softened mood gave me the idea that she should have another conversation with Chad.

I mentioned this to her and she agreed. I suggested that she speak with Chad about her alcoholism. She started out the dialogue saying, "I am realizing that we are more alike than I cared to admit, than I've ever cared to see. I became an alcoholic too, and I even drove drunk. I feel terrible about it. Why did you start drinking?"

I asked her to switch and answer for Chad. "I lost my wife from cancer." She knew this from the trial. "She was the love of my life. I will never forgive myself for what I did to you and your family that day." (Victoria told me this was something else Chad had actually said at the trial.)

I said, "Change again. Be yourself."

As Victoria, she paused. "I understand," she said. "I've been there myself."

We wrapped up the dialogue and then discussed the experience. Victoria said she felt something freed up inside of her. She went on to say, "I'm just realizing that I had an unenforceable rule that said this kind of thing wasn't supposed to happen to me and my family. I know that sounds crazy. Why should we be exempt from things like this? There's no denying it, we weren't, and it was foolish to think we might be."

I told Victoria that I thought what was happening to her was positive, but I still thought she was being a bit hard on herself. "You've forgiven Chad," I said, "but not yourself. We've got one more dialogue before you call it a night. I want you to talk to your alcoholic self."

Victoria now spoke to her alcoholic self and forgave it in the same way she was able to forgive Chad. Victoria realized that neither she nor her alcoholic self knew how to cope with this devastating experience and that the unconscious unenforceable rules she had established made coping impossible.

Through these conversations, Victoria was able to forgive herself and left the weekend alive and hopeful, eager to return to her husband and make amends to him.

The building blocks of emotional sobriety make forgiveness possible. Our self-awareness helps us become aware of our unenforceable rules. Taking responsibility for ourselves prevents us from playing the blame game. If we do get lost in it for some time, we can stop blaming and start owning. We learn to surrender our expectations so we can deal with whatever challenges life has set before us.

> Forgiveness is not found in simple platitudes but is a powerful set of actions that enable us to let go of our grievances, write a new story for ourselves, and claim our emotional independence.

Victoria and Billy both had some years of physical sobriety under their belts. I think this was necessary before they began this process of forgiveness. They needed to have at least begun the process of developing self-awareness, of uncovering unenforceable rules, of taking responsibility, and of learning other important lessons of recovery before they could tackle the deep practice of forgiveness. As we describe it here, forgiveness is not found in simple platitudes but is a powerful set of actions that enable us to let go of our grievances, write a new story for ourselves, and claim our emotional independence. If you've been working through the suggestions in this book, you may well be ready too; just don't force it. You can't forgive a harm unless you are prepared to release your grievance and tell yourself a new, more honest story about how you've framed the events of your life.

Sentence Completion Exercise

Use these incomplete sentences to explore forgiveness and what it means in your life. Take each sentence stem below and write it at the top of a piece of paper. Next, repeat it silently (or aloud) to yourself, and then complete the sentence stem with the first thought that comes to mind. Do six to ten completions for each, or as many as come to mind.

> The events that I lack words for are _____.
> The unfinished business and grievances that I hold on to are _____.
> To speak about these events, I can _____.
> The unforgivable events of my life are _____.
> I would have a hard time forgiving _____ because _____.
> The stories I tell to support my grievances include _____.
> The unenforceable rule that was violated for each situation I mentioned is _____.
> The grievance stories or resentments would change in these ways if I rewrote them to release the grievances: _____.
> For me, forgiveness is false when _____.
> For me, forgiveness is real when _____.

The steps you've taken throughout the book should be bringing you to an ever-greater grasp of emotional sobriety. This gives us a sense of freedom. What can we do with that freedom? We can turn to another very important aspect of emotional sobriety, living life with purpose. This is the subject of our next chapter.

**Chapter 13:
Living a
Purposeful Life**

I want to start this chapter with a brief look at Step Twelve: "Having had a spiritual awakening as the result of these steps, we tried to carry this message to alcoholics, and to practice these principles in all our affairs."

Step Twelve helps us maintain sobriety by reminding us of our earliest days in recovery, keeping us inspired, helping us be accountable to recovery principles, helping us regain integrity and trustworthiness, asking us to stay in contact with others, and giving us a sense of purpose.

These important benefits of Step Twelve can see us through life. But as we solidify our recovery and practice emotional sobriety, the psychological and spiritual applications of Step Twelve expand. Emotional sobriety urges us to move outside ourselves, drop any remaining narcissistic tendencies, find emotional freedom, and share that freedom with others, either through action or by example. It asks us to continue an internal practice of "peeling back the onion" to recover our true self. As we do this, we maintain recovery principles in all our affairs. Our practice of the Steps helps us recover our lost true self, if we attend to our inner development. We can then act with integrity in the outside world because we are internally aligned with our true nature.

Some refer to the expansive, sharing aspect of Step Twelve with the adage "To keep it, you have to give it away." That is, as we discover our human potential through the Steps, we find our gifts. We cultivate them and then give them away. We seek to be of service to others.

This does not mean that we find wholeness and then turn to service. Nor that we must seek service in order to become whole. Rather, the two work in tandem. The inner life, our search for wholeness or integrity, energizes our purposeful actions in life. But the reverse is true too; our purposeful actions in the world inform our inner life, our search for wholeness. We act in the world, we have successes and we have failures, we learn from both, and we move forward. Remember, we are hardwired to move toward wholeness. We seek to unite our many selves, to be one, to be integrated. We seek an appropriate balance, coordination, and harmony of all that we are. This is self-actualization.

I firmly believe, as a therapist and a recovering person, that self-actualization is a basic human need. When a basic human need is deprived or neglected, we suffer. Take our basic human need for oxygen. What happens if we aren't getting enough oxygen? The first sign of anoxia (oxygen deprivation) is mood and personality changes. We are no longer able to support who we are because we can't support our existence without oxygen. As oxygen deprivation continues, we suffer memory loss, poor judgment, and slurred speech. We forget words, have trouble walking, lose control of our limbs, feel weak and dizzy, and become disoriented.

If we don't get oxygen, we will die.

When a basic human need — in this case, oxygen — is restored, we become whole again. Of course, oxygen deprivation is a dramatic example, but this is also the case for the basic psychological and spiritual human need for self-actualization. When we cut off our true self, we become emotionally and spiritually unwell — and it can actually feel like a kind of suffocation. When we restore the basic human need to actualize who we really are, to be whole, to feel integrated, we flourish. This is what happens to so many of us who are first trudging, then walking, and finally bounding along the road of recovery. We actually are recovering our human potential, and as we do, we become healthier than ever before. We are recovering our buried, true selves. We are peeling back the onion.

I have used the words integrate, integration, and integrity often in this book. Integration is the coordination or unification of our once disharmonious self-parts into a totality so that they become joint contributors to our choices and behaviors in the world. When these self-parts act in harmony, we are acting with integrity. We are acting in accord with our true self. We are honoring ourselves.

Remember, we buried our true self early in life. We shifted our energies toward actualizing a concept of who we thought we should be. This was tantamount to depriving ourselves of oxygen. Our alcoholism, addiction to drugs other than alcohol, our emotional dependency, our unconscious compromises, the disowning of self-parts that didn't fit with the blueprint of our false self, our dishonesty, our lack of integrity — these were all symptoms of our true self's "oxygen deprivation." Though some parts of us appeared to thrive, we had choked ourselves off from our most human potential, and we suffered dearly.

In a broad sense, Step Twelve asks us to use our life experiences to be of value to others, to function with integrity, and to carry a message of hope to others. In the context of emotional sobriety, I interpret "carry this message" as an urge to be of loving service, to have a purpose beyond self-serving aims, and to help others achieve emotional sobriety. Being of service to others is a critical part of recovery. In the practice of emotional sobriety, this means we live our lives with a purpose greater than ourselves. To do this, we must find our gifts and cultivate them—a process that happens naturally as we integrate our parts—and then give our gifts away. Because our gifts are talents, not material objects, we can only give them away by using them with others. If we are emotionally sober, we no longer feel compelled to manipulate others to make our talents "real" in the world. Emotional sobriety offers us the opportunity to leave the tricks and tools of manipulation behind and to make our gifts and talents real in the world through service.

> Paradoxically, the more we give away, the more we grow and the stronger our practice of emotional sobriety.

Paradoxically, the more we give away, the more we grow and the stronger our practice of emotional sobriety. Emotional sobriety is like chlorophyll to a green plant. All the plant needs is sun and water and it will grow. All we need is a purpose greater than self to serve, and we will grow.

I would like you to see what this insight has meant in the life of someone very important to me — my long-term AA sponsor, Tom.

A Man beyond Hope

Tom has been my sponsor since I began my journey in recovery in August 1971. He has been in my life and in my family's life, and he has guided us through many trials and tribulations. I am filled with gratitude and respect for his wisdom, love, and guidance. I am grateful that he took time to tell me his story and has given me permission to adapt it for this book.

As you will see, Tom found a purpose in life and has lived that purpose for many decades. He has helped literally thousands of men and women find freedom from their addictions and has helped the growth of Narcotics Anonymous on every continent.

Tom has been in recovery since December 17, 1968. He sums up his experience in recovery with the following statement: "Time is free. What we do with it is what makes it priceless."

Tom was born in 1947 and grew up in Boston. His childhood was filled with trauma. Drinking and drugs became a part of his solution to the trauma, but the bottom line is that he was lost from his youth long into his adulthood. Addiction ruled his life, made every decision for him, controlled his thoughts, stole his integrity, made being in a loving relationship impossible, and eventually led to his being locked up in California's Atascadero State Hospital for the criminally insane. Tom told me that during this time he wondered, Is this all there is to my life? If so, it doesn't seem to be a life worth living.

After he was discharged from Atascadero, Tom moved to Venice Beach in California. His drug addiction was in full force. His life was in shambles, and he tried desperately to fill the holes in his soul with sex, alcohol, and other drugs. He started running with a very rough group of people — so rough that Tom grew afraid he was going to be killed. He realized he needed to leave Venice, or his crazy and dangerous lifestyle would catch up with him. He was desperate, thinking to himself, I'm beyond help. How could anyone help me?

Tom had a friend, a man we'll call Bert, who had met an older hippie woman who lived on the North Shore of Oahu. He showed Tom a picture of this older woman, said her name was Flobird, and mentioned that she was living with a bunch of alcoholics. Bert said she "was quite spiritual," but that didn't mean anything to Tom. He imagined that she was partying with them and having orgies. That sounded better than getting killed in Venice, California.

Tom decided to flee to Hawaii and thought that maybe he'd look her up at some point. He scraped together $75, which in those days was enough to purchase a one-way ticket to Hawaii. He rounded up a little more cash and packed his belongings in a couple of suitcases, and off he went. He landed on Oahu with $40 in his pocket.

Tom had no real plan except to go to the North Shore of Oahu, an area on the island known to surfers and snorkelers. On the plane he befriended a guy and later smoked a joint with him outside the airport. The man told Tom that he and his girlfriend could give him a ride most of the way to the North Shore. When they dropped him off, he was miles from the North Shore beaches. So there he was, dragging his suitcases in the dark, down a dirt road. A pickup truck stopped to pick him up. This was unusual, but Tom didn't know it. The locals really didn't care for people who came to freeload off them. Tom had what turned out to be one of many fortunate experiences, but in his mental state, he couldn't recognize it.

They dropped him off at a beach, and that night he crashed there. He slept in the sand, sheltering beneath a bush. He woke up to his first clear look at Hawaii. It was so much cleaner than California. The surf smelled of salt and seaweed, and as the waves crashed, droplets of seawater sparkled in the early sunlight. The sand, like sugar, clung to his clothes and hair. He was amazed to wake up on this strange, beautiful shore. But within moments he started to question himself. "What the hell am I doing here?" he said aloud. "How am I going to survive on forty bucks, a few candy bars, and half a bag of peanuts?" Only the surf, shorebirds, and sand crabs could hear him.

He rummaged through one of his bags and found a bunch of pills. He decided he couldn't afford to get strung out, so he flung them into the ocean. He also found a bag of pot and considered tossing it, but his addict self told him, "Keep it, Tom. It's natural. Maybe you'll need to mellow out."

In the back of his head, he thought if things got bad, he could look up this lady, Flobird, whom Bert had mentioned. Tom wandered around a bit and then returned to the spot where he'd slept the night before. He settled back down to rest beneath the bush. A car pulled up and a lady got out of the car. She walked to the top of a small dune and gazed at the ocean, then walked down to the beach near where Tom was sheltering. She was wearing a bikini and had long gray hair that hung past her waist. He instantly recognized her as the lady Bert had told him about.

Tom approached her and asked her if her name was Flobird. She said it was. Tom mentioned that he had heard about her from his friend Bert. He described him. The woman said yes, she remembered him. She looked Tom up and down, then unexpectedly said, "Why don't you put your things in my car and come back to the house?"

Something inside of him felt compelled to comply. He surprised himself by simply accepting her invitation.

They drove back to her house, and Flobird introduced him to a guy and gal his age. It turned out the young man was a famous musician from a Southern rock band. Tom tried to converse with them, but they just gave him puzzled looks. He later learned they couldn't understand a word he was saying. His body was still getting over the countless drugs he had consumed over many years. He stuttered and mumbled incoherently and feared making eye contact. Tom told me, "I remember staring at the floor and talking. I was a broken and lost man."

Flobird invited him to get some rest in one of the back rooms. Tom slept for more than a day. When he woke up the next morning, his whole body was buzzing. Something was happening to him, but he had no idea what it was. He walked into the living room. Flobird sat in an old chair, talking on the phone. As he looked at her, he felt something he'd never felt before. Tom told me, "I don't know what this was, but there was a presence in that room that was powerful and good."

Flobird got off the phone and greeted him. He tried to give her the forty dollars in his pocket, and she touched his hand and told him to put the money away. She said, "We are just going to take this one day at a time and keep it simple, honey."

There seemed to be a number of people in the household. Still detoxifying from his drug and booze binge, Tom took a stroll down to the beach with one of the women from the house. He remembers spontaneously saying to himself, Thank You! Thank You! Thank You! Moments later he thought, What the hell is going on here? He felt something was changing.

When he got back, Flobird offered him some food. As he ate, the woman talked about her alcoholism and recovery in AA. When she was talking to him, he looked into her eyes and saw freedom. Tom told me, "She was absolutely free from fear. She was free from her demons. She had found something very important in her life. You could feel her honesty and purpose. I thought, If I could get what she's got, I could make it in this world."

> "Find a power greater than yourself and trust it, clean up the wreckage of your past, and get out of yourself by helping others."

Tom discovered hope at that moment. He saw the possibility of another way to live life, a life that would be free from fear and the insanity of constant drug use. Tom shared what he was feeling with Flobird. She smiled at him and said, "Here's what you need to do, honey: Find a power greater than yourself and trust it, clean up the wreckage of your past, and get out of yourself by helping others. It is that simple. You clean house, trust God, and help another addict."

And so, with this direction from Flobird, my friend Tom's recovery journey began.

The Attraction of Purpose

Flobird's theme was loving action, love without a price tag. Her approach to recovery was based on the Twelve Steps of Alcoholics Anonymous. Keep in mind that in this era, there was a lot of stigma attached to alcoholism. Drug addiction was considered even worse, and not all people in AA wanted to associate with drug addicts. Often, AA members resented the attendance of addicts at meetings. But Flobird was different. She had seen and helped many alcoholics and drug addicts. She aimed to help the addict move beyond selfishness and self-centeredness. She freely shared her deep understanding of addiction and recovery with anyone who seemed open to her help. Her sole purpose in life was to help the alcoholic or addict who was still suffering. She radiated an inner peace and serenity. She had found her purpose in life, and she pursued it with a whole heart.

Flobird's serenity, love of life, and compassion for others attracted many addicts to her. They sensed she had discovered the key to living a good life. Unlike them, she had put many demons to rest and was no longer torn to pieces. She had found emotional freedom. She had found her purpose in life.

The late Dr. David Viscott, a well-known radio personality and psychiatrist, had a remarkable insight about purpose. He noted, "The purpose of life is to discover your gift. The work of life is to develop it. The meaning of life is to give your gift away" (1993, 87). This is how Flobird lived her life, and it explains the feeling Tom had when he first met Flobird. He could feel her serenity, emotional freedom, and sense of purpose. Purposeful behavior attracts other people, and the person who has purpose also serves as a role model for others.

The psychological value of living purposefully was described by Dr. Nathaniel Branden, whom I've referenced several times in this book.

> To live purposefully is, among other things, to live productively, which is a necessity of making ourselves competent to life. Productivity is the act of supporting our existence by translating our thoughts into reality, of setting our goals and working for their achievement, of bringing knowledge, goods, or services into existence . . . . It is not that achievements "prove" our worth but rather that the process of achieving is the means by which we develop our effectiveness, our competence at living. (1994, 130–131)

Tom felt the power and pull of Flobird's purposeful life. He realized he desperately needed his own sense of purpose. He wanted someone to see that he was more than his addiction. Flobird was able to look deep down inside of Tom and have faith that he had gifts to offer this world.

Flobird ushered Tom into recovery. Her love for him was unconditional but also tough. She would challenge him when he was feeling sorry for himself and encourage him to do something to get out of his self-centered trance.

Gradually, Tom started to grow up. He started to recover his lost, true self.

In his early recovery, Tom struggled with connecting to a Higher Power. He shared this with Flobird, and she told him, "The absence of the presence of God is the presence of God. Spirit means unseen. The true you is unseen, but it already exists. The Twelve Steps help you reveal your true nature."

The concept was liberating for Tom. It made sense to him, even as it demanded a major shift in his consciousness. This is possible, he thought. I have to become something I already am. I don't have to become something I am not.

Tom realized he had been sleepwalking through life. Now he was waking up. He was choosing to live a conscious life. He was choosing to peel back the onion, quit his servitude to the demands of his false self and his addict self, and align his actions with his true self.

During this time, Tom moved from Oahu to the Big Island of Hawaii and joined Flobird at Spencer Beach Park, where a recovery community was sprouting. The Beachcombers Spiritual Progress Traveling Group was the AA meeting that Flobird started and toured with worldwide. The members lived in tents, held meetings, worked the Twelve Steps, functioned as a recovery commune, and practiced the principles of recovery in their daily affairs.

This was a very important time for Tom. Flobird's philosophy was "God will provide where he guides." Her faith ran deep and fed the faith of those around her. The foundation for Tom's recovery was being strengthened. He began to develop a sense that there was something happening here that was much bigger than a single self.

Around this time Flobird gave Tom the Narcotics Anonymous White Booklet, which was one of the first NA publications. NA was a newcomer at this time—it had only been around for seventeen years or so. She also told Tom that there were only a handful of NA meetings worldwide — and no NA meetings on the islands of Hawaii.

This news planted a seed in Tom. The purpose that filled and fueled Flobird's life had spilled over into his own. He wanted to share the benefits of recovery with other drug addicts. He saw how helping others helped Flobird, and he wanted to help too.

Tom eventually returned to the island of Oahu. He learned about a drug clinic that had just opened up, in Kailua, called The Place. Tom volunteered at this program. He went through extensive training in running encounter groups and sensitivity groups (two forms of group therapy made popular by the Human Potential Movement). He also volunteered in other capacities around the island, always helping addicts who were still suffering. He had embarked on a purposeful life.

It was during this phase of Tom's recovery that he and I met. He volunteered to speak at the Kaneohe Marine Corps Air Station Drug Exemption Program. This is where I was receiving treatment for my drug addiction.

I met Tom on a Tuesday night. He was the speaker. The meeting was called the Drug Rap Session. The purpose of this meeting was for us to get an understanding of what it meant to be in recovery. Eventually this Tuesday night meeting became the first Narcotics Anonymous meeting on the island of Oahu.

I will never forget the night he spoke. There were about twenty marines in the room. We were dressed in our combat fatigues. As we said back in the corps, we were "squared away," which meant our shirts and trousers were starched, our boots were shined, our hair was regulation length, and our belt buckles gleamed with polish.

And there was Tom: long hair stuffed in a ponytail, sloppy Hawaiian print shirt, wrinkled khaki shorts, Birkenstock sandals. He was a hippie and we were marines, many of us combat Vietnam veterans.

We distrusted Tom immediately; judgment and disdain spread across the room like a thick fog. What could this weak hippie dodge drafter (of course we didn't know if he was a dodge drafter or conscientious objector we just imagined this because it helped us distance ourselves from him) say to us that would make a difference in our lives?

My personal skepticism lasted no more than five minutes. Once he started to share his life experiences, I was mesmerized. I had never experienced such honesty. It was refreshing and inspiring.

Tom didn't speak to us as some authority on addiction and recovery. He talked to us from his heart. He approached us eye-to-eye, and as he did so our surface differences melted away. We identified with him as he talked about the feelings he had while he was using—terror, insecurity, inadequacy, fear, and anxiety. He shared things that we all felt but didn't want to admit.

Tom spoke with intensity and courage that night, but most important, he showed us what emotional freedom was really like. He was free from all the internal nonsense telling him that he shouldn't be himself or that he needed to present an artificial persona to us. His false self was gone. We were seeing the true Tom, warts and all. Prior to that moment, the only time I felt something close to that kind of freedom was when I used alcohol and drugs, but even then I knew that freedom was false, fleeting, and externally induced. What Tom had was authentic and emerged from within.

I wanted what Tom had, just as Tom wanted what Flobird had. I wanted to be released from the cell that my false self and my addiction had constructed around me.

Tom was a living example of what it meant to be authentic, to be real. To be rigorously honest and vulnerable. To have emotional sobriety. To have a purpose that emerged from within. Yes,

I wanted what Tom had, and I told him so. He told me to stick close, and so I did — since 1971.

When we humans see true purpose, the kind that springs from an honest inner spirit, we are attracted. We want the same thing — we want to find a purpose of our own, and we want to live it. We seek purpose the way plants seek the sun.

Purpose but Not Perfection

There is much more to Tom's story. His path was not easy, and I can tell you that in the years I've known him, he has had many travails as well as joys. A high point for Tom was when he met his first wife. I was honored to attend the wedding. They had three beautiful children together, and Tom told me he was frightened by having them. His own childhood was, in his words, "messed up." Fortunately, his wife had confidence about how to raise children. He told me that together, they were able to "raise them without fear and shame, unlike the way I was raised. They got to unfold and realize their own potential. We broke the multigenerational pattern of shame and abuse that I'd experienced. This goal, to raise my children free, so they could become who they wanted to be, filled me with a life purpose."

It is not as though Tom lived an ideal life since he began to pursue his purpose. He struggled with perfectionism, shame, inferiority, and painful childhood traumas. He contended with divorce, learning to set boundaries, and other issues. In these ways, he was and is like all the rest of us. But he continued to inspire me and others around him, even during these difficult personal times. Throughout these struggles and stages in his life, he gained in his practice of recovery and emotional sobriety. I firmly believe that his devotion to trying to be true to himself while being of service to others is what helped Tom, my sponsor and friend, do so much for so many and to do so much to repair himself.

Eventually, Tom began to serve on the board for the Narcotics Anonymous World Services organization. He traveled to other countries to conduct NA workshops on how to start meetings and manage the NA fellowship.

One event that he described to me captures the spirit of his work. He was in Iran — a country that does not have a good relationship with the United States — and was to share his recovery story at a special meeting. When he was taken to a soccer stadium for the meeting, he was thinking there'd be a couple hundred members of the fellowship. To his surprise, there were thousands of NA members in attendance. About halfway through his story, the NA members began chanting. The interpreter turned to Tom and asked, "Do you understand what they are chanting in Farsi?" Tom said no. The interpreter explained, "They are chanting 'May God never take your recovery away from you.'" Tom started to cry. When he shared this experience with me, I cried too.

During the interview that became this chapter, Tom told me, "One of the fundamental issues for all human beings is to know that they are useful. Without that you are a shell of a person. Every day I pray, 'Please guide me in any way you can. Please make me a channel of your love and grace.' I was created to be a unique expression of God. I believe that God is love, and I want to be an open channel for that love. If it was just me, the magic wouldn't happen. God in me, as me, but greater than me. The spirit within me does the work. I am right where I need to be. I don't need to identify any more issues. Life does it for me."

Tom found his purpose in life, which was to be of value or, as he said, "to be love in action and in service of others." Tom's discovery of purpose was an emergent feature of his emotional sobriety. It is important to recognize that his very human life continued, uneven and imperfect, even after the seed of his purpose began to take root and grow and touch the lives of others. At times, doing his work helped him get through rough patches, and at other times, rough patches interfered with his work. This is how emotional sobriety works. It is a practice that is ongoing, not something we attain and check off a list.

Tom's story is inspiring; it echoes the popular "rags to riches" story in American life — although in this case, "riches" refers to his life's accomplishments. We like this kind of story. But Tom's work, which ultimately resulted in him spreading the benefits of Narcotics Anonymous around the world, is not the same as his purpose, which was to be loving action in service of others. This purpose could have been expressed in other work and in many ways. Tom found a way that was in line with his interests and gifts.

Each of us can find our own purpose in life. It may not be of the same magnitude as Tom's work. It doesn't have to be. As we do our own work we, too, can be of value. We can bring love where there is none. We can bring harmony where discord exists. We can bring maturity where there is reactivity. We can bring serenity where there is anxiety. We can bring perspective where others lose theirs. We can serve a purpose greater than ourselves where others serve only themselves. All the while, we are modeling and practicing emotional sobriety. We are, as Step Twelve says, practicing "these principles in all our affairs."

Dr. Viktor Frankl argued that we are responsible to actualize the potential meaning in our lives. He revealed the importance in serving a cause greater than ourselves:

> I wish to stress that the true meaning of life is to be discovered in the world rather than within man or his own psyche, as though it were a closed system. I have termed this constitutive characteristic "the self-transcendence of human existence." It denotes the fact that being

human always points, and is directed, to something, or someone, other than oneself — be it a meaning to fulfill or another human being to encounter. The more one forgets himself — by giving himself to a cause to serve or another person to love — the more human he is and the more he actualizes himself. What is called self-actualization is not an attainable aim at all, for the simple reason that the more one would strive for it, the more he would miss it. In other words, self-actualization is possible only as a side effect of self-transcendence. (1984, 115)

Tom is a living example of someone who actualized his potential as a side effect of transcending his false self. He really was, for a long time, a messed-up guy who did some crazy things and was at risk of completely losing himself to insanity and addiction. But he found recovery, he found a purpose in life, and he followed sobriety and purpose wherever they took him. This has included being a sponsor, helping get NA groups started, and eventually representing NA throughout the world. Wherever his purpose led, he followed his heart. What an amazing connection I feel: from Flobird, to Tom, to me, and, I hope, to you! That is the beauty of emotional sobriety.

The Sufi poet Rumi from the thirteenth century wrote a story about a cook and a chickpea. I will paraphrase it for you. The cook is preparing a batch of chickpeas for a meal. One chickpea keeps trying to leap out of the pot of boiling water. (Who wouldn't?) The cook keeps knocking the chickpea back into the boiling water with his ladle. The desperate chickpea says to the cook, "Why are you doing this to me?" The cook answers, "Because you are being prepared for something great. You are going to be mixed with fine spices and become a great nourishment for a hungry soul. Remember," the cook says, "when you drank the water from the garden, it was preparing you for this."

> When we look back at our lives in ten, fifteen, twenty years, we will be able to see more clearly what our life experiences were preparing us for.

When we look back at our lives in ten, fifteen, twenty years, we will be able to see more clearly what our life experiences were preparing us for. We will have words to describe the purpose that was unfolding right before our eyes. We know from our history that there are some things we just couldn't see until we gained some perspective. Tom found his purpose by behaving with increasing emotional honesty and sobriety. As he began to peel back the layers of the onion to reveal his true self, his purpose emerged naturally. This is the path to emotional sobriety and to realizing our human potential.

Sentence Completion Exercise

Take each sentence stem below and write it at the top of a piece of paper. Next, repeat the sentence stem silently (or aloud) to yourself, and then complete it with the first thought that comes to mind. Do six to ten completions for each.

> My life is meaningful when I _____.
> I am of value when I _____.
> What stops me from being of service to a purpose greater than myself is _____.
> The idea about myself that I'd need to give up to be

more loving toward myself is _____.

Being of value to another means _____.

I lose myself when I _____.

One thing I could do to bring a higher degree of self-awareness to living with a purpose greater than myself is _____.

My self-centeredness still shows up when I _____.

Our purpose emerges in relation to what the world demands of us. This most often manifests in the needs of the people about us. We humans are social creatures who are always acting in relation to others. We crave close relationships. Our relationships are crucibles where emotional dependency is exposed. In that crucible, emotional autonomy may be forged or lost. Close relationships put our practice of emotional sobriety to the test. But our practice of emotional sobriety can help us experience better relationships. We explore the nature of healthy relationships in the next chapter.

Chapter 14: Holding On to Ourself in Relationships

I've saved the toughest insight for last. And yet, it's also potentially the most rewarding. Loving relationships give us remarkable potential to grow, but they also test our practice of emotional sobriety like nothing else. You see, the thing about emotional sobriety is that it's not really something you do on your own that much. Most of the practice is about how we relate

> to the hard facts of the universe;
> to ourselves, our fortunes and misfortunes, and our
> history;
> to family and friends; and, most difficult of all,
> to the people we love.

Only the first item in that list does not involve other people. If we lived alone in the world, we might be tested by the weather, an earthquake, a wildfire, a hurricane, or that mountain lion chasing us. But we live in a social world. Humans need to be together, and most of us crave the closeness of a loving relationship. The tough thing is that the closer we get to someone, the harder it is to hold on to ourselves — to keep our values intact, to know who we are, to not get hooked by our emotional dependency. A loving relationship challenges every aspect of our emotional sobriety, as you will see.

I want you to meet Martin and Serena. When I met them, Martin had six years in Narcotics Anonymous, and Serena had four years in Overeaters Anonymous. They attended four or more meetings every week. They were very sophisticated; they had both worked hard on themselves, understood a lot of the principles of recovery, and were well-versed in recovery jargon. But though they were working hard on their drug and food dependencies, there was another dependency that was destroying them: emotional dependency.

They lacked emotional sobriety. Their dependency on each other caused constant squabbles that erupted into shouting and tears.

Serena and Martin thought they understood what it takes to have a healthy relationship. They sincerely believed they were following relationship practices that would improve their connection, but they were wrong. Their relationship was riddled with unenforceable rules that were choking it.

Martin and Serena seemed unusually confident, grounded, and comfortable during our first appointment. I commented to them about their comfort, and both said they'd worked hard at their recovery and their relationship. But then Martin said, "Don't let us fool you, Doc; it doesn't mean we aren't going to be quibbling with each other in a couple of minutes. That's all we seem to be able to do when we talk to each other lately."

Serena jumped right in. "That's probably the one and only thing we agree on."

No warm-up was necessary with this couple. We were off to the races.

I asked them what they wanted from each other. Serena was

the first to respond, "I want more real, honest talk."

Martin chimed in and said, "That's very much what I want from you too." But then he elaborated, "I need to be able to say what's on my mind. It's hard for me to just do that, so instead I make jokes. And I feel that you make jokes too. A lot. And nothing's serious. I'd like to be able to bypass all that and just talk to you, with no double meanings. Just good, honest, straight communication."

Serena echoed his position, "That sounds great."

"It does," I said. "So where are you disagreeing with each other?"

Martin turned to Serena and said, "Well, it's hard for me to be honest with you when you run out of the room in tears and you tell me you don't want to talk about it. I think you take things personally. You react all the time. When we try to discuss things, we come to a point where you just say, 'I don't want to deal with this.' We just come up against a wall. You shut me down."

Serena tried to clarify her position. "I feel like you just want to be right, and I come up against a wall. It's impossible for me to get my point across, because you won't cop to what you did wrong. I think to myself, Why am I even wasting my breath? Then you start shouting and I start crying and the best thing is just to run to some other room."

I asked them if they could give me a specific example.

Serena responded. "Last week I had a video call with my mother. She lost her husband, my dad, four months ago. It's been very hard on us. Mom always said she wanted to go before Dad. Now she's living her worst nightmare, marching on in that house with all his things around her."

She had more to say. "Martin joined in the call. But he never asked Mom how she was. He just made small talk with her. I was so upset I could barely keep it together. After the call I said, 'How can you be so cold? I know you didn't like my dad, but it seemed like you had a pretty good relationship with my mother. How selfish!'"

Martin jumped in to defend himself. "You always assume the worst about me. You think that because I had trouble with your father, who wouldn't accept me, that I'd be cold to your mom. I didn't want to upset your mom, and that's why I didn't talk to her about her loss," he explained. "I thought it would be better to keep the conversation light with her. I told you that, but you won't believe me. You always think the worst of me."

Serena countered, "I can't stand when you start yelling at me. You're doing it now, and soon, like always, you'll threaten me with breaking up. That's why I leave the conversation. I feel scared. It seems like you are trying to control me. I've told you many times before; I can't handle it when you're angry and raising your voice."

Interestingly, both Martin and Serena made sense. But what they were missing was the recognition that they were emotionally dependent on each other. Each reacting, one to the other. They shared an unspoken unenforceable rule: Both believed that for the relationship to work, it had to be on their own terms.

Martin demanded that Serena stay engaged in the conversation. She couldn't get scared or angry and leave it. She had to stay until he was satisfied that she agreed with his point of view. He wasn't really concerned with Serena, just with what he wanted.

Serena was equally outrageous in her demands. Martin needed to cop to what she thought he did wrong. There was no room for his point of view. Moreover, if he got angry or upset, she emotionally cut him off. Serena was concerned only with what she wanted.

Each demanded that the other live up to unspoken expectations. And each reacted when the other failed to respond in precisely the right way. They then tried to leverage what they wanted by getting angrier, or crying more, or distancing. Each only had room for one thing: winning. Their shared and impossible rule was, "I'm gonna have things my way or I'm not gonna play at all." This left no room for the other person, which makes a relationship untenable.

I confronted them. "Neither of you really want to talk. You both want to win, meaning you want the conversation to be on your own terms. That's the rule that's operating here, and it stinks," I said, then continued. "Neither of you will state your rules in the open, probably because saying them out loud would reveal just how ridiculous the rule is. You're each reacting to the other, trying to manipulate each other to make yourself feel okay and to win. He shouts, you cry, and then you both shut down because that's the only way to win. You are emotionally dependent."

Martin and Serena needed to make a significant change in the way they were dealing with each other. That's normal when you're stuck! Sometimes we need new information to begin to change unhealthy habits and patterns. So I suggested a new, healthier rule.

"How about this?" I said. "You each get to say whatever you damn please whenever you please, and you get to walk away whenever you please. And you don't have to like what the other person does or what they say. But they get to do it, regardless of what you want."

They looked confused, so I gave an example. "I had an experience recently that I shared with my therapist that may help you understand what I mean. I was on the phone with a contractor who was working on our house, and he was giving me the runaround. I was upset because of his excuses and deflection of responsibility. I started expressing my dissatisfaction with him, and he hung up on me without warning! He can't do that!"

My therapist asked me what I did. I responded incredulously, with "Well, of course, I hung up too."

She pointed out to me that I didn't have to hang up. I could have kept on talking or yelling or saying whatever I needed to say to restore my equilibrium. "You think you need the contractor to stay on the phone to take care of your emotional business, but you don't!" A lightbulb went on for me. I was starting to see what emotional autonomy looked like.

After I shared this story with Martin and Serena, I said, "This is exactly what you two are doing with each other. You require that the other person stay on the phone with you until you take care of your business. That's your rule, and it is unhealthy."

Growth through "Grinding"

Throughout this book, I have been discussing the effects of emotional dependency. Emotional dependency creates toxic rules. These rules, most of which exist on a subconscious level, are designed to manipulate others to behave in specific ways that make us feel loved, validated, and emotionally secure. Toxic rules take many forms but in a loving relationship generally state, If X loves me, then X would willingly and joyfully do A, B, and C. (A, B, and C are always some version of "submit to my will.") Toxic rules are direct or indirect attempts to control the people around us, either through coercion or manipulation. They diminish our connection—especially with the people we claim to love most.

In case you're patting yourself on the back, stop now. Let me assure you, these rules exist in every relationship.

When a relationship is healthy, it facilitates growth. My mentor, Dr. Walter Kempler, and I developed the term grinding to refer to this aspect of relationships. (And no, we're not referring to the kind of lovemaking that grinding may first bring to your mind!) Grinding occurs when we struggle with our differences in a loving relationship. To grind like this, we must find the courage to say what we want and what we don't like, even when it is emotionally risky. We also encourage our partners to declare what they want and don't like. We create an atmosphere that has room enough for two. We don't try to manipulate them to get what we want. We struggle with our differences. We honor what we want—and we equally honor what our partner wants.

The goal of grinding is the victory of all at the expense of no one. When we grind in a healthy way, it's like polishing a diamond. We take off the rough edges and bring out the stone's beauty. When we grind with our partner, we polish and strengthen the bond that exists between us. We grind off the unpleasant shoulds of our own and our partner's false selves and inspire self-actualization and autonomy.

> The goal of grinding is the victory of all at the expense of no one. When we grind in a healthy way, it's like polishing a diamond. We take off the rough edges and bring out the stone's beauty.

Toxic rules interfere with grinding because they make it impossible to find a mutually satisfactory solution. Toxic rules are based on should demands. If our partners act the way we think they should, we think of them as good partners. If they always act the way they should, we nominate them for sainthood. "Isn't my husband or wife wonderful!" When they don't act the way we think they should, they are bad partners. If they never act the way they should, then clearly, they must be the devil.

When we label our partners as good or bad, we are manipulating them. Think about this for a moment. There's a difference between saying, "I like what you just did," which is more personal and direct, and "You are not a very good person," which is indirect and manipulative. We know that most people (especially our partners, who crave our approval) want to be seen as "good." So, when we directly or indirectly call them "bad" in order to change their behavior to align with our needs and desires, we are manipulating them.

The problems that toxic expectations cause in relationships have been discussed by many psychotherapists. Relationship author Dr. Jerry Greenwald warns us about the effects of expectations on a relationship: "Expectations lead to the erosion of any relationship. The myth that the resolution of loneliness will result because we have found an intimate one-to-one relationship is a cop-out. It begins a toxic process which dissipates the mutual nourishment that occurs when both people are committed to sustaining a nourishing interaction and growth of their separate selves" (1980, 130–31).

The toxic rules that Martin and Serena had for each other interfered with their ability to enjoy the natural therapeutic value of a partnership. Rather than helping each other become more whole, they were emotionally fused to each other. They expected each other to behave in specific ways before they could speak their minds. Every time they attempted to "grind," sparks flew.

To put it simply, their toxic rules were breaking their hearts.

Surrendering Expectations

Here's one way to state the rule that Martin and Serena had tacitly agreed to: In a loving relationship, everyone has to be an angel. This idea needed to be challenged. I said to them, "You both expect your partner to be a perfect angel. But we're not angels. You don't have to be perfect to have a loving relationship.

You have to be able to own your issues and surrender the expectations that you have for each other. You have to gain emotional independence from each other, so you can say and do what you need to."

"So, Martin," I said, "are you going to let Serena be who she is and not be an angel?"

"Yeah," Martin said. "I get that."

"Not so fast," I said. "Just think about it. Once she starts crying, you cut her out."

"No, I don't," Martin said. "I don't cut her out."

"You say that, Martin, but then when she cries, you shut down. You clam up, don't you? Because why would an angel not do what you want? Why would an angel cry at what you have to say?" I asked. "You see, even if you pretend to give her space, when you shut down, you're trying to make it look like she's bad. You're excluding her from your life because she doesn't act the way you want her to."

Serena sat back in her chair, her lips together, pulled tight. She looked thoughtful.

Martin said, "I don't know what to do when she does that, when she cries because I'm mad."

"Just speak your mind," I told him. "Say what you have to say. And stop letting her reactions control you."

Now Serena's brow crinkled. She looked puzzled.

"Look," I said, keeping my attention on Martin, "here's a healthy rule for you to have with Serena: 'Anytime you don't like what I have to say, you can leave, you can go to another room, you can do whatever you want. And I'm just going to sit here and talk or shout until I'm done. Then if you want to talk again later, we can.'"

"That's a healthy rule?" Martin asked. He almost jumped out of his chair, then sat back, arms crossed. "I don't get it. When she walks out of the room, she's not participating in the conversation."

"That is participating, in her way."

"I'm calling bullshit on that," said Martin, a bit louder. "That's total B.S. When she leaves, she's not taking an active part."

"Yes," I said. "It is active, because she is taking care of herself. Look, your rule is that she should put up with whatever you have to say to her and stay engaged with you as long as you want her to. There's no room for Serena in your rule. A healthy rule would be that you say what you want to say regardless of what Serena is doing," I explained. "Just like my therapist told me about that phone call. You can just keep talking. When you get silent after she leaves the room, you've essentially run out of the room too. If you have something to say, say it. But you can't require that she listen in the way you demand. That's the condition you've tacked onto it. That isn't going to work, no matter what tricks you try."

Martin looked over at Serena. He leaned forward, all but pleading with her. "But for me, if you leave, then you're not hearing me." He stopped abruptly, went quiet, and gazed up at the ceiling.

Serena had moved to the edge of her seat.

"Ohhhhh," Martin said. He sounded like he'd finally found a missing puzzle piece. "That's my condition—she has to stay!" His shoulders slumped and he seemed to fade back into the chair. "Man, that's not fair. I want her to stay. But that's my demand. That just sucks that I can't make her stay."

"It has nothing to do with being fair," I said. "Your rule is toxic because you are trying to make Serena 'behave.' The rule has to go if you want to have a better relationship with her. It's a new way of thinking for you. I can see that."

I let that settle in for a moment. Then I glanced at Serena; I thought maybe she'd be looking smug. But I could see that the wheels were spinning for her too. "Martin," I continued, "the magnificent thing about this kind of rule is that it applies to you too. You don't have to listen to her crap either. You can walk away whenever you want to. Here's the thing we all need to learn: Good, nourishing rules can be used by everyone. That's how you tell the difference. Toxic rules are one-sided."

"I've always been taught that you should spill everything out and if you walk away, you're a wuss; you're giving up," Martin said.

"I hear you, but it's not working. It might be difficult for you to give up that idea," I said. "But consider this. Serena's tears, leaving the room, shouting—none of that really matters. When you clam up, you've walked away. Speak your mind, whether she's there to hear you or not. That's what really matters. You need to hear yourself state what you need. Get it out in the open, and you might do a better job responding appropriately to your needs instead of demanding that Serena takes care of you."

As the session continued to unfold, more of their unenforceable rules surfaced, and Martin and Serena got better and better at realizing how and when they had been trying to manipulate each other. Eventually, we got to the critical goal for these two and for most people in loving relationships.

"Here's what I hope you both will work on," I said. "Learn to say what you mean. Learn to enjoy what there is and grieve what there isn't. It sounds like you guys do a lot of crying and yelling. Fine. Those are incidentals. Those aren't central to the relationship. What is central to the relationship is surrendering your expectations for each other."

"Because the feelings are just part of the process," said Martin.

"Exactly," I said. "The feelings are part of the process. That's beautifully put. They're incidentals. People think that crying or yelling is the important issue, but it's not."

Earlier Serena had said to Martin, "I just think you should be crying when you're hurt instead of yelling at me." I reminded them both of her statement and said, "See, Serena has a rule that crying means vulnerability, and that means love. That's just another should, a toxic rule. Don't get caught up in those ideas. Learn how to say what you want and encourage each other to do the same."

I continued, "Just don't think for a minute that you have to give each other what you want, because that's not love either. Give yourselves the right to have your say. Like I said a minute ago, enjoy what is and grieve what isn't. If you can do those things, then you won't be doing so much yelling or crying."

As Martin and Serena became aware of their unreasonable expectations, they became more reasonable. This is what happens when we own what we are doing. It creates new possibilities.

Serena turned to Martin near the end of the session and told him, "I can see that I missed your true intention with my mother and accused you of something that wasn't true. I am sorry, and I do appreciate that you were trying to protect her from her grief by making small talk. I couldn't see that before."

Martin appreciated what Serena said to him. He also realized that his expectation that Serena should behave the way he wanted her to be was something he needed to let go of. They were letting go of their expectations and creating room for each other.

This seems to be the process of change. We own what we are doing, we take 100 percent responsibility, and then something new becomes possible. This requires rigorous self-honesty and humility. Demanding that things go our way is a surefire way of turning any relationship into a power struggle.

There's an adage that says, "Do you want to be right or be happy?" Most of us choose being right because we think we need our partners to behave a certain way to make us happy. That is emotional dependency. In a loving relationship, the practice of emotional sobriety urges us to unhook that dependency by expressing the wishes of our true self without expecting that our partner will fulfill them. They may or may not join us in our wish; we can be happy or sad about that as needed.

We replace our toxic expectations with healthier, more nourishing ideas that will create genuine happiness and freedom. This is critical to the process of emotional sobriety. Rumi wrote, "Out beyond ideas of wrongdoing and rightdoing there is a field. I'll meet you there." It's in that field that loving relationships meet.

I would be remiss here if I did not raise the problem of physically abusive relationships. If you are in a relationship where you are physically hurt, look to your physical safety first. If your household includes children or other vulnerable people, be sure they are safe. Besides tending to your safety needs, seek counseling. Physical abuse is an obvious "leave now" indicator. The guide is, if you are not feeling safe, seek help and seek counseling!

Immature Love

It's easy to get caught up in the image of an ideal relationship. We fantasize, either consciously or subconsciously, that our partner will help us in our quest to create a future that reverses the painful or traumatic experiences of our past. Phrases like "a match made in heaven" reinforce the idea that a heaven-sent partner will magically deliver us from our pain or suffering.

Good luck with that idea.

Our partners cannot do that for us. No one can. Our job is to create the life our true self urges us to own and enjoy. It is great when our partners encourage us in our journey of self-discovery, but we cannot require this type of attitude from them. Much of the time we set unrealistic expectations on our partner, as we saw with Martin and Serena. When our partner does not live up to our expectations, we have an opportunity for "good trouble"— for the kind of grinding I described earlier. We can use the discord and discomfort in the relationship to help us face ourselves with honesty.

Grinding often reveals the ways our emotionally dependent perfectionism emerges. Dr. Fritz Perls discussed this issue in great detail:

> One can observe in marital difficulties that either one or both of the marriage partners are not in love with the spouse but with an image of perfection . . . . The mutual frustration of not finding perfection results in tension and increased hostility which results in a permanent status quo, an impasse or, at best, a useless divorce . . . . Though perfection is generally labeled an "ideal," it is actually a cheap curse which punishes and tortures both the self and others for not living up to an impossible goal. (1975a, 3)

We saw perfectionism in the interaction between Martin and Serena. Martin expected Serena to do things exactly the way he prescribed; then she'd be the perfect mate. Serena had a similar expectation: Martin should be the perfect partner and always take her feelings into consideration. They resented each other for failing to live up to these expectations. This is the reason that their rules needed to go. If there was going to be room for each other in the relationship, they had to surrender their immature fantasies of perfection.

Virginia Satir, a pioneer in working with families and couples, offered an antidote to the toxic rule demanding the perfect partner: "If your rules say that whatever feeling you have is human and therefore acceptable, the self can grow" (1972, 101). Toxic rules dismiss our emotions and make us feel ashamed of ourselves for being who we are. Martin's and Serena's rules justified them dismissing each other's feelings while also making them feel ashamed of themselves. In essence, they took each other hostage.

Unfortunately, we are often more committed to our rules than we are to having a relationship with our partner. This is a serious problem and interferes with creating a healthy climate for two people to grow and enjoy one another. This is the essence of immature love. It leaves no room for differences. It's our way or the highway.

When I was twelve years old, The Beatles released "You Can't Do That." This John Lennon–Paul McCartney tune was sung by my favorite Beatle, Lennon. You've probably heard it, even if you're young. I thought it was a great love song. It filled me with what I thought were romantic notions. I carried them well into my thirties. (Finally! I figured out who's to blame for all my screwed-up relationships! The Beatles. It's their fault!)

> Our job is to create the life our true self urges us to own and enjoy. It is great when our partners encourage us in our journey of self-discovery, but we cannot require this type of attitude from them.

Today, I see this song in a totally different light. If you've got three minutes, go listen to it. I hope you'll hear that it is a recipe for emotional dependence. In fact, I think we should nominate it as the theme song for immature love. John demands that his girlfriend behave the way he wants so that he won't feel insecure or jealous. He gives her a list of things she can't do—hence the song title from the repeated line "You can't do that." If she breaks his rules, he threatens her with abandonment as a way of controlling her. Over the course of the song, he takes no responsibility for feeling insecure and makes her responsible for his feelings. He tells her that his well-being and sanity are dependent on her submitting to his rules. There isn't room for the girl to be herself. She needs to live up to his expectations if the relationship is going to be all right.

This is the same kind of thing we heard from Martin. He demanded Serena behave the way he thought she should, or else.

We all sing you can't do that at various times in our lives because we are all emotionally immature. Oftentimes we don't realize it. Our rules seem normal to us, like "This is the way a relationship is supposed to be." The rules make up the air we breathe, so we don't see them.

Immature love is a form of emotional dependency. It is anathema to emotional sobriety. "I love you because I need you" is the dominant theme of this type of love. Immature love is rooted in selfishness. People who are selfish are interested only in satisfying their own needs. They may give the appearance of being interested in what the other person needs, but this is only a ruse to camouflage the underlying selfishness. Self-effacing people (see chapter 3) who erase themselves to gain the love and validation of a partner are an example of this deceit. Their personal sacrifices are not made out of love for the person. Rather, they are driven by a selfish belief that such a sacrifice will win them love and acceptance.

Selfish people don't love themselves too much, as some people think. Selfish people actually hate themselves. This is what makes them emotionally dependent. They feel empty and frustrated, which makes them demand that someone else step in to make them whole, provide them with emotional security, and validate them.

> Selfish people don't love themselves too much, as some people think. Selfish people actually hate themselves.

Emotionally dependent people see the world in terms of what they can get out of it. In relationships, they see partners as sources of approval or disapproval rather than for the unique individuals they are. This motive overpowers any positive instincts to respect the needs, interests, dignity, and integrity of others. This is why people who are emotionally dependent aren't bothered when their expectations demand that their partners disregard or sacrifice their own needs to make them happy. To justify this, they point to the toxic rule that love means sacrifice.

Immature, emotionally dependent love is riddled with rules:

> If you love me, you won't do anything without me.
> If you love me, you will do what I want.
> If you love me, you will show me that you live for me.
> If you love me, you will think the way I want you to think.
> If you love me, you will feel the way I think you should.
> If you love me, you will read my mind and give me what I want.
> If you love me, you will anticipate my every need.
> If you love me, you will give my feelings privilege over yours or anyone else's.

Immature, emotionally dependent love takes hostages. It turns a relationship into a prison in which there is no room for people, only rules.

We need to admit our emotional immaturity before we can

do something about it. As Greenwald writes, "Awareness of what we do to poison our intimacy and how we do this is the royal road to the discovery of the antidotes to toxic patterns in our intimate relationships" (1976, 146).

Mature Love

What does a relationship look like when its partners are practicing emotional sobriety? This is where mature love blossoms. Mature love says, "I want you because I love you." The connection is not motivated by dependency but by desire. Mature love is based on wanting our partners to do what they want to do rather than living up to our expectations. Mature love is rooted in one's own capacity to love, and the partners in such a relationship cooperate and coordinate their behavior as needed for growth and happiness.

Emotionally independent people are able to love in an affirming way. Their capacity to love is an affirmation of their own self-love, their love for life, their commitment to emotional growth, and their own emotional freedom or emotional sobriety. Greenwald recognized the importance of our relationship with ourselves and how it impacts our capacity to love. He writes, "It is not possible for me to relate to others intimately and allow (and enjoy) their full expression of themselves if I have not yet discovered how to do this for myself. An intimacy of two begins with an intimacy of one" (1976, 63).

Greenwald's concept is an elaboration of the idea that if we don't love ourselves, then we will not be able to love someone else. Generally, people follow a sad sort of "not-so-golden rule" that says, We treat others the way we treat ourselves. In action that means, if I don't accept me, then I won't accept you. If I don't enjoy and support my full expression of myself, then I won't be able to enjoy or encourage your full expression of yourself. If I don't love myself, then I won't be able to love you. If I don't live by my true desires, I won't be able to enourage you to live by your true desires.

Mature love is created by having a loving relationship with ourselves. How do we do that? Awareness (in chapter 4) opens us up to emotional sobriety and therefore to the possibilities for healthy relationships. Emotional sobriety allows us to sense our expectations of others and unhook them from our demands.

To awaken this awareness, we need to think about how we talk to ourselves, which is a clue to how we feel about ourselves. We need to get rid of our top dog bully (see chapter 11) so we can develop a better relationship with ourselves. We need to become aware of and work through whatever messages we received in our childhood that said we weren't okay or we weren't lovable or we were ugly or we should be ashamed of ourselves. These toxic messages are injunctions and act as impediments to our intimacy with self and others. These messages are clues to the ways in which we expect our future (and those in it) to reverse the negative experiences of our past.

It boils down to this: solid, authentic self-esteem (based on an honest self-appraisal)

> leads to a stronger self-identity, which
> leads to a deeper intimacy and connection with ourselves, which
> leads to a greater capacity for an enduring, growing, intimate relationship with another person.

An intimacy of one becomes an intimacy of two as Dr. Greenwald observed. A loving relationship between two people who have this kind of emotional independence is not a house of straw, sticks, or even brick. Its strength comes from its flexibility. It has room for both partners; its rules include rather than exclude each partner. It has very few expectations about the fulfillments and gratifications that the other partner may bring. This house has plenty of room for the partners to seek to get their needs met, to appreciate what is available, to express regret or disappointment about what is not available, and to grieve its absence if need be. Such a house can withstand quite a bit!

> # Healthy rules help us love what is, understanding that it is not our partner's job to make us whole.

What kind of material is this magnificently flexing house built of? Healthy rules form its beams, trusses, and walls. The rules promote emotional freedom and experimentation. They open things up rather than close things down. Healthy rules enhance our relationships and interactions. They encourage authenticity and support integrity. Healthy rules help us realize the full potential and value of our relationship. Healthy rules help us love what is, understanding that it is not our partner's job to make us whole.

Healthy Rules

So, what do these rules look like? Obviously, books and books can and have been written on this. For our purposes, practicing emotional sobriety, I feel the following guidelines can help us love what is.

1. Make room for people, not rules.

I also think of this as the no shoulds rule. Expectations are incredibly destructive to an intimate relationship. They diminish our experience in these relationships because they create resentments and interfere with spontaneity. Some say that "expectations are resentments under construction." Surrendering our expectations is extremely important if we are going to have a healthy relationship.

When our partners do not live up to our expectations, we try to control them. We may do this by shaming them, silencing them, by bullying them, or by withdrawing. The trouble is, even if we get what we want, we pay a terrible price. We damage the relationship. We treat our partner as an object rather than as a person. This is the reason Martin and Serena had to release their rules — to make room for each other.

Letting go of our expectations creates a safe and loving atmosphere that supports the growth of both partners as well as the growth of the relationship. Think of your relationship as a child. The way you and your partner care for and manage the child/relationship determines if it will thrive and flourish.

Letting go of our rules encourages our autonomy. As Dr. Nathaniel Branden noted, "Autonomous people understand that other people do not exist merely to satisfy our needs. They have accepted the fact that no matter how much love and caring may exist between persons, we are each of us, in an ultimate sense, responsible for ourselves" (1980, 137).

A word of caution is vital here. Letting go of our expectations does not mean that we don't ask our partner for what we want. In a healthy relationship we are authentic with each other and ask for what we want. But this doesn't mean we will get what we want. If we are demanding that the other person give us what we want, we will get angry and manipulative in response to not getting what we want. When we are genuinely asking our partner for what we want and we don't get it, we feel disappointed. It was a preference or desire, not a demand. An appropriate response is to grieve what is not (what we could not get from our partner) but appreciate what is (their honesty).

2. Differences are desirable and need to be respected.

It is easy to respect someone who thinks the same way we do. After all, isn't good taste any opinion that agrees with mine? Usually we disrespect differences because we experience them as a threat. Differences can feel like threats because we have the immature belief that when we love someone, that person will think and feel the same way we do. This is not true.

Mature love is grounded in the awareness of and appreciation of our partners as unique individuals. To respect our partners, we must see them as separate from us and not as a projection of our needs or desires or an extension of our beliefs. They are special. There will never be another person on this planet exactly like them. Emotionally autonomous partners can see each other with a sense of wonder. They appreciate that both see the world through their own eyes, filtered by their life experiences. They realize that each may assign a different meaning to the same situation or event.

Serena interpreted Martin's behavior as uncaring and cold. She couldn't see that Martin was avoiding discussing a heavy topic with her mother as his way of showing his concern for her. For Serena it meant that Martin didn't care, but for Martin it was an act of love. When Serena gave up being right, she could put herself in Martin's shoes and understand his motive. She could appreciate what is.

When we respect our partner's differences, we are making

an emotional deposit in the relationship's bank account. We are strengthening the bond that exists between us.

3. Struggle is beneficial.

When we embrace struggle as beneficial, we understand that trouble doesn't mean something is wrong with our relationship. We endure discomfort and don't press our partner to submit to our view or our suggestion as to what is wrong or what needs to be done to make things better. We embrace the conflict we are having because we know that dealing with it can be meaningful to our personal development and to the integrity of our relationship.

If, on the other hand, we treat trouble as an unwelcome guest, it will motivate us to identify who is at fault. We will either blame ourselves or others. Blame is disempowering and toxic to a relationship. Taking responsibility, on the other hand, is empowering.

Emotional sobriety requires that we take responsibility for our thoughts, feelings, and actions. We must be willing to look squarely and honestly at ourselves when there is conflict or tension and see what that trouble says about us.

When we step back and look at what the trouble shows us, we begin to live in the space between the stimulus and the reaction (see chapter 10). Remember it is in this space that we recover balance and discover the best response. It is in this space that we have the time to grow up and become emotionally mature. In this space we discover new possibilities.

Satir suggested that when something goes wrong in a relationship, we should ask and answer a few questions:

> What part in my problem are my expectations playing?
> What part in my problem are my thoughts playing?

What part in my problem are my fears playing?
What part in my problem are my interpretations of what is going on playing?
What part in my problem is my lack of faith in being able to grow or cope with what is going on? (1978, 106)

These important questions can help us grasp what we are doing to contribute to the trouble in our relationships. From there, we can imagine what we can do to turn things around.

I especially like the last question—do I have faith in my ability to grow or cope with what is going on? If we are honest, most of us lack faith in ourselves. This is because we tend to play it safe. We don't take risks and try things on to see if they fit. We get stuck in a rut. If we can let go of the need to play it safe and find the courage to take risks, then we can go a long way in creating a healthy relationship.

A word of caution—almost a sub-rule: Struggle doesn't always have to be serious and heavy. We can have fun as we struggle. We can learn to laugh at ourselves too. Emotional sobriety helps us tolerate discomfort and welcome struggle instead of avoiding it.

4. *Grief is necessary.*

Grieving is our way of integrating a loss. When we allow ourselves to grieve—that is, to get angry or sad or to feel empty or sick—we begin to digest the painful experience. As we digest it, we integrate it.

An analogy might help. If we take a bite of an apple, at some point during the digestive process the apple has been assimilated. The apple becomes us. This is what happens when we digest a loss. If we chew up the experience we are having and let ourselves feel what we need to feel, we can begin to integrate the loss. Don't let anyone ever tell you how long this process takes. No one really knows. Some of us will digest a loss and integrate it rather quickly. Others need time.

In healthy relationships, we encourage our partners to grieve as long as they need to. We offer our support but only if it is necessary or desired, and we don't take it personally if our partners don't want our comfort. We all process loss and seek support in whatever way we need to. Emotional sobriety emerges as we face and integrate painful experiences, and as we respect the differences between how we might grieve and how our partner is grieving.

5. Cooperate with integrity.

Some say that you need to compromise to have a healthy relationship. I say this is nonsense. That way of talking about compromise is a myth derived from the idea that love is about sacrifice.

Mature love is togetherness with the preservation of integrity. This means we don't accept anything that is not freely given, nor do we offer anything that we cannot freely give. We join with our partner, but we don't lose ourselves in the connection. We hold on to our individuality.

Most of us do not know how to cooperate with integrity. We have never had the experience, and we don't know what such cooperation looks or feels like. We typically cooperate out of duty or obligation. We may compromise, giving up something to get something, and mistake that for cooperation. But such "cooperation" is just transactional. We don't want to do what our partner is asking for, so we do it out of a sense of duty or obligation or to get something in return. We don't do it freely, wholeheartedly.

Compromise is a corrupted form of cooperation.

Here's a related rule worth thinking about: If I really love you, I don't want you to do something you don't want to do. That's really what cooperation with integrity means. Some of you might be thinking that if this is true, then no one will ever cooperate in a relationship. My experience as a therapist leads me to disagree. We all have a desire to cooperate. We are social animals, and cooperation is a part of our genetic heritage. The belief that no one will ever want to cooperate without being obligated or duty-bound to do so is utter nonsense. It sells us short.

In loving partnerships practicing emotional sobriety, our relationships are grounded in who we are rather than who we should be. That's why we offer to do something only if we really want to. Similarly, we refuse to do something we don't want to do. Then our choices are not based on rules but on who we are.

6. *Ask for what you need; when it is unavailable, appreciate what is.*

As we relinquish our rules, we can handle situations in a different and refreshing way. Let's say I need my partner's encouragement for something I want to try differently at work. She responds that she is too busy to discuss what's going on with me right now. I could get angry at her for refusing to help me and try to emotionally blackmail her into doing what I want. But I want to cooperate with integrity. I want to practice emotional sobriety. So here, I need to appreciate what is: She is being clear with me about what she cannot do. While I might be disappointed, I am also genuinely grateful for her honesty and integrity. See the difference? One leads me to manipulate and corrupt the relationship. The other leads me to accept and appreciate the situation, which also enables me to move forward in search of some other solution.

When our partner cannot give us what we think we need, there is always something we can appreciate, even as we feel disappointed. Most of the time we can appreciate our partner's honesty and authenticity. This reinforces our agreement that we don't damage integrity in our relationship. It sends the message that our partner's integrity is important and that we can find another solution to our desire.

A word of caution: This doesn't mean that if we don't want to cooperate with a request from our partner, we can't change our mind. If our partners turn to us for something they need, and we don't want to do it but we see they are deeply disappointed, we might explore (ask them) what makes our cooperation so important to them. If their explanation is compelling, we can choose to change our mind and cooperate. But only if we want to. If we decide to change our mind, then we keep our autonomy and cooperate with integrity. That's what emotional sobriety looks like.

7. Don't press; inspire.

This rule has two parts that work together. Let's look at the "don't press" part first. In a healthy relationship, our primary focus is on ourselves. If we are too focused on what our partners need to change, then we are out of balance. Typically, this means we are being intrusive and sticking our nose into their business. Being in a relationship does not give us a license to tell our partners what we think they should be doing.

The dynamic that is operating here is a psychological mechanism called projection, which, as discussed in chapter 3, occurs when we attribute unwanted traits of ourselves to another person. Typically in a relationship, "What we want to change in someone else is a reflection of a lack of full acceptance of ourselves," as Greenwald states (1976, 99).

If we are pressuring our partner to change, then we are not fully accepting ourselves. We are not taking responsibility for what we need to change. The first thing we are not taking responsibility for is staying on our own side of the street.

What does this look like? Sometimes I'll I confront my clients about how they are too focused on what their partner needs to change. Often, they'll respond with something like, "I am hoping they are finally going to hear me." My response is, "It is more important for you to hear what you are concerned about rather than hoping your partner will hear you." This is what I mean by "staying on our own side of the street." The hope that our partners will finally wake up and smell the coffee is a cop-out. We need to listen to ourselves and take the appropriate action rather than defer to them.

Why do we want them to change? Because we aren't willing to. We don't want to suffer the pains of growing up and taking care of ourselves, of becoming emotionally independent, so we continue to try to change our partners. We hope that will keep us from having to change ourselves.

If there is something happening in your relationship that you don't like, it is important to let your partner know what you don't like and what you want. This is more important than telling your partner what you think. Read these statements aloud and listen to the differences:

> I feel hurt when you put me down in front of our friends.
> You are so cruel. You are always putting me down in
> front of our friends.
> I don't like it when you put me down in front of our
> friends. I want you to stop it.

The first two statements conceal an expectation that your partner will change because of how you feel (in the first one) or because your partner is bad (the second statement). Only the third statement directly states what you don't like and what you want. That is straight and healthy communication. But let's take this further. You go out to dinner with friends again, and your partner puts you down again. You need to stand up for yourself and say in front of your friends, "I won't tolerate you putting me down in front of our friends. I imagine it makes them feel as uncomfortable as it makes me feel. I am leaving and I will see you at home." If someone is disrespecting us, it's important for us to respect ourselves and to address the situation directly.

This brings us to the "inspire" portion of the rule. Our honesty is how we stir and inspire someone to change. It's important to note that when we stand up for ourselves, we are not trying to get the other person to change. We are standing up for ourselves, not against someone else. This distinction matters. If we stand up for ourselves to change the other person, it is nothing more than a manipulation, trying to change our partner instead of changing ourselves.

In the practice of emotional sobriety, we need to take responsibility for our side of the street. We don't press our partners to change; we say honestly what we don't like and what we want. Our honesty may (or may not) inspire a change in them.

8. *Let love be the result of who we are with each other.*

As we make progress toward more and more nurturing attitudes and behavior, we give up our expectations that anyone or anything should be different from what it is at that moment. In practice, this means that instead of focusing on love as a plan or a commitment, we shift our focus on the process between us. If the process in our relationships is a healthy one, then our relationship will be secure and grow.

Awareness is the key to a healthy relationship. Fortunately, our practice of emotional sobriety involves employing our awareness to live consciously, as we discussed in chapter 4. Our awareness includes a sense of our own needs and desires and also includes a sense of our partners' needs and desires. We create a loving relationship when we use the information we have received from our awareness to seek a mutually satisfying relationship with our partners. This comes down to what we do at our point of contact—that is, our connection.

A healthy connection involves our authentic presence and integrity. We strive to bring ourselves fully to our connection, and if we are having trouble being present, we tell our partners. Then they don't have to guess where we are at or whether we're trying to manipulate them. It is our responsibility to be clear and present, and when we are not, to admit and declare that too. That may sound a little like "therapy gobbledygook," but in practice, it means saying something along the lines of, "I can't talk right now. My mind is elsewhere, and I can't participate. I'd like to do this another time. Does that work for you?"

> Rather than placing our faith in love as a plan or a commitment, we place our faith in creating a nourishing emotional climate for our relationship.

Rather than placing our faith in love as a plan or a commitment, we place our faith in creating a nourishing emotional climate for our relationship. When we do this and we are honest with each other, emotionally independent and profoundly satis-fying love may result. This kind of loving relationship emerges in the absence of shoulds, rules, and expectations.

•••

Rule 8, letting love be the result of who we are with each other, is the whole point of this chapter. In a relationship between two people who are seeking to be authentic with themselves and each other—that is, who are practicing emotional sobriety—love emerges, as a by-product of connection. Martin and Serena were having trouble letting love emerge because they were never honest in their relationship. Rather, they both saw each other as an object to manipulate to help themselves deal with unfinished personal business. As our therapy progressed, they unraveled and unhooked themselves from all their shoulds, rules, and expectations. When they did this, they saw each other as the extraordinary people they were.

And it was in that moment that love emerged.

When we love our partners in this way, we see them as they really are, instead of as who we need them to be. We see our differences and respect them. We struggle with them construc-tively, grinding away toward solutions that may take startling and delightful turns. In such grinding, the idea of blame becomes ir-relevant. We encourage our partners to cooperate, but not at the expense of their integrity, and we do the same. We guard against transactional sacrifice and compromise. We give with an open hand and refuse to take anything that is not given with an open hand. We ground our relationships in personal language. We say what we want or don't want or what we like or don't like. We challenge our rules, and if they are not nourishing or nurturing, we surrender them and replace them with healthier alternatives.

This was the journey Martin and Serena began.

This is how we create an emotionally free climate in which

love may emerge.

Sentence Completion Exercise

Take each sentence stem and write it at the top of a piece of paper. Next, repeat it silently (or aloud) to yourself, and then complete the sentence stem with the first thought that comes to mind. Do six to ten completions for each.

> The rule I have that has been harming my relationship with my partner is _____.
>
> I lose my integrity in my relationship when I _____.
>
> A rule that would enhance my connection with my partner would be _____.
>
> To cooperate with integrity, I need to remind myself to _____.
>
> What stops me from telling my partner what I want is _____.
>
> My emotional dependency shows up in my relationship with my partner when I _____.
>
> To give up my toxic relationship rules, I need to remind myself that _____.
>
> The best way to encourage my partner to not compromise who he or she is might be to _____.

We have been on quite a journey as we have explored these twelve essential insights. In our final chapter, I'd like to share a vision of what is possible through emotional sobriety.

Chapter 15: Paddling Your Own Canoe

If you have ever paddled a canoe, you know how unstable these boats can be. A canoe is relatively narrow and shallow, and that makes it easy to tip. Just a slight shift in your weight from one side to the other will cause it to rock in the water. If a canoe is turned broadside to a wave or a strong current, the force of the wave or the current will rock the boat hard, possibly even capsizing it. An experienced canoeist knows this about these boats and knows how to anticipate and accommodate the craft's unsteady nature—either through engineering or skill. When you widen the canoe, or add some outriggers, it becomes much more stable. As we improve our skill in handling the canoe through practice (as well as trial and error), we can reduce how unsteady the boat feels.

Before coming to recovery, we were all paddling highly unstable canoes, and most of us didn't know what we were doing. Even the best among us were, at most, mediocre canoeists. Our stability required the cooperation of the forces of nature. We could manage fairly well if we stayed dead center in the middle of our canoe. As long as we were paddling in calm waters, we could maintain our balance and enjoy the ride. Conditions had to be near perfect, though. If the current or wind picked up or we started to hit some whitewater, we were challenged to keep our balance. If conditions got too difficult, stability seemed impossible, and capsizing felt inevitable

Fear of capsizing turned us into control freaks! We tried to take control of the conditions surrounding us to ensure we'd always be paddling along in flat water and perfect weather. But, of course, we looked and sounded liked crazed old sailors, yelling at the wind.

Our life in addiction and recovery is like a journey through waters both calm and rough. Our psychic lives, the canoes. Our coping skills like paddles and canoeing knowledge. On this journey, we have some tough waters to navigate and a long way to travel. Too often we try to change life to meet our conditions instead of changing ourselves to meet the conditions and requirements of life. Our complaints amount to nonsense. "This isn't the way the river was supposed to run." "These waves can't do that!" "Life is unfair, and that's why we're tipping." "Who built this stupid canoe?"

Rarely did we consider that the problem was that we had never learned how to deal with the ever-changing conditions and requirements the river of life presents. Even in recovery, we struggled to manage our boat and learn better paddling techniques.

The reality was that we had designed and built a highly unstable canoe. It was constructed using a blueprint drafted by our false self. The ribs and hulls of our canoe were made of narrow, rigid, and often unspoken demands. Our vessel was leaky and unsteady, and we blamed the water for that! Life had to conform to our expectations if we were going to enjoy what we unconsciously hoped would be a leisurely paddle along a quiet river.

We are told in recovery that "some of us have tried to hold on to our old ideas and the result was nil until we let go" (Alcoholics Anonymous World Services 2001, 58). The first thing we needed to let go of was this old, highly unstable canoe. We realized we had to replace it with a more stable model—we had to rouse ourselves from our sleepwalking state. As we became more aware and as we started our journey of emotional sobriety, we began to live our lives more consciously. This allowed us to see what we could not before: Our canoe needed to be wider; maybe we even added an outrigger for our journey. We admitted to the truth that our skills were poor; maybe we needed more help, even guidance from an experienced canoist. After a time of trial and error and ongoing practice, we developed a more stable design, capable of navigating the conditions we were going to encounter on the river of life. We began to learn how to manage this vessel too. We even started to find joy in this boat on the water—no matter the weather. Our faith in ourselves and in our ability to cope were growing.

> In our lives, emotional stability is achieved by becoming aware of our toxic beliefs and unenforceable rules, the ideas that make our emotional balance dependent on external conditions.

In our lives, emotional stability is achieved by becoming aware of our toxic beliefs and unenforceable rules, the ideas that make our emotional balance dependent on external conditions. We start to see how these ideas and rules emerge in our relationships with others ("If you love me, you will do what I want you to do") as well as in the lies we tell ourselves ("The right person can rescue me from my troubles").

Once we become aware of these unenforceable rules, we must surrender paddling them. We need to move toward an attitude of "I am okay even if this or that happens," and away from the idea that "I am okay only if this happens or that happens." This is emotional freedom. This freedom brings more stability to our canoe; we find we might even dance in it if we wish!

As we paddle forward in emotional sobriety, we become aware of our emotional dependency and surrender its hobbling expectations. These expectations made our life unstable. Tossing them overboard was an important step toward achieving emotional sobriety. But even this isn't enough. We also need to learn how to cope with life on life's terms.

Learning to live life on life's terms is really a lot like taking paddling lessons. We learn how to handle the canoe when the current picks up or we hit a tough patch of whitewater. We learn what to do when the waves kick up or when we experience high winds that threaten to capsize us or blow us off course. We learn that the river is in charge, and we learn how to respond to its rules and stay afloat. The skills we learn to handle these tough times include using our awareness to help us regulate and respond in the best possible way to the situation at hand—whether that means genuine rough water or the rampages of our emotional seas. We may feel stuck and scared, but we quit hoping for the river to calm down. We realize no one is coming to help us, so we stick our paddle in the water again and get back into action to see what we can do to steady the canoe. Lo and behold, we make it through a rough patch of water! But soon enough, rocks crop up to knock us about. We may wish to take personal offense at the rocks and get mad at Mother Nature or God — Why are you doing this to me? — but our growing practice of emotional sobriety reminds us that even this is not about us. We deal with life as it is, on its terms. We stop objecting to the strong current in the river and get busy coping with it — even riding it and enjoying it as it flows us toward the future.

All the tools and skills we learn in our practice of emotional sobriety help us keep the canoe stable and on course. We learn to manage and care for ourselves during rough waters. As our competence grows, so does our self-esteem. As our skill in handling difficult situations grows, we develop a greater faith in our ability to cope with life. We've made our canoe more stable, and we've grown better at paddling it.

To develop these new skills and become competent at using them, we need to practice their application, especially when we feel unstable. We stop blaming ourselves or others, and we get on with the business of growing up, of paddling our own canoe. When we are stuck or stalled or unable to recover our balance, we get help. We don't get caught up in the idea that "we should have known better." Instead we realize that we are and will always be learning how best to cope with the ever-changing waters of life.

> To develop these new skills and become competent at using them, we need to practice their application, especially when we feel unstable.

As we learn to canoe better, we realize that everything becomes more complex when we add another person to the boat. Now, we not only need to manage our relation to the canoe and river, but we also need to cooperate with our partner as we journey down the river together.

Much of what we learned in canoeing by ourselves applies to canoeing with two. We will encounter trouble, and we need to realize that the trouble we encounter in our relationship doesn't mean something is wrong with our recovery program or with the relationship. Quite the opposite is true. Our trouble merely indicates that we have more growing up to do, more paddling skills to develop, more balance to find. Our relationships will evoke and reveal their own versions of rapids and whitewater, as well as warped hulls and busted struts—a whole new set of toxic expectations and rules that we need to become aware of and release.

Now we need to learn how to keep our balance in relationship to our partner in the boat. We focus on what we need to learn so we can canoe together. We focus on how to best cooperate, synchronize our movements, and not criticize what our partner is or isn't doing. We learn to communicate with our partners in a clear and straightforward manner, and we encourage them to do the same. We get better at listening. If we fall short of our goal to operate from the best in us, we own our mistake and get on with the business of understanding the lesson we just learned. We realize that we are both doing the best we can, and therefore there is no need to criticize or demand more. Accepting that we and our partners are doing the best we can is a key to holding on to ourselves while in a relationship.

> Emotional sobriety is a practice, a set of skills we learn by doing and develop only by living them out.

Acceptance turns out to be extremely important in the process of achieving emotional sobriety. In relationships, we have to accept that we are not here to live up to each other's expectations. If by chance we come together and can enjoy what we have together, grieve about what we don't, and love each other regardless of having a relationship that is less than perfect, we are experiencing emotional sobriety. There's always going to be more to learn. Emotional sobriety is all about how we build our canoe and how we learn to paddle it. Emotional sobriety is a practice, a set of skills we learn by doing and develop only by living them out. That's true for all the insights in this book.

As we paddle down the river of life, we will encounter many unexpected events. Purpose can drive us forward, and forgiveness can help us heal the wounds we sustain. From time to time, we will lose control of our canoe. We may even capsize because we have not yet learned how to best respond to a new or unexpected challenge, but we don't have to drown. Emotional sobriety also provides us a life vest. Humility can bring us back to the surface where we can catch our breath, swim to shore, right our canoe, climb back in, and learn from what just happened. This is emotional sobriety: continuous learning and integration that leads to more and more emotional maturity.

Bill Wilson had a vision for us:

> Sobriety is only a bare beginning, it is only the first gift of the first awakening. If more gifts are to be received, our awakening has to go on. And if it does go on, we find that bit by bit we can discard the old life — the one that did not work — for a new life that can and does work under any conditions whatever. Regardless of worldly success or failure, regardless of pain or joy, regardless of sickness or health or even of death itself, a new life of endless possibilities can be lived if we are willing to continue our awakening. (1988, 234)

Emotional sobriety continues our awakening and opens us to the discovery of new possibilities as we navigate life's waters. For me, it holds the key to peace of mind, fulfillment, and authentic happiness. I firmly believe it will for you too.

My hope for you is that you will embrace emotional sobriety in your recovery and begin to discover its incredible gifts.

Appendix A
Bill Wilson's Grapevine Article
Emotional Sobriety: The Next Frontier

JANUARY 1958
The Next Frontier--Emotional Sobriety
BY: BILL W.

I THINK THAT MANY oldsters who have put our AA "booze cure" to severe but successful tests still find they often lack emotional sobriety. Perhaps they will be the spearhead for the next major development in AA--the development of much more real maturity and balance (which is to say, humility) in our relations with ourselves, with our fellows, and with God.

Those adolescent urges that so many of us have for top approval, perfect security, and perfect romance--urges quite appropriate to age seventeen--prove to be an impossible way of life when we are at age forty-seven or fifty-seven.

Since AA began, I've taken immense wallops in all these areas because of my failure to grow up, emotionally and spiritually. My God, how painful it is to keep demanding the impossible, and how very painful to discover finally, that all along we have had the cart before the horse! Then comes the final agony of seeing how awfully wrong we have been, but still finding ourselves unable to get off the emotional merry-go-round.

How to translate a right mental conviction into a right emotional result, and so into easy, happy and good living--well, that's not only the neurotic's problem, it's the problem of life itself for all of us who have got to the point of real willingness to hew to right principles in all our affairs.

Even then, as we hew away, peace and joy may still elude us. That's the place so many of us AA oldsters have come to. And it's a hell of a spot, literally. How shall our unconscious--from which so many of our fears, compulsions and phony aspirations still stream--be brought into line with what we actually believe, know and want! How to convince our dumb, raging and hidden "Mr. Hyde" becomes our main task.

I've recently come to believe that this can be achieved. I believe so because I begin to see many benighted ones--folks like you and me--commencing to get results. Last autumn, depression, having no really rational cause at all, almost took me to the cleaners. I began to be scared that I was in for another long chronic spell. Considering the grief I've had with depressions, it wasn't a bright prospect.

I kept asking myself, "Why can't the Twelve Steps work to release depression?" By the hour, I stared at the St. Francis Prayer. . . "It's better to comfort than to be comforted." Here was the formula, all right. But why didn't it work?

Suddenly I realized what the matter was. My basic flaw had always been dependence--almost absolute dependence--on people or circumstances to supply me with prestige, security, and the like. Failing to get these things according to my perfectionist dreams and specifications, I had fought for them. And when defeat came, so did my depression.

There wasn't a chance of making the outgoing love of St. Francis a workable and joyous way of life until these fatal and almost absolute dependencies were cut away.

Because I had over the years undergone a little spiritual development, the absolute quality of these frightful dependencies had never before been so starkly revealed. Reinforced by what Grace I could secure in prayer, I found I had to exert every ounce of will and action to cut off these faulty emotional dependencies upon people, upon AA, indeed, upon any set of circumstances whatsoever.

Then only could I be free to love as Francis had. Emotional and instinctual satisfactions, I saw, were really the extra dividends of having love, offering love, and expressing, a love appropriate to each relation of life.

Plainly, I could not avail myself of God's love until I was able to offer it back to Him by loving others as He would have me. And I couldn't possibly do that so long as I was victimized by false dependencies.

For my dependency meant demand--a demand for the possession and control of the people and the conditions surrounding me.

While those words "absolute dependency" may look like a gimmick, they were the ones that helped to trigger my release into my present degree of stability and quietness of mind, qualities which I am now trying to consolidate by offering love to others regardless of the return to me.

This seems to be the primary healing circuit: an outgoing love of God's creation and His people, by means of which we avail ourselves of His love for us. It is most clear that the real current can't flow until our paralyzing dependencies are broken, and broken at depth. Only then can we possibly have a glimmer of what adult love really is.

Spiritual calculus, you say? Not a bit of it. Watch any AA of six months working with a new Twelfth Step case. If the case says "To the devil with you" the Twelfth Stepper only smiles and turns to another case. He doesn't feel frustrated or rejected. If his next case responds, and in turn starts to give love and attention to other alcoholics, yet gives none back to him, the sponsor is happy about it anyway. He still doesn't feel rejected; instead he rejoices that his one-time prospect is sober and happy. And if his next following case turns out in later time to be his best friend (or romance) then the sponsor is most joyful. But he well knows that his happiness is a by-product--the--extra dividend of giving without any demand for a return.

The really stabilizing thing for him was having and offering love to that strange drunk on his doorstep. That was Francis at work, powerful and practical, minus dependency and minus demand.

In the first six months of my own sobriety, I worked hard with many alcoholics. Not a one responded. Yet this work kept me sober. It wasn't a question of those alcoholics giving me anything. My stability came out of trying to give, not out of demanding that I receive.

Thus I think it can work out with emotional sobriety. If we examine every disturbance we have, great or small, we will find at the root of it some unhealthy dependency and its consequent unhealthy demand. Let us, with God's help, continually surrender these hobbling demands. Then we can be set free to live and love; we may then be able to Twelfth Step ourselves and others into emotional sobriety.

Of course I haven't offered you a really new idea--only a gimmick that has started to unhook several of my own "hexes" at depth. Nowadays my brain no longer races compulsively in either elation, grandiosity or depression. I have been given a quiet place in bright sunshine.

Appendix B
The Emotional Sobriety Inventory
Revised 2021
Allen Berger, Ph.D.

Describe What Happened	Describe Your Reaction	Identify Your Expectation	Identify Your Unhealthy Dependence	Claim Your Emotional Autonomy
Describe an upsetting event in as much detail as possible.	How did you respond to the situation? What did it mean to you? What did it say about you? What was your reflected sense of self?	To identify the underlying expectation complete this sentence: What they should have done or what was supposed to happen was ___.	The unhealthy dependence that is underlying my emotional reaction and unenforceable ruse is ___.	To achieve emotional freedom add more self and stay connected during trouble. To hold on to myself I need to ___.

* To Identify Your Unenforceable Rule, Answer the Following Question: What ought to have happened or what should they have thought, or done, or said, or felt to make you feel more loved, more self-esteem, more respected, etc.?

References: Berger, A. (2010). 12 Smart Things to do When the Booze and Drugs are Gone. Hazelden: MN.

Berger, A. (2021) 12 Essential Insights for Emotional Sobriety. 4th Dimension Publishing: CA.

References

Alcoholics Anonymous World Services. 1981. *Twelve Steps and Twelve Traditions*. 3rd ed. New York: Alcoholics Anonymous World Services.

2001. *Alcoholics Anonymous*. 4th ed. New York: Alcoholics Anonymous World Services.

American Psychological Association. 2015. APA *Dictionary of Psychology*. Edited by Gary Vandenbos. 2nd edition. Washington, DC: American Psychological Association.

Branden, Nathaniel. 1971. *The Disowned Self*. Hardcover ed. Los Angeles: Nash Publishing.

1980. *The Psychology of Romantic Love*. New York: Bantam Books.

1994. *The Six Pillars of Self-Esteem*. New York: Bantam Books.

1996. *Taking Responsibility: Self-Reliance and the Accountable Life*. New York: Simon and Schuster.

Frankl, Viktor E. 1984. *Man's Search for Meaning: An Introduction to Logotherapy*. Newly revised and enlarged 3rd ed. New York: Touchstone / Simon and Schuster.

Goodreads. n.d. "G. I. Gurdjieff: Quotes." Accessed December 30, 2020. https://www.goodreads.com/quotes/872730-in-order-to-awaken-first-of-all-one-must-realize.

Greenwald, Jerry. 1974. *Be the Person You Were Meant to Be*. New York: Simon and Schuster.

1976. *Creative Intimacy: How to Break the Patterns That Poison Your Relationships*. Hardcover ed. New York: Simon and Schuster.

1980. *Breaking Out of Loneliness*. New York: Rawson, Wade Publishers.

Horney, Karen. 1991. *Neurosis and Human Growth*. Paperback ed. New York: W. W. Norton.

Kerr, Michael, and Murray Bowen. 1988. *Family Evaluation*. New York: W. W. Norton.

Larsen, Earnie. 1985. *Stage II Recovery: Life Beyond Addiction*. New York: HarperSanFrancisco (a division of HarperCollins).

1987. *Stage II Relationships: Love Beyond Addiction*. New York: HarperCollins.

Lowen, Alexander. 1975. *Bioenergetics*. New York: Coward, Mc Cann and Geoghegan.

Luskin, Fred. 2002. *Forgive for Good: A Proven Prescription for Health and Happiness*. San Francisco: HarperCollins.

Perls, Frederick S. 1969. *Gestalt Therapy Verbatim*. Moab, UT: Real People Press.

1975a. "Gestalt Therapy and Human Potentialities." In *Gestalt Is*, edited by John O. Stevens. Moab, UT: Real People Press.

1975b. "Group vs. Individual Therapy." In Gestalt Is, edited by John O. Stevens. Moab, UT: Real People Press.

Ruiz, Don Miguel. 1997. *The Four Agreements*. San Rafael, CA: Amber-Allen Publishing.

Satir, Virginia. 1972. *Peoplemaking*. Palo Alto, CA: Science and Behavior Books.

1978. *Your Many Faces: The First Step to Being Loved*. Berkeley, CA: Celestial Arts.

Siegel, Daniel. 2011. *Mindsight: The New Science of Personal Transformation*. New York: Bantam Books.

Siegel, Daniel, and Tina Payne Bryson. 2012. *The Whole-Brain Child*. New York: Bantam Books.

Viscott, David. 1993. *Finding Your Strength in Difficult Times: A Book of Meditations*. New York: McGraw-Hill.

Welwood, John. 2000. *Toward a Psychology of Awakening*. Boston: Shambhala Publications.

Wilson, Bill. 1988. *The Language of the Heart: Bill W.'s Grapevine Writings*. New York: AA Grapevine.

About the Author

Allen Berger, Ph.D. is a leading expert in the science of recovery from addiction. Sober since 1971, Berger was part of a pioneering recovery program for marines returning from Vietnam with alcohol and other drug addictions—first as a participant, then as a counselor. Since then, he has become a thought leader in the field, working in clinical settings and private practice. In demand as a speaker, workshop presenter, and interviewee, Berger is well-known in recovery circles among those in recovery as well as therapists and clinicians around the world. He has lectured and written extensively on the process of recovery, emotional sobriety, and the therapeutic value of the Twelve Steps. You can learn more about Dr. Berger and his work at www.abphd.com.

Made in United States
Cleveland, OH
28 November 2024

11029426R00171